Persuasion IQ

Persuasion IQ

The 10 Skills You Need to
Get Exactly What You Want

Kurt W. Mortensen

⊿AMACOM

AMERICAN MANAGEMENT ASSOCIATION

New York • Atlanta • Brussels • Chicago • Mexico City • San Francisco
Shanghai • Tokyo • Toronto • Washington, D. C.

Special discounts on bulk quantities of AMACOM books are available to corporations, professional associations, and other organizations. For details, contact Special Sales Department, AMACOM, a division of American Management Association, 1601 Broadway, New York, NY 10019.
Tel.: 212-903-8316. Fax: 212-903-8083.
Website: www. amacombooks.org

This publication is designed to provide accurate and authoritative information in regard to the subject matter covered. It is sold with the understanding that the publisher is not engaged in rendering legal, accounting, or other professional service. If legal advice or other expert assistance is required, the services of a competent professional person should be sought.

Library of Congress Cataloging-in-Publication Data

Mortensen, Kurt W.
    Persuasion IQ : the 10 skills you need to get exactly what you want / Kurt W. Mortensen.
        p. cm.
    Includes bibliographical references and index.
    ISBN-13: 978-0-8144-0993-0
    ISBN-10: 0-8144-0993-8
    1. Business communication. 2. Persuasion (Psychology) 3. Influence (Psychology) 4. Success—Psychological aspects. 5. Success in business. I. Title.

HF5718.M664 2008
651.7—dc22   2007049174

Printing number

10 9 8 7 6 5 4 3 2 1

I want to express my love and appreciation to
my loving wife Denita. She is the main reason
for my success. I also want to thank my children
Brooke, Mitchell, Bailey, and Madison
for their love and support throughout this project and
throughout my life. Family is what makes life a joy
and our dreams worth pursuing.

Contents

Preface

What makes someone successful? Why do some people achieve wealth, while others don't? How can we predict who will make it big, who will barely make ends meet, and who will fail? How do we quantify the characteristics of highly successful people?

It all started in 1905. French psychologist Alfred Binet developed one of the first IQ (intelligence quotient) tests. Throughout the years many scientists have tried to predict future educational achievement and life performance by using tests to measure intelligence. The hitch was that a high score on this type of measured intelligence was no guarantee of life success.

Intelligence is an important trait, but there are many types of intelligences. Howard Gardner found there were multiple types of intelligences, with each individual exhibiting varying levels of these different intelligences. What types of intelligences did the successful and ultraprosperous have? Which ones were they born with and which ones were learned?

Eventually, the concept of emotional intelligence (EQ) was developed. Daniel Goleman's groundbreaking book, *Emotional Intelligence*, showed the world that success was determined not only by IQ, but also by EQ. Emotional Intelligence, often measured as an Emotional Intelligence Quotient (EQ), describes an ability to perceive, assess, and manage the emotions of one's self, of others, and of groups.

My research on what makes people successful has revealed that success depends on something beyond IQ and EQ. My studies show that those who enjoy greater happiness and wealth in life possess a high ability to persuade, influence, sell, negotiate, motivate, lead, and understand human nature. These are not abilities learned in school, yet they must be mastered to achieve major success in life. Some call this "street smarts;" I call it your "Persuasion IQ" (PQ). Studies show that those who generate wealth and success always possess a high PQ.

Given that, increasing your PQ is critical for your success and this book will help you do just that. This book can change your income, your relationships, and even your entire life. Each chapter reveals the traits and characteristics of top producers in every aspect of life. This is based on over seventeen years of research. Not just theory or hearsay, but proven techniques that work in real life. In this book I've taken all the results of my research and made them easy to understand, easy to apply, and easy for you to use.

Deep down we want everyone to listen and do exactly what we want. Every day you either persuade others to your point of view or they persuade you to theirs. We have learned from society to use intimidation, coercion, control, force, or sometimes compromise to get what we want. Why settle for short-term compliance when you can have lasting long-term influence? Persuasion has changed and we must change our persuasion skills to adapt ourselves to the new world. Top persuaders persuade without detection and they persuade others the way they want to be persuaded. In today's skeptical world any old-school persuasion attempts will be resisted.

Lack of persuasion, lack of trust, old-style persuasion, and lack of people skills cost business billions of dollars a year in lost revenue. How much has lack of persuasion or a low PQ cost you? Now is the time to upgrade your skills instead of relying on techniques of the past.

—Kurt W. Mortensen

Acknowledgments

Grateful acknowledgments and deep appreciation are due to all of the people who helped make *Persuasion IQ* a reality.

I want to express special sweeping thanks to all my customers and clients of the Persuasion Institute who made this research possible. I appreciate all my colleagues, parents, friends, teachers, examples, and associates who helped me along the way. Thanks for your help in teaching and testing these ideas every step of the way. Thanks to all of you who believed in me and all of you who didn't.

Deepest appreciation also goes out to Steve Olson, Mike Ray, Tyler Ruby, Ellen Kadin, Dan Merrick, David Bird, Jake Simpson, Jason Denney, Jill Waters, John Sorenson, Russ Voght, Kiona Teo, Loren Peterson, Natasha Marcon, Perry Wakefield, Rob Wheeler, Seth Ellsworth, Kim Scott, Gavin Poulton, Mike Carter, Judd Simpson, Jarad Severe, Kurt Jacobson, Michael Jackson, and Jim Brewster.

CHAPTER ONE

What Is Your Persuasion IQ?

The New Rules of Success and Wealth

W hat does it take to persuade with power in any encounter? Think about it. When was the last time you didn't get something you wanted? What happened? Did you fail to get your point across? Were you persuaded by someone else? Our understanding of persuasion and influence has changed dramatically over the past twenty years. In the past, we did not know or care how consumers thought or what prompted them to buy or take action. Most people in sales and marketing were shooting in the dark. We hoped that what we were doing was working. Dr. Antonio Damasio of Iowa College of Medicine sums it up best: "More may have been learned about the brain and the mind in the 1990s—the so-called decade of the brain—than during the entire previous history of psychology and neuroscience."[1]

At some point, every persuader has lost a client, a customer, or even a friend, has failed at a business, or has blown a new account. Setbacks of this kind have no doubt happened to you. Sure, it hurts, but the question is: Who or what did you blame? It cost you money, embarrassed you, upset you, and someone must be blamed for your discomfort. However, when you embark on a new career, start a new business, or attempt something new, there are risks involved. When things don't work out as expected, the knee-jerk reaction often is: "Well, this doesn't work." I say, "No, it didn't work for you this time. But I know you *can* make it work." There are thousands of people in your field or industry, in the same (or worse) circumstances as yours, with the same intelligence (and often less) who have made it work. It is not the *vehicle* (whether business, real estate, network marketing, the Internet, commissioned sales, or any other endeavor) but the *gas* (persuasion, people skills, self-mastery) for the vehicle that makes the difference between mediocrity and success.

The power of persuasion enables and empowers you to:

- Read people instantly.
- Create instant trust.
- Get others to take immediate action.
- Close more sales.
- Win over your adversaries.
- Earn what you are worth.
- Get others to accept your point of view.
- Repeatedly hear the magical word "yes."
- Accelerate the success of your business.
- Enhance your relationships.
- Win negotiations.
- Get your way.

Persuasion is the number one skill possessed by the ultra-prosperous. If you stop and think about it, everything you want in life comes as a direct result of persuasion. Brian Tracy, a renowned expert in persuasion, says, "People who cannot present their ideas or sell themselves effectively have very little influence and are not highly respected."[2] The converse of this statement is that if you can effectively present your ideas and persuade others, you will be highly influential and highly respected.

Did you know that more CEOs of major U.S. corporations come from sales and marketing backgrounds than from any other discipline?[3] Being the CEO of a major corporation may or may not be your goal, but no matter what your career choices, dreams, or goals are, persuasion is the key to your success. Persuasion professionals—sales and marketing experts—are the most sought-after employees.[4] Parents, teachers, leaders, managers, entrepreneurs, employees, and sales professionals all need persuasion skills. Regardless of our actual job title, we all persuade—we all sell—for a living.

Napoleon Hill spent twenty years researching success and prosperity, during which he uncovered the skills and habits of millionaires and discovered what the ultra-prosperous were doing that the average person was not. What habits, skills, and traits did the successful all have in common? Following the release of his famous bestsellers, *Think and Grow Rich* and *Succeed and Grow Rich Through Persuasion*, Hill dubbed the ability to persuade as the most important skill for reaching one's "greatest potential."[5]

Your area of persuasion might be selling a product, presenting an idea effectively, negotiating a better deal, getting a raise, influencing someone to become a better person, or reaching a troubled teenager. No matter what the setting, success in all these situations depends on persuasion. Persuasion is key in every aspect of life. Consider the following ways we use persuasion every day:

Role	Persuasion	Audience
Parents	Guide	Children
Sales professionals	Close	Prospects
Account reps	Sell	Clients

Role	Persuasion	Audience
Managers	Recruit	Employees
Leaders	Influence	Followers
Coaches	Train	Teams
Advertisers	Educate	Shoppers
Lawyers	Sway	Juries
Presenters	Inspire	Listeners
Entrepreneurs	Win over	Customers
Marketers	Convince	Consumers
Mentors	Advise	Students
Politicians	Urge	Constituents
Corporations	Assure	Shoppers
Clergy	Enlighten	Members
Doctors	Counsel	Patients

The list could go on. The point is we constantly find ourselves in persuasive encounters, in every sphere of life, both publicly and privately. What is *your* persuasion IQ (PQ)? Where do *you* rank in the world of persuasion and influence? And how do you move from persuasive mediocrity to persuasion mastery?

The Man and His New, Shiny SUV: A Fable

After the purchase of a shiny red SUV, the new vehicle owner felt excited about his purchase but, at the same time, nervous about the large investment. It was a financial stretch to buy the car, but he felt so good behind the wheel. It just felt right. He was sure that this new car would open many doors—that it would be the start of something great. Things would be tight financially, but he felt the investment was worth every penny. Two weeks later, the gas light illuminated, and he automatically pulled into a gas station to fill up the tank. To his great dismay, he watched the counter on the pump go to $20, then $30, then $70 . . . it finally stopped at $82.77. "That's highway robbery!"

he thought. It wasn't fair that gas was so expensive! He vowed never to buy gas again, and he never did. There his car sat, parked in the driveway, shiny and new and never moving because of his headstrong refusal to put gas in his car.

Meaning: No matter what type of vehicle (business) you have, it will go nowhere if you do not have the gas (persuasion and people skills).

Just as gas is critical to your car (regardless of cost), persuasion is critical to your business. Most people would love to be able to know how to persuade and influence others, on the spot, in any situation. Suppose you are talking to a friend, a client, or a prospect, and you can't get your point across. Now imagine you could buy a spray can of persuasion, spray that person, and have her instantly change her mind to your point of view. What would that be worth to you? How much would you pay for such a spray can of persuasion? Imagine being able to persuade others with such power and ease.

YOU CAN MASTER THE ART AND SCIENCE OF PERSUASION

The good news is that persuasion skills can be learned and mastered. It's amazing how little effort, time, or expense that individuals, companies, and corporations would have to spend on sales and persuasion training to equip themselves with these vital skills. Armed with such knowledge, the persuader's income and the company's profitability increases dramatically, and the client, customer, or friend is yours for life. The question I always get at this point is: "How much will it cost me to acquire, learn, and master these persuasion and life skills?" I want to shift the focus of that question. How much will it cost you if you don't? As the billionaire

Donald Trump said, "Study the art of persuasion. Practice it. Develop an understanding for its profound value across all areas of life."

Why have I dedicated my life to understanding, mastering and teaching persuasion and life mastery? The reason is that I was mad I hadn't learned these critical life skills while earning my college degree or advanced business degree. Who/what had failed me? If persuasion is the skill of success, why hadn't I learned it from school, or anywhere else for that matter? Why had I been given a pocket knife to chop down the tree of success and wealth? Why had I been given the wrong tools? Why did these critical life skills have to be learned through the school of hard knocks?

I desperately wanted to master the priceless skill of persuasion. I read every book on the subject that I could get my hands on, attended countless persuasion, leadership, negotiation, and sales seminars, read thousands of studies on human behavior and social psychology, listened to every audiotape or CD on persuasion, motivation, and influence I could find. I gleaned lots of great information, but found something was still missing. All the studies, programs, books, and speakers touched on good ideas, but I couldn't find a source that tied it all together.

Frustrated, I decided to take my research to the next level. I sat through countless sales presentations, consumer intercepts, and surveys. I listened to telemarketing scripts, endured many offensive old-school persuasion tactics, and witnessed innumerable closes. I took sales and sales management positions to find what was working. I sought out the top professional persuaders to learn what makes them tick. I monitored not only top persuaders, but their audiences as well to determine what they did and did not like, why they were or were not persuaded.

Overflowing with my research results, I founded the Persuasion Institute to catalog my findings and share the secrets of persuasion with others who desire to reach their greatest potential. Since its inception, the Persuasion Institute has administered over 20,000 Persuasion IQ assessments. My role is to teach you the skills of top persuaders. What talents, traits, characteristics, habits, and mindset do top persuaders possess? How can an average persuader become a great persuader? I also help persuaders understand their audience. I talk to your customers, clients, and prospects after you do. Why are they lying to you, not calling you back, avoiding you, running away, or not buying? I find out exactly what happened and what you can do to improve your ability to persuade and influence.

Learning how to persuade and influence makes the difference between hoping for a better income and actually *having* a better income. Ask yourself this question: How much money and income have I lost with my inability to persuade and influence? Think about it. Sure, you've seen some success, but think of the times you just couldn't get it done. Has there ever been a time when you did not get your point across? When you were unable to convince someone to do something?

I have asked the question, "How much has your inability to persuade cost you or your business?" across the world, online, and in seminars. The answers are staggering. Across the board, the average amount people felt they had lost totaled $4.3 million. Over time, all those lost opportunities—relationships, business deals, or promotions—take their toll. As I delved deeper into the subject, I realized that those who had mastered persuasion and influence were able to dictate their income and could almost effortlessly find employment, start a business, or lead others anytime, anywhere.

CRACKING THE PERSUASION CODE

Based on seventeen years of study, research, and experience in the field, the Persuasion Institute's Persuasion IQ assessment has cracked the code. Our findings and information will equip you with the essential habits, traits, and skills you need to become an unstoppable power persuader. The intelligence gathering, conceptual organizing, and explaining are all done for you. It is the most comprehensive persuasion resource available today.

Do you think you are already persuasive? Think again. Research shows that most persuaders use only three to four persuasive techniques, over and over again. Even high producers typically use only seven or eight persuasive techniques. What a waste of talent! Did you know that there are over one hundred persuasive tools and techniques that you can have readily available, right at your fingertips?

If you look at persuasion as if it were a piano, then most people only use a few piano keys and are playing "Chopsticks" when they could be using all the keys and playing Mozart.

Understanding that yesterday's persuasion training no longer applies in today's fast-paced, educated environment is the first step to mastering persuasion. Your audience does not want a product pusher, and they don't want to hear those cheesy one-liners. True persuasion is about creating customers and friends for life; it's not about getting that one quick sale that's all too likely to turn into a dissatisfied customer, a return, or a refund. It's not about getting short-term compliance. That type of persuasiveness will generate long-term resentment, rebellion, and frustration.

People aren't won over by tactics and gimmicks. In fact, they're all too weary of them. A *New York Times* poll found that 56 percent of respondents felt you can't be too careful in dealing with most people, and 34 percent said that most people would try to take advantage of you if they got the chance.[6] When asked what they thought about persuaders or salespeople, only 32 percent of respondents said, "I have a positive attitude toward salespeople."

The challenge is that most persuaders are certain they possess most of the persuasion traits they need, but when you ask the people and prospects they interact with, you get a completely different picture. Whatever your area of persuasion, most of your audience (whether prospects, employees, or clients) will describe you as:

One-sided	Loud	Condescending
Time waster	Exaggerator	Poor listener
Fake friend	Pushy	Deceptive
Greasy	Fast-talking	Manipulative
Dishonest	Devious	Self-centered

Or they'll complain about your:

Poor communication	Getting personal too fast
Being misinformed	Blaming others
Lack of followthrough	Not really caring
Overpromising	Asking offensive questions
Badmouthing the competition	Attempts to get their wallet
Lack of interpersonal skills	Not understanding their business
Useless small talk	Employing obvious closing tactics

Why all this negativity? First of all, the general public is more educated now than ever before, which means they are more discerning. Secondly, all of us are bombarded by countless persuasive messages every day. We don't have to go looking for them—they find us. By the age of twenty, the average American has been exposed to approximately one million television commercials.[7] With such a constant marketing onslaught, who wouldn't be sick of it? Everyone starts to go numb with the sheer volume of daily persuasive attempts.

So it's best to know the facts up front. Most people think persuaders talk too much, overpromise, fail to follow through, are only looking out for themselves, and are greedy or manipulative. Sorry, no sugar coating.

What does all this mean for you as a persuader? It means out with the old and in with the new. Forget about the old tactics, clichés, and stereotypes. It's not about having tricks up your sleeve and pulling a fast one. It's not about coercing, nagging, bullying, or begging. These forms of "persuasion" are not really persuasion at all. They may work initially, but their effects are only temporary and your audience quickly becomes desensitized. As a society, we've grown to be more demanding and less patient.

Instead of learning techniques and strategies, think in terms of transforming yourself into a naturally persuasive person. *You* are what's persuasive, not some tactic you employ. You're the real deal. You are persuasive because of the traits, talents, and characteristics you have integrated into your life. Persuasion is the critical skill, and it's transferable in any situation or career. Cultivating your natural persuasiveness will bring you success in any job, setting, or business.

While traveling on an airplane, I remember talking to a gentleman who was faced with a significant, but very common challenge. He had always wanted to be an entrepreneur and to own his own business. He knew that having his own business and being his own boss were the keys to his personal freedom and financial independence. He'd earned his college degree with honors and had done extensive research on his great business idea. He wrote the perfect business plan. Everyone said it was a great idea. It seemed he could not fail. But he made one vital mistake, which was thinking that his college degree and extensive research were enough to ensure success. As it turns out, studies show that there is no correlation between college grades and lifetime earnings.[8]

Furthermore, this airplane seatmate of mine had forgotten one crucial element—the one thing he had skimmed over in his haste to get to the "good stuff," the nuts and bolts of his business—and it proved to be a major stumbling block. He thought he possessed persuasion and people skills, but that is not what his potential clients thought. He did not have the ability to connect with people. He could not persuade others to believe in his ideas or services. He told me he had suffered huge financial losses because of this one issue. It was extremely frustrating for him, because he'd gotten his degree, done his homework, and wanted to be successful. Every single possible detail was in order, but without persuasion, people skills, or communication skills, none of it mattered. We can be experts in our field, but still never see great success without these core skills we will be talking about in this book.

This oversight is a common trend in corporate America, and in particular in the entrepreneurial world. Did you know that 96 percent of all business start-ups fail within five years? [9] Why is this so? The U.S. government's Small Business Administration and the Persuasion Institute (independently) set out to discover why. Both organizations spent considerable time and money trying to uncover the root of the problem, and in the end, they both came to the same conclusion: businesses fail because of lack of sales. Dun and Bradstreet found similar results and called this failure "managerial incompetence," meaning that the individuals running these businesses did not know what they were doing. More specifically, they found that the number-one area of incompetence was sales and marketing.

Those entrepreneurs who had failed did not know how to persuade others to take action and to use their product or service. In other words, sales fixes everything (assuming you have a good product or service). What's more, it is no secret that the majority of people who are fired or downsized are let go because of their inability to work and communicate with people. In other words, they lose their jobs because they lack people and persuasion skills.

The greatest ability in business is to get along with others and influence their actions.
— JOHN HANCOCK

Ironically, many of the business owners and upper management executives who fire these individuals themselves do not know what would make the situation better. They think they do, but often it is the wrong solution. When asked what the essential attributes of great persuaders are, they name many great skills and qualities, but surprisingly, not the ones that head the list. We hear that it's all about persistence, communication, intelligence, aptitude, people skills, product knowledge, and organization, but these things still don't explain why some people are great persuaders and others are not.

TRAITS OF TOP PERSUADERS

When the public is asked to identify the common traits and characteristics of great persuaders, the resulting responses are interesting. Some are self-evident, while others may surprise you:

Informed	Great communicator	Determined
Educated	Hardworking	Accurate
Knowledgeable	Punctual	Humble
Honest	Solution-oriented	Admits mistakes
Organized	Empathic	Sincere
Cooperative	Candid	Creative
Adaptable	Dependable	Pleasant disposition
Good listener	Friendly	Great personality
Resilient	Proactive	Continuous learner

Sure, this list sounds great. Anyone would love to possess all these talents or traits. The shocking news is most great persuaders don't possess all these talents or traits. What consumers define as a great persuader, or what you think constitutes a great persuader, could be far from reality. So, what talents and traits do great persuaders possess?

Many people are like the man I met on the airplane. They have great intentions, they work hard on their career or business, they put in the hours, but all that energy and effort aren't going to the right place. All the other stuff doesn't really matter if you don't have the right mindset, persuasion, or people skills (PQ). K. A. Ericsson's studies show there is no correlation between your ability to persuade (performance) and your intelligence (IQ).[10] And why are the majority of individuals not persuasive? For most people, persua-siveness is not innate. It is a learned skill. Unfortunately, many of the major universities don't teach persuasion, sales, or interperson-al relations, so it is hard to turn to formal education to help rein-force these most fundamental business necessities, even in a busi-ness program!

The *Wall Street Journal* reported on the importance of persua-sion and sales training in MBA programs. It found that this train-ing usually ended up as a footnote at most graduate schools. How can you be ready for success, life, and business without being trained in these basic skills? The ability to sell, market, close deals, communicate your ideas effectively, understand consumer behav-ior, give presentations, influence people, get clients, or raise money is the ticket to success. If you are good at persuasion you can write your own ticket.[11]

So if you're going to put time, energy, and effort into honing your skills, be sure to focus on the ones that will give you the fastest and most dramatic improvements first—your persuasion skills. If you can hone your persuasive abilities, your natural gifts and abilities will emerge and blossom even more because your per-suasiveness will help get more people and more resources on your side. When this happens, your hard work won't feel so hard any-more. Instead of killing yourself to make things happen, you'll find that your work becomes fun. In our persuasion workshops, I ask persuaders and entrepreneurs if they want to double their income. Of course, they always answer in the affirmative. They then quick-ly realize that the only way to double their income is to double their effort, or double their ability to persuade and influence.

Why haven't most persuaders caught up with the times? Why are so many still using the old tools that should have been put to rest long ago? Are you one of them? When you are meeting with prospects, clients, or employees, are you a guest? An enemy? A pest? A product pusher? A pushover? Are you welcome or are you annoying? Think twice. Most people think they are a welcome guest, but the reality is—and the research shows—that you are more likely to be an annoying pest. They just never tell you. Times have changed, and we are no longer able to push people into buying a product or service. We need to be able to help them persuade themselves. To be an effective persuader, you must be able to bring your audience around to your way of thinking.

How often have you faced someone who needed, wanted, liked, and could afford your product, service, or idea but wasn't buying, simply because you were unable to persuade him? It was a perfect fit for both parties. What happened?

We have all seen great persuaders in action. We have been in the presence of persuasive experts who automatically attract everyone to them. Wherever they go, people are captivated and influenced by such individuals' radiant energy and dynamic personality. People just naturally want to be persuaded by them. Most people wear an invisible badge that says, "Convince me! Help me make the right decision!" They are thinking, "There is too much information. I need someone to trust, someone to guide me in the right direction."

All this takes us back, full circle, to the challenge. Where do master persuaders learn the skills, habits, and traits to reach the top? Are these capabilities acquired through osmosis? Are they ingrained in the persuader? Can they be learned? The answer to all of these questions is a resounding yes; these learning methods are all part of the persuasion formula.

How do you (1) discover the skills you need to become more persuasive, (2) begin to embody these skills so that they are a natural part of who you are, and (3) create massive success? Here is the first step you need to take: Take the Persuasion IQ Test in Appendix B or online for instant results and analysis.

(For a more detailed breakdown of your persuasive abilities, go to www.persuasioniq.com and take the comprehensive persuasion skills assessment. This will help you—and it helps us with our research. I will even give you free persuasion software (a $197 value). This persuasion software systematizes the persuasion process for you. Wondering what to say or do next while you are persuading others? What law of persuasion should you use? Find out and follow what great persuaders do and say.)

When you have your Persuasion IQ results you will have a clear understanding of your starting point, you will know just what steps to take next, and you will make faster progress. It will make the skills, traits, and characteristics of this book come alive. The Persuasion IQ evaluation is based on research compiled by the Persuasion Institute. We have gathered and analyzed information from all over the world about how and why persuasion works. As a result, the Persuasion IQ assessment will help you discover point-by-point and step-by-step what you need to do to transform yourself into a master persuader. Where do you rank, what are your strengths, and what are your weaknesses?

ARE YOU READY?

*If we do not change our direction, we are likely
to end up where we are headed.*
—**Chinese proverb**

In the course of this book, I will use the words "persuade" and "influence" to deal with all forms of persuasion. I will also alternate the use of product or service to indicate the persuader's topic, bearing in mind that persuasion applies to so many situations beyond sales. Instead of using prospect, client, customer, or consumer, I will usually use the word "audience."

I am not going to be concerned with being politically correct, tactful, or gentle. I won't sugarcoat reality. My job is to take your life, career, and income to the next level by teaching you the powerful skills of persuasion and influence. I am going to be blunt. I will tell the truth, even when it hits you over the head! It is time to get past old habits. I know you have heard about obtaining closing

"THE COMPUTER SAYS I NEED TO UPGRADE MY BRAIN
TO BE COMPATIBLE WITH ITS NEW SOFTWARE."

skills and finding common interests. I know you've been told to sell benefits, not features, or to answer a question with a question, to handle objections, to create interest with WIIFM. Without the fundamental skill of persuasion, however, none of these tips and tricks means a thing. It's a new world out there. It's time to raise and upgrade your Persuasion IQ. It's time to master the world of persuasion.

After you've completed the Persuasion IQ assessment, you'll know what areas you need to pinpoint to become a master persuader. Mastering the world of persuasion and influence is an open-book test. Remember those tests in school? They were my favorite type of test, because all the answers were right there in front of me. Sure, I had to find them, but I also knew exactly where to look. I've applied that same open-book theory to this book. Within these pages, I have provided all the guidance and areas of expertise you need to master to take your life and income to the next level. You can raise your Persuasion IQ. As you cultivate these skills and attributes, you will see dramatic results in all aspects of your life. Are you ready? Then let's go!

CHAPTER TWO

Persuasion Resistance

*Ten Common Obstacles That Limit
Your Persuasion Success*

The worst time to learn a persuasion skill is when you need it. Persuasion must be mastered before it is needed, or the opportunity is lost forever. In all the years that I have worked in persuasion, sales, influence, and leadership, I have never yet found a perfect persuader. I have met many very skilled persuaders, but none that have completely mastered all that they were capable of achieving. This is understandable. It's demanding enough just to keep up with the bills, maintain existing customers, lead the organization, prospect for new customers, outmaneuver the competition, and increase product knowledge. Faced with so many tasks, it's difficult to find the time to spend on developing yet another skill.

Ironically, one area of persuasion that is easily overlooked is the very one that would make everything else fall into place. You've probably heard the old adage, "Dull knives work the hardest." Working hard is not the same as working smart. Are your knives sharp? Are you working smart? If you sharpened up in this one area, you'd likely be working more efficiently overall. Check yourself. Are you just going through the motions? Are you still using the same old tools over and over again without seeing the desired results? Or worse, are you making the same old *mistakes* over and over again? Are you making less than you could because of common "old-school" persuasion mistakes?

© Randy Glasbergen.
www.glasbergen.com

"You've been shaking my hand for six minutes, said my name 19 times in a single sentence, and mirrored every gesture I've made including the nose pick I did just to test you. I'm guessing you're here to sell me something."

There are things you are doing right now that cause people to resist you and your message. My research shows that there are ten common obstacles mediocre persuaders make that limit their success and income. Each obstacle is like driving around town with your emergency brake on. You are wondering why your car never has much power. These problems are simple to fix, but expensive to have.

OBSTACLE #1: THE WOBEGON EFFECT

Radio humorist Garrison Keillor coined the term "Lake Wobegon Effect" to describe the tendency most people have to see themselves as better than average. In his book, *Lake Wobegon Days*, Keillor depicts a town where "all the women are strong, all the men are good-looking, and all the children are above average."[1] Like the Lake Wobegon folks, we all have a natural bias to see ourselves as above average. It's really hard to admit it when we just don't cut it, especially when it comes to skills that we regard as basic or common. Psychologists call this tendency "cognitive bias," or the "better-than-average effect." It is also called "The Wobegon Effect."

When I teach persuasion, negotiation, or mastery seminars, sometimes I ask my students to list the top ten reasons why they are not more successful. They find plenty of reasons for their lack of success, but the notion that their own shortcomings could somehow be responsible hardly ever makes it onto their radar screen. We always feel we must gloss over our weaknesses to make things seem better than they really are. We lie about our incomes, our ages, and our weights.

The reason the Wobegon Effect has such a negative impact, not only on our persuasive abilities but also in our lives, is because we are lying to ourselves. That's the bottom line. We're lying to others, and we're lying to ourselves. We are investing in hopes and dreams that are not based on honest evaluation. It might seem nice to view the world through rose-colored glasses for a while, but in the end, you're setting yourself up for failure. The Wobegon Effect ultimately gives us a false sense of security. When afflicted by it, we become numb to reality and fail to see exactly where we stand and what we need to improve. This tendency can lower our expectations about ourselves and falsely improve our confidence.

> *A hyena cannot smell its own stench.*
> —AFRICAN PROVERB

I'm not recommending a doom-and-gloom attitude, but how can you expect to set goals—modest or lofty—if they are all built on false skills and presumptions? Great persuaders are able to take a good, hard look at themselves and come to grips with the facts, both the good and the bad. This is when you will be able to make real progress.

The Wobegon Effect manifests itself when we are evaluating a skill or talent that we expect ourselves to have or when others expect us to have a particular skill. When social pressure or social validation is involved, we make higher-than-expected evaluations. For example, if you were in sales and you were asked to rate your ability to connect with people or your product knowledge, you would be 90 percent likely to rate yourself above average, even though mathematically the validity of your assertion would be less than 50 percent.[2] Among managers, 90 percent will rate themselves better than the average manager.[3] We tend to overestimate everything from grades and physical appearance, to the possibility of divorce.[4]

To drive home the Wobegon Effect's prevalence, one study found that most people believe they are more _____ than the average person.

- Athletic
- Intelligent
- Organized
- Ethical
- Logical
- Interesting
- Fair-minded
- Attractive[5]

Things change, however, when people start evaluating themselves with respect to skills that are not part of their everyday world. Individuals tend to rate themselves below average in such areas as acting, mechanics, juggling, nuclear fusion, or computer programming—things our employer or society at large does not expect us to know and understand.

My research has shown the following to be the top five strengths persuasion students say they have mastered, but rate themselves higher than they actually are:

1. People skills/empathy

2. Persistence/determination

3. Communication/listening

4. Personal mastery

5. Closing skills

Do you suffer from the Wobegon Effect? What is it that you've been telling yourself and everyone else you do really well, when in fact you don't do it well at all—or at least you're not above average, as you've been trying to convince yourself and everyone else? Did you accept your Persuasion IQ test results or did you rationalize why they were not higher? Where do your talents and traits compare to the real world? If you really want to know, go to www.persuasioniq.com and click on free reports.

OBSTACLE #2: THE BRICK WALL OF RESISTANCE

Has this ever happened to you? You enter a retail store and you're approached by a sharply dressed persuader. You are interested in buying, but the salesperson is a little aggressive. You get an alarming feeling in the pit of your stomach and then do what many of your customers do to you. You lie! You say, "I'm just looking; I'll come back later," or "It's too expensive," or "I have to talk to my spouse before I decide." What you're really thinking is "I don't like this guy," or "I don't trust her," or "Something didn't feel quite right." In the end, you never go back to this store, you never recommend it, and neither the store owner nor the persuader ever knows why. This is a large brick in the Brick Wall of Resistance.

This obstacle is truly a silent persuasion killer. Most people will never say anything to you to alert you to the fact they are feeling this way. They are more comfortable lying to you—so they don't hurt your feelings. They walk away and simply never deal with you again. The reason this obstacle is such a killer is because we don't even realize we're doing it. We are offending people and don't even know it. You may think you're just being friendly or enthusiastic, but be careful. While friendliness and enthusiasm are great attributes, if there is even so much as a hint of force, deception, hype, or selling underlying any of it, you've pretty much sunk the deal.

Audiences are tough. Ever-smarter consumers have built a lot of resistance to the old style of persuading; many people have a brick wall of resistance up before you've even started your presentation. They assume you're going to be the sleazy, manipulative sales guy before you've even had a chance to speak. They are all ready to resist you before you start.

What do you do to overcome this tendency? Your persuasion attempts must be nonthreatening and very natural. Forget loud and flashy. That strategy only encourages resistance. And most definitely forget about high pressure. Not only does that solidify the wall of resistance in that particular moment, but the wall will increase in size. When people feel they have been pressured, bullied, or coerced into buying or doing something they don't need or want, they are resentful. They will never do business with you again. They will detest you for "tricking," "manipulating," "selling," or "forcing" them. They will bad-mouth you to all of their friends and family—even to people they don't know! You can end up losing not only this one person but, as the grapevine goes, potentially hundreds of others as well.

The moment people sense that you are attempting to persuade them, the brick wall increases in size and strength, and they will resist you. To counter this tendency, persuasion and sales must take place below the conscious radar.

The following are common mistakes that will create large bricks in the wall of resistance.

What You Do	How Your Audience Feels
Cover every single possible detail.	Overwhelmed, confused, stressed out.
Incessantly ask unnecessary questions.	Antagonized, annoyed.
Say, "Honestly . . ."	Persuader is getting ready to lie.
Take excessive time with the person.	You don't respect their time.
Demean or belittle the competition.	Lack of confidence.
Exaggerate the details.	Mistrustful and more skeptical.
Try to show off your impeccable skills, know-how, and experience.	Annoyed, that you're arrogant and egotistical, condescending.
Say, "Are you prepared to buy today?"	Incoming, here come the old-style tactics.
Overly friendly or happy.	Insincere and *fake*.
Say, "How are you doing today?"	"Now what are you trying to sell me?"
Employ coercive tricks.	Manipulated, turned-off, tense.

Great persuaders have cultivated a sixth sense when it comes to the "push and pull" aspect of persuasion. You must encourage without pushing. Entice, but don't ensnare. You have to sense and then predict—based upon knowledge, instinct, experience, and nonverbal cues—what you can do and how your audience will respond. With this sensitivity, which you can learn, there won't be any smacking head first into the brick wall of resistance.

OBSTACLE #3: THINKING LIKE AN EMPLOYEE

Most people think of themselves as employees. They make their hourly wage or their annual salary; they get their fixed amount. The truth is we *all* are paid for our performance. We are *all* really on commission, whether we realize it or not, whether we like it or not. The path to success is often blocked by our inability to take full responsibility for our current situation.

We really are paid exactly what we're worth, or what others feel we are worth. (Remember I am not going to sugarcoat this.) If we don't like our mediocre incomes, but do nothing about it, we really are just getting exactly what we've asked for. If we stopped complaining and began proactively seeking to enhance our knowledge, skills, and talents, we'd see an increase in opportunity and income. It is in this sense that we are all on full commission. We get out of life what we put into it. We are rewarded precisely for our skills, talents, and abilities.

Consider your current situation and ask yourself, "Am I happy? Am I doing all that I can? Is there more out there?" When we are honest with ourselves, we often find that the status quo is set where it is because we are either comfortable or lazy, not because we honestly believe it's ideal. If you know you've reached a plateau and you're ready to break through, it's time to step up to the plate and take on a new do-it-yourself project. Do you know what that project is? Building a better *you*. Roll up your sleeves, because you and you alone will decide what your income will be. What are you really worth? Does that amount match your current paycheck?

I think the whole world should be paid on commission. You decide, based on your skills, mindset, and talents, how much you are going to get paid. Owning your own business, working on commission, wanting incentives or bonuses based on performance— these desires usually mean an increase in income. After the second or third year, most commission-based persuasion professionals are making more than those who started with a straight salary.

This increase in earnings is also true of entrepreneurs. In 2004, for example, the average income ($141,500) for families headed by a self-employed person was roughly double the average ($70,100) for a household headed by someone who is working for someone else, according to the Federal Reserve survey of consumer finances.[6] It is time to earn what you are worth.

OBSTACLE #4: TALKING TOO MUCH

Being an extrovert, having the gift of gab, or being able to make small talk with anyone you meet can definitely be used to your advantage, but watch yourself. How can you persuade if you are always talking? It will be very annoying to your audience if they sense that you like hearing yourself talk more than listening to their concerns. Remember, it's about *them*, not you. Great persuaders listen more than they talk. In fact, great persuaders use their listening and questioning skills to get their audience to persuade themselves.

Often when someone comes to you, she already knows what she wants. She already has something in mind. She just needs to talk through it with someone. Which approach do you think will have better, longer-term results: you persuading your audience, or you helping them persuade themselves? It's much better if your audience feels as if they have made the decision themselves, without perceived external influences. When you do have to talk, be succinct and to the point. A good rule of thumb is not to talk more than 30 percent of the time.

Now, with these general guidelines in place, it is worth pointing out that you must always be prepared to adapt and adjust to the personality type of your audience. For some people, talking 30 percent of the time will still be too much. Discussing only what is relevant to the matter at hand and keeping chit-chat to a minimum is best for these no-nonsense types. Your attempts at being their buddy will likely annoy and maybe even offend them. Some people feel that being overly warm and personable is not appropriate when you have just met someone for the very first time. Polite and professional, yes, but warm and fuzzy, no. The bottom line is, don't get too friendly too fast.

OBSTACLE #5: AN AVALANCHE OF INFORMATION

Many times, when we are trying to be persuasive, we want to highlight all the perks and plusses. It's only natural. Wouldn't helping someone see the potential gains of your product or service be a good thing? Yes, but here is the issue: Your audience will buy for their own reasons and only their reasons. They don't care about why you like the product or service. They don't care how much you know about it—don't bury them in detail. The more you spout off about features, the more your audience mentally checks out.

When you want to draw attention to the benefits of a product or service, the best thing to do is uncover the features or benefits your audience is looking for *first*. Why spend precious time and energy highlighting things they don't care about? Let them tell you what they're looking for, and then center your discussion around those few key points. It is critical to remember that most people already know what they want. In fact, your audience's mindset often is looking for reasons *not* to buy. It is a natural defense mechanism. They're thinking, "How do I make sure I'm not getting myself into something I'll regret? What could go wrong?"

There is another way spouting and spewing too much information can backfire: You might actually feature something they're not interested in or something they even see as a drawback. Why give them reasons not to buy? Again, let them tell you what they're looking for. *After* you've discussed what they care about, after they've made the decision to buy, then and only then should you fill in any remaining blanks with other benefits or features. Don't oversell by cluttering or distracting the few most important key points.

Overpersuading your audience is in this same category. Many times, our impatience to impress our audience with our knowledge and wisdom leads to overpersuading. When you overpersuade, you give your audience no room to ask questions or make a decision. You come across as forceful, aggressive, and obnoxious. Do you really think you can convince someone by interrupting them? Research demonstrates that 81 percent of persuaders talk more than necessary during the persuasion process. They are talking too much,[7] and you are likely talking too much.

When we talk too much and fail to allow our audience to ask questions, it increases the thickness of the brick wall of resistance. Consider the doctor analogy to persuasion, meaning you have to listen and ask questions before you can diagnose the problem. The doctor does not come into the examination room and try to sell you on a prescription without first asking questions or trying to discover what you really need. Like a physician, you need to step back and be able to absorb and evaluate everything your audience is saying. While monitoring persuaders, I have found a constant epidemic of overpersuasion and regurgitating too many features.

Ask yourself the following questions to determine whether or not you ever overpersuade or flood your audience with too much information:

- Do you interrupt your audience in your eagerness to highlight another point before they have finished?

- Are you worried about making the sale or satisfying a new customer?

- Do you ever lose their eye contact or get a glazed look?

- Do they seem stressed, indifferent, or agitated?

- Does your audience seem overwhelmed or confused?

- Are you concentrating on what you need to say next instead of listening?

- Is your audience giving you excuses and objections that you've already covered or that you know aren't really true?

- Do their nonverbal signals tell you they are getting ready to run?

- Are you talking about yourself instead of discovering their needs?

OBSTACLE #6: BEING MOTIVATED BY DESPERATION

Do you think it feels good to be a wild animal's prey? Are you coming across as a ravenous wolf or a shark after the smell of blood? Would you want someone stalking you who doesn't have your best interests in mind? This is how your audience feels when they can sense you are desperate for their compliance. My research shows that people can sense when a persuader or salesperson is uneasy, nervous, or tense. In other words, if you're uncomfortable, your audience is uncomfortable. There's no way around it. They will see past your gleaming smile, and even if they don't understand it, they'll start to get the feeling that you're a wolf in sheep's clothing.

How do you know when you're in desperation mode? You can recognize the mentality:

"I have to get this sale or else."

"I have to get his business or it's over."

"I have to negotiate the deal today or I can't pay the bills."

Usually this desperation is rooted in fear. If you ever find yourself slipping into desperation mode, ask yourself what you are so afraid of. What's the worst thing that can happen? Is it really that bad? What if the worst really did happen? You've got to face your fears, because despair-driven persuasion rarely works. Even if you get your way, it will hurt you in the long run. Your audience will not appreciate feeling that you pressured them. They will resent you, harbor negative feelings toward you, and never do business with you again. Desperation leads to poor decisions, forces unwanted choices, reduces options, and spawns regret.

OBSTACLE #7: FEAR OF REJECTION

In the last section, we talked about how despair is rooted in fear. In this section, let's discuss the fear of rejection because it is one of the most common fears. Of all the things that we might fear, most of us will have a bout with this one at some time. We all experience rejection in small doses every day. But what about when we persuade for a living? Rejection seems to take a higher toll. We avoid rejection like the plague, but it affects your income. Running away from the rejection solves nothing. Letting our fears overtake us and paralyze us also solves nothing. Ironically, whether we run or succumb, neither option helps the situation.

When we don't handle our fears appropriately, we inadvertently end up being the ones passing out the bricks for that wall of resistance. How excited would you be to buy from someone who seemed nervous, tense, and demanding? Or, what if he seemed overly eager for your approval? Even if his awkwardness were totally unrelated to the product—the product is great, let's say—you would probably still feel uneasy buying from this particular person. Fear of rejection can also affect the bottom line by inhibiting you from getting out there and approaching people in the first place. If you are so incapacitated by fears of rejection that you retreat from attempting persuasion at all, then you have sealed your own fate.

So we can hate and fear rejection all we want, but it's still going to happen. What do great persuaders do about this? How do great persuaders respond so that their fear of rejection doesn't paralyze them and affect their performance?

The first thing to keep in mind is that even if your audience ultimately concludes that your product or service is not the right fit, they are not rejecting you personally. We generally understand this concept on a superficial level, but I ask you to give it some thought and really let it sink in. Great persuaders think through the reality of the situation in a rational, unemotional way: "This person just met me. She doesn't even know me. She knows nothing of my background, personal interests, hopes, or dreams. It is not me, personally, that she is rejecting." Once you have established this concept, then it naturally follows that your audience's rejection has no bearing on your worth or value. It is totally irrelevant to such matters. Do not allow yourself to feel inferior, embarrassed, or depressed based on somebody else's opinion.

The ability to bounce back after being faced with rejection on any scale is critical in the persuasion world. Great persuaders have the ability to erase the negativity from their minds at will and move on with a clean slate in a matter of minutes. This tendency is worth noting considering the fact that most of us hang on to negativity and use it to nurse our wounds or make excuses for weeks, months, and sometimes even years. Another way to hasten your rebound from rejection is to realize that your worst fears are probably not even realistic. Suppose a sweet deal slipped through your fingers. No matter what you said or did, the client's words were final. In other words, you were *rejected*. Is your life really over? Does your audience now hate your guts? Are they going to smear your good name and come after your family in a mad rage? Are they going to spray-paint the office with slanderous, hurtful remarks? Of course not. The truth is, it just wasn't a good fit. They'll have forgotten about it in a matter of minutes or hours, and you should too.

OBSTACLE #8: LACK OF PREPARATION

Another reason our persuasion power weakens is that we get lazy and don't take the time to prepare. After acquiring a certain amount of experience, we take for granted that we're pretty smooth and that we can always wing it or go through the motions. Well, maybe you'll get away with that kind of approach every now and then, but I'm here to tell you it's a bad practice.

If you catch yourself feeling this way, it's time to take a personal inventory. First of all, you are going to come across as unprofessional, too laid back, or too relaxed. These perceptions are all turnoffs, making your audience feel like the encounter is not important to you. If you're going to be persuasive, you have to do your homework. Furthermore, if you aren't up on critical details, you risk coming across as uninformed. How can your audience take you seriously if you aren't taking them or the situation seriously?

There are four areas in which great persuaders prepare. They are:

1. Knowing your product or service inside and out.

2. Knowing your audience and what their needs and wants are so you can tailor your presentation.

3. Having several tools in the toolbox so that you can present them with options and alternatives.

4. Knowing how to customize your presentation.

OBSTACLE #9: PREJUDGING AND MAKING ASSUMPTIONS

Have you ever caught yourself saying, "Oh, great. Look at that strange person. He's never going to buy," or "I can just tell she's not going to like what I'm offering," "They don't seem that smart," or "I can't change their mind." We do it all the time. We qualify our audience or clients based on only a thumbnail sketch of information, how they look, or worse, no information at all. The problem with this qualification is that we make up our minds before even attempting persuasion, and we end up losing deals, negotiations, or clients because we've already decided our persuasion wouldn't work. This is one of the most devastating mistakes you can make, because you really cannot judge a book by its cover. Many, many times we find that the people who seem to be the least likely candidates are the ones who become a big part of your business.

Your audience can sense when they don't really matter to you. If the ship wasn't sinking already, your lack of interest will definitely sink it fast. Give your audience the time and attention they deserve each and every time. Wouldn't it be a shame to lose a deal because you judged someone wrongly, only to learn later that he ended up going to your competitor with a big order when you had exactly what he needed all along? Furthermore, even if it turns out that what you have to offer is not right for him, he still probably knows someone who does need it. If you've treated him right, he may well send you word-of-mouth referrals. Finally, whether you are consistently successful or not, every time you interact with someone, you're gaining invaluable experience and honing your skills—and you start to become a great persuader.

OBSTACLE #10: ASSUMING CLOSING SKILLS ARE THE MAGIC CURE-ALL

Closing skills were the big thing twenty years ago. We were taught that closing skills were all you needed. If you did not persuade enough people, you had to learn more closing skills. Nowadays, sure, it's nice to have a few closing skills in your persuasion toolbox, but shouldn't you spend more time opening up your audience before you even think about closing a deal with them? In fact, great persuaders don't even have to use closing techniques. That's because their audience is ready to purchase before the end of the conversation has even been reached. You need to be able to connect with your audience, to be sincere and empathic, and to show them you have their best interests in mind. When dealing with a potential client, you should spend more time on connecting, building rapport, and uncovering needs and wants than gunning for a close.

Your audience is tired of those old phrases. You know the ones—tired sales phrases like:

- "The truth is . . ."
- "Trust me on this one."
- "Nobody cares as much as I do."
- "Off the record . . ."
- "I'll treat you right."
- "Call me anytime."

- "Everybody uses it."
- "That looks perfect on you."
- "I'm looking out for you."
- "I'm your friend."
- "I think there is one left."
- "This is a perfect fit."

There is only one way to get anybody to do anything. And that is by making the other person want to do it.
—**DALE CARNEGIE**

Persuading your audience on a product, service, or idea occurs throughout the entire persuasion process, not just at the end of the encounter. In fact, studies show that how you open your presentation is much more important than how you close it. Research also shows that hard closes not only offend, but that over time, they have also lost their effectiveness. And of those that do work, over half the persuaded audience later have buyer's remorse, with many wanting to return the product they felt pressured to buy.

When closing skills are used at the wrong time, in the wrong place, or with the wrong person, another brick is added to the wall of resistance. When people sense that they are about to be hit with a hard close, the wall starts to increase in thickness and strength.

"PERSUAD*EES*" WEIGH IN ON PERSUAD*ERS*

If you don't understand yourself, you don't understand anybody else.
—Nikki Giovanni

We have spent this chapter understanding obstacles and mistakes in the world of average persuaders. Now I want to look at the flip side. We'll look inside your audience's mind and reveal all the things that Persuasion Institute research tells us "persuad*ees*" love about their persuad*ers*. Please notice that most of these qualities are all emotion-based. You made your audience feel good about themselves or comfortable about you. There's nothing here about price, quality, or warranties. These traits keep the brick wall of resistance from forming.

1. *"He kept his promises."* Promises made during the persuasion process are fulfilled. Persuaders are honest and realistic in what they promise—they don't build false hopes or expectations. They "underpromise and overdeliver"—not the other way around!

2. *"She's really dependable."* Successful persuaders proactively give their audience the attention they deserve, doing everything in their power to resolve any problem or concern. They are reliable; nothing stops them from getting the job done or from getting a call back.

3. *"He's clearly very well trained."* Successful persuaders know the ins and outs of their product, including its strengths and weaknesses and how it stacks up against the competition. A great persuader is always an expert on the product, service, or idea he is handling.

4. *"She was very sincere, very genuine."* Real persuaders don't act like they're just out for a hefty commission. They are sincerely interested in their audience and have their best interests in mind.

5. *"I consider him a friend."* Taking the time to build rapport pays off. Personable, likable, caring, and friendly persuaders make the grade. They know that people buy from people they like.

6. *"She'd never argue with us."* A good persuader is not so bent on making a point that she argues with her prospects. She is not consumed with her own need to be right; she knows she will not persuade by demonstrating that her audience is wrong, misinformed, or uneducated.

7. *"He provides solutions that work!"* Helping an audience visualize their success brings the persuader and audience together to illustrate how the product or service will get them there.

8. *"She always takes 100 percent responsibility."* No matter what happens, a great persuader accepts full responsibility for results. When challenges present themselves, she deals with those challenges rather than making excuses.

9. *"I can tell he is really behind his products."* Successful persuaders love what they offer. They know they cannot get someone to believe in their product more than they do.

10. *"She is honest."* It is always clear where a great persuader stands. She is always honest with herself and with others. From this position of strength, she is the audience's friend, advisor, and advocate.

11. *"He's really entertaining—his visits are always a treat."* Winning persuaders are fun and enjoyable to talk to. They help others feel good about themselves and put smiles on people's faces. They are full of charisma, love to be around people, and are the ones to bring light to a room. Their presentations are lively, engaging, and informative.

The Sun and the Wind: A Fable

The sun and the wind were always arguing about which of them was the strongest. The wind believed he was stronger because of his destructive power in tornados and hurricanes. He wanted the sun to admit he was stronger, but the sun held fast to his own opinion and could not be convinced.

One day, the sun decided he wanted the matter settled once and for all, so he invited the wind to compete with him in a contest. The sun chose the contest carefully. He pointed out an old man taking a walk, and challenged the wind to use his power to blow the man's jacket off. The wind felt this would be an easy contest to win and began to blow. To his surprise, each gust of wind only made the man cling more tightly to his jacket. The wind blew harder, and the man held on tighter. The harder the wind blew, the more the man resisted. The powerful blows of wind even knocked the man down, but he would not let go of his jacket. Finally, the wind gave up and challenged the sun to succeed in getting the man to take off his jacket. The sun smiled and shone radiantly upon the man. The man felt the warmth of the sun, and sweat began to appear on his forehead. The sun continued pouring out warmth and sunshine upon the man, and at last, the man took off his jacket. The sun had won the contest.

Meaning: If you push, they will resist. Your goal is to help others want to do what you want them to do and to like doing it.

ALWAYS SEEK TO IMPROVE YOURSELF

Deep doubts, deep wisdom; small doubts, little wisdom.
—**Chinese proverb**

When we take an honest look at our persuasion methods, we often find that what we think we need to work on and what we actually need to work on are two different things. The truth is, even in our areas of strength, there is still always room for improvement. I have never met a top persuasion professional who felt he or she had every single skill perfectly mastered. Great persuaders are always open to new ideas, and they're always willing to look for ways to improve even the most basic skills. Remember, success starts with learning and mastering the fundamentals. If you want to become a better persuader, first master the fundamentals. Know them inside and out and cultivate the ability to execute them flawlessly. Then, as you gain mastery over the basics, you can incrementally add new tools to your toolbox. Whatever skill you are focusing on at any particular time, always be a professional and strive to be the best at what you do. Now, let's talk about the ten traits, habits, and characteristics of top persuaders.

CHAPTER THREE

PQ Skill #1

*Mental Programming of
Top Persuaders*

The psychological edge gained by top persuaders cannot be overemphasized. How do great persuaders prepare their minds for success? What is their mental process before, during, and after the persuasion cycle? This mental aspect is one of the most important (and usually neglected) traits of success.

Almost everyone wants to accomplish their dreams, achieve more, become a better person, or pursue bigger and better goals. And we often know exactly what we need to do to make these things happen. So why don't we do them? Why do we fall short of our dreams and aspirations?

Writing down your goals coupled with a strong desire to reach them won't automatically bring success if you overlook this one vital detail: Successes are not achieved if they aren't first conceived mentally. We are told all the time to be positive, to change that attitude, to have a good outlook. In fact, we are so bombarded with these messages that they are easy to tune out. We gloss over "think positive" messages, saying, "Yeah, yeah, yeah, I've heard that before. Now get to the meat."

In this chapter, we're going to talk about much more than just positive attitudes—I call it "mental programming." This mind training or self-persuasion is what gives great persuaders the psychological edge. It's true that "you'll only achieve it once the mind believes it." By "programming" our minds, we dictate our future. It's just that simple. Think of your loftiest goals, your greatest aspirations. Do you really believe you can achieve them, deep down? Do you? If you can't visualize your success, you are unlikely to ever experience it in real life. We are always thinking and processing information, and our thoughts either propel us closer to our goals or drive us away from our dreams. We have a choice. It is critical that our "mental programming" is always geared to our advantage.

Great persuaders have to forget their past mistakes and focus on their future potential. Rest assured that this is something you can reprogram yourself to do. We all try to hide our mistakes and shortcomings, but you can only bury them for so long before they come back to haunt you. Identify your feelings and where they are taking you. Learn to handle those feelings, thoughts, and emotions on your own. Don't bury them; understand them, master them, and adjust them.

The first step in adjusting your mental "settings" is to take an honest look at where you are now and where you could use some work. Typically, we turn our minds off for subjects and topics that make us feel uncomfortable. But when we are in a state of denial, nothing can change. It's time to blow the dust off of the "Needs Work" files that you've stashed away in the dark corners of your mind. Pulling them out will be a bit like exercising again for the first time in years. In the beginning, it will be quite uncomfortable—maybe even painful. But it's necessary in order to get back in shape. Ultimately, you will be much better off for having dealt

Great persuaders share a "psychological edge" or a "mental program-ming" commonality with great athletes. Here are some examples of what athletes and top persuaders have in common. They both:

- Maintain self-discipline.

- Are able to rebound after a loss.

- Are always learning and growing.

- Continually improve—they can ask tough personal questions after a loss.

- Constantly practice the fundamentals.

- Determine issues that caused mistakes, deal with them, and move on.

- Become stronger with fierce competition—they are strengthened by adversity.

- Visualize success/mental rehearsal of winning.

- Replace negative thoughts with positive thoughts.

- Enjoy the mental/psychological pressure of the game.

- Have the ability to change the way they are feeling.

- Possess a strong self-image and self-esteem.

with your issues. The things that were once so difficult will even-tually become easy.

I have devised two formulas that help illustrate the importance of mindset, or mental programming. If your thoughts are set on cruise control—whether negative or just neutral—then all the training and tools in the world are not going to yield great results. Multiply anything by zero, and what do you get? Zero. The expo-nential success that is possible will not happen. Tools, experience, and training won't do a thing if your mindset is set at zero or even below zero.

Success Equation

(Tools + Training + Experience) × Mindset = Success/Wealth

(100 + 100 + 100) × 0 = 0 (Failure)

Here's another way of thinking about mindset in terms of "pro-gramming." You could buy the most incredible computer. It could be top of the line, with the fastest processing chip available. Let's say you get it with all the bells and whistles, sparing no expense for an ergonomic keyboard, a wireless mouse, and a 32-inch flat-screen monitor with built-in speakers. You get a perfect desk to put it on, and you're ready to go. But without the right software, all the fancy external features are of little value in and of themselves. What good is the hardware if it is sitting there collecting dust and there's no software to run the computer?

EFFECTIVE MENTAL PROGRAMMING IS YOUR FOUNDATION

Anytime we consider a major project in its ultimate and final form, we have to acknowledge the steps that will be necessary to get us there. Becoming a master persuader is no different. Just like build-ing a house or even a skyscraper, you cannot go about it haphaz-ardly. If you were building your home, you would not just go out and get lumber and cement and then start building. You would start out with a visual representation of the finished product. You would turn that into a blueprint. Then you would carefully follow prescribed steps to ensure a safe, functional, and beautiful home, starting with the foundation. Make sure your mental program-ming is built on cement, not sand. Make sure your foundation will withstand the storms that are bound to come.

TIME TO DREAM BIG

What are your wildest dreams—the ones that are exciting to dream about, but seem unrealistic? Is it okay to dream big? I love what Henry David Thoreau had to say about this: "If you have built castles in the air, your work need not be lost; that is where they should be. Now put foundations under them." Yes, it is okay to dream big. In fact, we *should* dream big. Don't give up on your dreams; let them become elaborate castles. This will help you stay motivated and excited about the future. Your job is to put a foundation under your dreams and turn them into a reality.

> *All our dreams can come true—if we have the*
> *courage to pursue them.*
> —**WALT DISNEY**

Your foundation is the mental aspect of the persuasion game. It's a critical skill for all successful persuaders, but it works equally well in all fields. You will not be able to achieve your goals and dreams until you believe you can achieve them. All the best influential techniques and tools in the world will not help you until you first believe in yourself and your future potential.

Unfortunately, no matter how lofty our aims might be, most people will tend to bring you down. When you tell people about your dreams, revealing to them the things you want to accomplish in life, they can have the tendency to be discouraging. Do you know people like that? With the right mental programming, you know where you're going and what you want to accomplish. Then, anything negative or derogatory people say won't matter. They won't be able to crush your dreams no matter how hard they try. The right mindset involves knowing what you want and having a plan to get it. When your psyche (mindset) is in the proper place, you will always follow your heart.

How do you use mental programming effectively? The first

step is to channel your emotional energies into specific desires. You're unlikely to get very far if you don't even have the desire in the first place. Embracing what's closest to your heart will unleash your greatest energy, imagination, and potential. And just like striking oil, you will experience a surge of greater productivity than you have ever had in your life. This burning desire will allow you to transform mediocre abilities into amazing successes... above and beyond what you ever thought possible.

After you have a specific desire in mind, let it simmer in your subconscious for awhile. Many great persuaders work on "programming" right before they fall asleep. As the conscious mind winds down, the subconscious mind kicks into gear. You can take advantage of this transition to turn your thoughts and desires over to the subconscious mind to work on. As you drift off to sleep, try to summon the feelings and emotions that will accompany your success. Vividly imagine the events, the people, and the places that will get you where you want to go. The subconscious mind cannot discern that which is real from that which is vividly imagined. It will accept the positive or negative suggestions that it is given, particularly if they are accompanied by and reinforced with relevant feelings, emotions, and vivid details. You can powerfully program your mind into believing certain things have actually happened. When your mind pre-accepts your victories as already won, you're halfway there. You'll find that promptings, instinct, and intuitions begin to emerge. You'll find yourself thinking, talking, and behaving in a more positive and productive way. In short, all of your energies will be aimed at your goals.

Understand that your conscious and subconscious mind must agree. The subconscious will accept what you feel to be true. The subconscious mind is real. As such, it is something you need to program. You need to look at some of your past programming and see if it is affecting your future success. Understand that when negative thoughts come into your mind, they will always have an effect on your future and what you will accomplish. Your job is to shift all those thoughts to serve your dreams, goals, and aspirations in a positive way. So let's talk about what it takes to strengthen your foundation. What are great persuaders doing to have a strong foundation of success?

FOUNDATION INGREDIENT #1: THOUGHT DIRECTION

I have already spoken at length about the necessity of positive mental programming and the initial steps one must take to put this powerful tool into practice. Great persuaders gain control over their destiny by controlling and directing their thoughts. Considering that our actions are emotion-driven, and our emotions are thought-driven, we've got to get our thoughts on track. They determine everything! You can always remind yourself of this powerful reality by keeping in mind the acronym TEA:

Thoughts → Emotions → Actions

It all starts with your thoughts. Your thoughts lead to emotions and your emotions lead to your daily actions.

Take an honest look at your life right now. Where do you find yourself? That place is the sum total of your thoughts over the course of a lifetime. Where have your thoughts taken you thus far? Where will they take you tomorrow, next week, or next year? It is only natural that negative thoughts will creep into your mind from time to time. As soon as they sneak in, escort them right back out. Don't entertain them. They are destructive. Some people use a rubber band to snap their wrist every time a negative thought comes into their mind. The pain associated with this technique fixes their negative thinking very rapidly. If you don't want to try the rubber band, you can send me a $2,000 check every time you have a negative thought. I am sure that would start to work for you real fast, because that is what it is probably costing you! Your thoughts are what programs your subconscious mind.

> *A man is what he thinks about all day long.*
> —RALPH WALDO EMERSON

Your thoughts are what program your subconscious mind. Your subconscious mind is the center of all your emotions. When your subconscious accepts an idea, it begins to execute it. And then your subconscious uses your ideas, knowledge, energy, and wisdom to find the solution. Now, it might occur in an instant, or it might take days, weeks, or even longer. Nevertheless, your mind will continue working on a solution. You need to understand that as you program your mind, you must ask yourself, "Do I program negative suggestions in my mind?" If you are telling yourself that you can't do it, you are right. When that inner voice tells you that you can't do something, it is important that you replace the thought or turn down the volume or intensity of the negative voice. Then you can change it to "I can do it," "I'm going to win," and "there's plenty for everybody." Altering your inner voice's perception is going to make a difference, and that's the important thing. That's because your subconscious mind will always accept what you program it to think. The bottom line is that you are what you think about, and you have the power to choose what you think. No one can do it for you. Great persuaders work on this mental training every day, while average persuaders think they have heard it all before and are doing OK.

If we are going to squash our negative thinking, we must replace those thoughts with new, positive ones. As you practice mental programming, new and inspiring ideas will intuitively and instinctively arise on their own. But give yourself specific goals and targets to keep your thoughts centered on—this type of focus will nurture and augment your newfound inner strength. Sure your logical mind will fight you on these new thoughts, but eventually your new programming will win. I love what Napoleon Hill, author of the classic *Think and Grow Rich*, had to say about this:

> Every man is what he is because of the dominating thought
> which he permits to occupy his mind. Thoughts which a man
> deliberately places in his own mind, and encourages with
> sympathy and with which he mixes any one or more of the
> emotions, constitute the motivating forces which direct and
> control his every movement, act, and deed.[1]

Ask yourself these questions: What is my dominant thought? What specific thoughts should I deliberately place in my mind? What thoughts are sabotaging my success? How can I encourage actions to arise from these thoughts? How can my rational, conscious thoughts come together with my emotions to complement and strengthen one another?

FOUNDATION INGREDIENT #2: SYNCHRONIZED BELIEFS

Very closely related to directing our thoughts are our beliefs or belief systems. Just as airplanes have guidance systems to direct them, so do we have systems guiding and shaping what we think, do, and believe. Without these influences, we will miss our intended destination, just like an airplane out of touch with the control tower would never be able to land.

What if you had two control towers telling the pilots what to do? The results would be devastating. What many of us don't realize is that we are tuned in to multiple guidance systems simultaneously. For example, we value the input of our parents, spouse, and close friends, and pay heed to rules of the community, society, and often religion. Since so many influences may conflict with one another, we have to prioritize who or what dictates our belief system. If we cannot synchronize these influences, we will wander through life, always missing the target because of our inability to synchronize our beliefs. Great persuaders hit their targets more often because of a well-synchronized belief system.

It may be a very helpful exercise to pinpoint the main beliefs that are shaping your life and to determine whether or not any of them are in conflict with each other. Consider the following possible conflicts of interest:

The pursuit of wealth	"Money is the root of all evil"
Job security	Entrepreneurial freedom
Making it to the top of your career	"Family comes first"
Love of eating	Healthy body
Adventurous	Ducks in a row
You only live once	Restraint, moderation
More free time	Pursue financial independence
Reduce debt	Start investing
Successful business	Successful parent
Spiritual	Wealthy

After you have identified which beliefs shape your life, you need to determine which beliefs represent personal truths for you and which ones you have simply acquired by social and cultural osmosis. Upon closer study, we often find that much of what we believe has not come through our own thoughtful searching. Rather, it comes through imitating what society teaches is appropriate, and what we have been exposed to at home, school, or work. In order to truly change, grow, and prosper, we need to be consciously aware of the rules we've made for ourselves, where they have come from, and what they're based on. Do they all serve you? Or are they sabotaging you? It is time to take ownership of your beliefs.

FOUNDATION INGREDIENT #3: CONFRONTING FEAR

Willingness to confront your fears is critical to mental program-ming. Great persuaders have mastered their fears. You will be tempted to leave your fears buried, but they will invariably come back to haunt you. It is much better to deal with fears directly, especially considering that whatever we fear most is never as bad as we think. Human infants are born with only two fears: fear of falling and fear of loud noises. A newborn baby fears nothing else. All other fears are learned. The good news is that if we can learn fears, we can unlearn them.

How do you unlearn a deeply ingrained fear? You must face it. That's right—you must deliberately put yourself in the situation where you are confronted with it and there is no escape. Any new skill comes only through extensive practice. There is no way around it. Let's say you have a terrible fear of public speaking. If you want to be a brilliant public speaker, then you've got a lot of public speaking to do. You must force yourself to present to others over and over again. Comedian Jerry Seinfeld jokes about how people are more afraid of public speaking than of dying. He says they would rather be in the casket than delivering the eulogy! The truth is, we usually find out, once we've stepped up and faced a fear directly, that it wasn't so bad. Most of our fears are exaggerat-ed doubts or they are based on unrealities. How will you ever come to this realization if you don't look your fears in the face?

Very closely related to fear is worry. While "worry" may seem a lesser emotion than "fear," it should still be avoided like the plague. Worry expends energy (needlessly), distracts you from your goals, disrupts momentum, and sets you back. It also wel-comes negative thoughts that can undo all the good mental pro-gramming you've done. Research tells us that fully 92 percent of our worries either will never come to pass or can't be changed.[2] Why spend time and energy fretting about the things that we are the least likely to be confronted with? It is much better to deal with the realities in front of you than with imagined obstacles.

Finally, even if you've had painful experiences in the past (and who hasn't?), your future is always a clean slate. Don't allow yourself to be immobilized by past mistakes. You are better off for the knowledge and experience you have gained from them. I know you wish you could see the future so you could feel assured that you wouldn't get yourself into a mess again, but unfortunately there are no crystal balls. Careful and effective mental programming is your best crystal ball. Once you've programmed your mind toward your true goals, you must learn to trust. Trust that things will fall into place and follow the best course of action. Dr. Martin Luther King, Jr. said, "Take the first step in faith. You don't have to see the whole staircase. Just take the first step."

FOUNDATION INGREDIENT #4: VIBRANT, FULL-COLOR VISUALIZATION

I can't say this enough: The subconscious mind cannot distinguish between reality and that which is vividly imagined. In a very real way, your future is foreshadowed by your ability to visualize. The more vivid and detailed you can imagine your future to be, the more likely it will be in your actual outcome. If success already exists in your mind, then you have already mentally achieved your goals. Your subconscious mind will then work to make your mental blueprint a reality. Always remember this adage: Winners win in advance.

Another way in which vibrant, full-color visualization is a major factor is that our mind is not a finite resource that will run out. It is not like a computer hard drive or compact storage device. We may have limited time, energy, or money, but we are not limited by our imaginative capabilities. And great persuaders know that you can program your thinking. We'll budget our time better because we are passionate about what we're doing. We'll find greater reserves of energy because the right programming will put a bounce in our step and fire in our heart. Our financial resources will expand because we'll be more productive. As Muhammad Ali said, "The man who has no imagination has no wings." Your vibrant, vivid visualization will give you the wings you need to soar over any obstacle. And since it has no limits, your unfettered imagination is wasted only if you don't use it.

FOUNDATION INGREDIENT #5: FINDING YOUR PURPOSE

I am a firm believer that we all have greatness within us. I believe that we each have within ourselves unwritten books, un-started businesses, brilliant ideas, great inventions, charitable ideas, and untapped energies. But sometimes we have a hard time knowing exactly what our purpose is. We may fill many roles—husband or wife, father or mother, school board member, coach, employee, or community advocate. How do we know which roles will give us the greatest joy and satisfaction? First and foremost, most of us would agree that investing in loving and fulfilling relationships with family and friends is most important. It is a critical part of emotional health and well-being. Beyond this fundamental basis, however, what is it that you live for? What is your purpose and passion in life? Where do your interests and gifts and talents lie? What is your mission in life?

Dare to dream big. Have a purpose that will make getting up in the morning a pleasant task. Know that you are going to become what you want and get what you dream. Don't create a lifeless or unexciting purpose. Many people already know exactly what their purpose is. If you don't know, now is the time to find out. Great persuaders have tapped into and are using their purpose. Understand that for many, the self-discovery process is like sculpting. All you see at first is a big rock and you're not sure what masterpiece lies inside. You know something is there, but you don't yet know how you'll get it out.

To help channel your thoughts on this topic, I've created some questions and exercises. They are intended to be thought-provoking and to stimulate new ideas toward finding out exactly what your purpose is. Give these questions serious thought and meditation. The answers might come right away or they might take days, weeks, or even months to reveal themselves. Stick to it, however, and the answers will eventually come:

1. You are ninety-five years old and have lived a great life. You have accomplished everything you wanted, more than you ever expected. How will you be remembered?

    Purpose Question #1: What is your eulogy going to say? Take the time to write your eulogy.

2. Imagine finding a lamp on a deserted beach. You rub it, and a genie magically appears, offering you a single wish. There is one condition, however: your wish must improve the world. How can you make the world a better place?

    Purpose Question #2: What is your one wish? How are you going to make the world a better place?

3. There are many things you have wanted to try in your life. Fears of failure and criticism, however, always seem to have prevented you from following through. The nagging questions, "What if I fail?" and "What will others think?" have always stopped you in your tracks.

    Purpose Question #3: If you knew you would succeed—if you knew you could not fail—what would you do if you were guaranteed success?

4. You get a phone call from an attorney informing you that a long-lost uncle has left you ten million dollars. You will never have to work another day in your life. What will you do with your time? What will you do with your life?

Purpose Question #4: What would you do with your newfound financial resources and free time?

FOUNDATION INGREDIENT #6: SELF-ESTEEM

Great persuaders enjoy healthy self-esteem. Studies show that high self-esteem strongly influences your success and your ability to persuade, lead, and influence. When your self-esteem (the measure of how much you like yourself) is unhealthy, it tends to trigger anxiety, worry, and fear. Egotism and pride (seemingly high self-esteem) usually reveal low self-esteem. When people exhibit this outward behavior, it is a false front to convince everyone (including themselves) that they are powerful and important. In other words, those who appear to have the highest self-esteem often have the lowest. The truth is, when we have a healthy self-esteem, we don't need to prove our worth to anyone. Worth is innate and has nothing whatsoever to do with external achievements and attainments, no matter how great they may be.

What about low self-esteem? My research has shown that 85 percent of Americans rate their self-image as good to excellent, a statistic that clearly demonstrates the Wobegon Effect. We often try to deny that we struggle with self-esteem, even when it is apparent to others. The fact is we all suffer from low self-esteem in some aspect of our lives. It is key to realize that it's an unproductive focus, because it's tough for us to be objective in such matters. We constantly make irrational and illogical comparisons, like rating our weaknesses against other people's strengths.

We decide that we don't measure up, so we look for inadequacies in others to make us feel better about ourselves. One study found that the majority of people with low self-esteem generally do not see themselves as worthless incompetent losers. Instead, they evaluate themselves neutrally, rather than either positively or negatively.[3]

The short list of symptoms attributable to low self-esteem includes the following:

- Inability to trust
- Compares self to others
- Gossiping
- Inability to take criticism
- Scarcity mentality
- Defensiveness
- Avoidance of rejection
- Avoidance of potential failure
- Resentment of others
- Tendency to tear others down
- Aggressive behavior
- Procrastination
- Concern with who is right
- Inability to accept compliments
- Unwillingness to take risks
- Quick to the offense

How does self-esteem affect persuasion? Self-esteem is like a mirror of what's going on inside. If you have a hard time maintaining a healthy and balanced degree of self-respect, you're going to have a hard time persuading others. You've got to persuade yourself first! It is only when you are truly happy and comfortable with yourself that you will you be able to influence others. You will find happiness will cause you to be generous, upbeat, open-minded, and just more pleasant to be around.

How do you boost your self-esteem and stop beating yourself up? The best advice I can give you is to watch your self-talk and stop comparing yourself to others. We are constantly bombarded by advertising messages telling us how we should look, dress, and smell, what we should eat, and what we should drive. We can never measure up to these standards because they are false hopes or expectations. We cannot expect exaggerated and misleading images and portrayals to be our guides. Stop using phantom measuring sticks. *You* are in charge of your life. *You* decide what matters in your life. *You* decide who and what you're supposed to be.

FOUNDATION INGREDIENT #7: HEALTHY HABITS

Your life is an accumulation of all your habits. Your ability to become a great persuader hinges on your habits and choices. Let's take, for example, some common life situations. We gradually put on weight over the years, but then we want to lose it in a couple of days. Similarly, we spend years getting deeper and deeper into debt, but we want to become financially independent overnight. We decide we want to run that marathon—when it's only a month away. We want to ace that exam, but we only allow ourselves an hour to cram all the material. We start thinking about retirement when it looms only five years out on the horizon. There are many things in life we want to attain in the shortest amount of time and by exerting the least possible effort, but success rarely happens that way. Success is a process, not a quick fix. Progress comes in steps, and the groundwork has to be laid.

So, it is time to take a look at your habits, to acknowledge any bad habits you have, and to understand that over 90 percent of our normal behavior is based on routines and habits.[4] You've picked up your habits somewhere—often without even thinking about it—and you're not even sure why. Great persuaders have spent the time and energy to analyze all their habits—good and bad. We talked earlier about beliefs. Beliefs influence habits. These beliefs are learned from society and from your parents. It often takes a while for the consequences of our habits to appear. Remember, overcoming debt, weight gain, and other addictions are all slowly evolving processes.

> *Three feet of ice does not result from one day*
> *of freezing weather.*
> —CHINESE PROVERB

Here is the key from great persuaders: Instead of trying to drop all of your bad habits at once, try replacing each of them with something else. Pick other activities that are enjoyable and fulfilling, but more productive.

Ask yourself the following questions:

■ Where are your habits taking you?

■ What habits are holding you back?

■ (Pick one bad habit.) How long have you struggled with this habit?

■ Why did you start this habit?

■ What are the long-term consequences of this habit?

■ How are you going to replace this habit?

FOUNDATION INGREDIENT #8: ACCOUNTABILITY

In spite of all our planning and preparation, unexpected challenges are certain to arise. The outcome will depend on your willingness to take responsibility for your success instead of blaming other people, events, and circumstances for your failures. You can't keep waiting, hoping, or wishing for external circumstances to change. Are you waiting for some terrible wake-up call to make you change your ways? Great persuaders take 100 percent responsibility for their destiny. Are you hoping for a miracle, like winning the lottery, unearthing a long-lost inheritance or being Publisher's Clearinghouse's latest multi-millionaire, to change your life and income? It's time to stop wishing and waiting. The bumps in the road are unavoidable, but you'll never get to your destination if you aren't willing to remain in the driver's seat and drive over them. The difference between catastrophe and triumph lies in whether or not you're buckled up, prepared and willing to weather the storm. If you're ready, those bumps will become stepping-stones. Though you will have to endure some discomfort along the way, you'll ultimately end up on higher and better ground.

I have identified three critical areas where you must be sure to take accountability:

1. Stop Rationalizing and Take Action

Are you stuck in neutral? Are you only using first gear? Is your car not getting you where you need to go? Do you resist leaving your comfort zone? You know what you want, but you don't take action. Much of the time, this inaction is due to a game we play with ourselves called "rationalization." See if you play any of these mind games with yourself:

- I just don't have time right now.
- I'll get to it as soon as (x, y, or z) is taken care of.
- I can focus on that after I've tucked away some more savings.
- I can't take on any more projects until I get caught up on what's in front of me.
- My spouse isn't enthusiastic about it.
- I'm too tired.
- I need to wait until the weather improves.
- I'll do it when I've lost twenty pounds and I feel better about my appearance.

■ I don't know where or how to start.

■ I don't know anyone to guide me or answer my questions.

■ I have to plan it out perfectly first, then I'll get to it.

■ I tried once before.

■ It is too expensive.

■ It just won't work.

When we use these excuses, even if only with ourselves, they start to gain some validity, and we start to lean on them too much. We use them to pardon our lounging in the comfort zone instead of giving them fair consideration and then actually doing something about the situation. Rationalization only encourages inaction, so stop the "I would, I could, I should" stuff and do something to take ownership. When you expand your comfort zone, you expand yourself.

Comfort zones are most often expanded through vision and discomfort. We have to go where we are unfamiliar and uneasy. The irony is that this is precisely why you will experience so much growth when you face these new challenges. You will want to do everything possible to balance and neutralize the discomfort. You will be motivated to overcome the obstacles, so that you can find comfort again. It is by pushing back the line again and again that you will grow to incredible heights. You can't ever let yourself get too settled.

2. Stop Blaming Everything and Everybody—Except Yourself

Great persuaders take full responsibility for every part of their lives. We are usually much better at finding fault in others than we are in ourselves. It is easy to get stuck in the blame game because it diffuses our sense of responsibility. If we can place the blame on

**"I do not blame others for my mistakes.
I blame the same people every time!"**

other people, events, or circumstances, we can relieve ourselves of the guilt we feel when we don't do the things we know we should be doing. We also use blame to heal our frustration and disappointment when things don't go our way. We delude ourselves by thinking that the apparent comfort of laying blame is going to make things better.

The truth is, placing blame outside yourself pacifies matters only temporarily and does little to correct the problems that are upsetting you in the first place. In the end, you will feel worse because, not having been dealt with directly, the same issues will continue to haunt and plague you. Elbert Hubbard once said, "It has always been a mystery to me why people spend so much time deliberately fooling themselves by creating alibis to cover their weakness. If your time was used differently this would cure the weakness; then no alibis or excuses would be needed."

Nobody is defeated until he starts blaming someone else.
—Coach John Wooden

These are some of the most common ways I hear people using blame to excuse their problems:

- If only I had better tools to work with.

- My training didn't prepare me for this.

- The economy isn't doing very well.

- The industry is slow right now.

- I got stuck with the worst territory.

- My boss just doesn't like me.

- The cost of living is too high.

- My spouse doesn't understand.

- No one supports me.

- They just don't understand.

3. Begin to Acknowledge and Own Your "Failures"

Sometimes, in spite of the best planning and the best effort, things seem to crumble around us. Things don't go our way. How do we respond? How do great persuaders respond? Most of us rationalize why the project went the way it did, or we try to downplay the shortcomings. We don't want to deal with the reality that maybe we blew it. But the best persuaders not only acknowledge where there was a failure, they're willing to step up to the plate and own their mistakes. As scary as this may be, it has the best long-term benefits. How can you learn from mistakes and failures if you won't even acknowledge them? The key thing to realize is that even though we often fail, that does not make us failures. Systems fail, or plans fail, but the individuals behind them are not failures. They just need to figure out how to adjust the system.

A fall into a ditch makes you wiser.
—CHINESE PROVERB

Failures and setbacks will either make you or break you. They will either give you grief or make you grow. They will either stretch your potential or cause you to stagnate. But a failure or setback is an event; it does not define the person facing it. A failure results from not learning from your mistakes and from not using that valuable education to invest in your future. Rest assured that the universe will test you to see if your goals and dreams are mere fads or a true, burning desire. No one is exempt. Don't ask yourself, "Why me?" Ask yourself, "Why not me? What do I need to learn?" We obtain great experience from our setbacks and our obstacles. We have to learn this way because it is essential for success.

Negative and bad things will happen to anyone. It is how you deal with those events. What will you learn from those experiences? Great persuaders know how to move on and make the next experience a better one.

Some reasons intelligent people fail:

- Lack of motivation
- Lack of impulse control
- Lack of perseverance
- Fear of failure
- Procrastination
- Inability to delay gratification
- Too little or too much self-confidence[5]

Failure is not an event that happens overnight. You don't fail in one sitting. A few different things happening every day are what make you fail. Failure and neglect happen over time. Neglect compounds itself exponentially. It's just like interest that compounds itself with other interest. Before you know it, you are deeper in debt. Over time, failure grows into a huge problem. Don't ignore the initial problem. Like with a small wound, if you ignore it, it may turn into a festering infection, and you could lose a limb.

The most successful people have been through multiple failed plans and endeavors. It is only by getting out there, rolling up your sleeves, and making a few mistakes that you're really going to figure things out. Life is not a textbook exercise. You have to learn by doing, and by risking the mistakes that will be an inevitable but necessary part of your learning curve. When you can learn and grow from your failures, then they will not be failures at all. Rather, they will be major building blocks in your climb toward success.

So how do you adjust your attitude about your "failures"? A huge step in the right direction would be to stop dwelling on the gloom-and-doom aspects and start thinking about solutions. Just because you have failed in the past does not mean you will fail in the future. Also, you may want to remind yourself of the fact that we are often way too hard on ourselves. Nobody gets it totally perfect the first time. I love what soccer coach M. H. Alderson said, "If at first you don't succeed, you're running about average."

FOUNDATION INGREDIENT #9: TRUE HAPPINESS

The great persuaders I have found and interviewed are happy people. They love and enjoy life. They are very successful. They attract people to them. How does society define success? By fame, fortune, achievement, or material wealth. Notice that every single one of these measures is external. None of them has anything to do with inner peace or purpose. We think we will be happy when we finally make our fortune, graduate from college, retire, are promoted, or end up at the top in business.

The truth is that none of these things will give us deep or long-lasting happiness. Numerous studies compare happiness in children versus adults. Why is it that children laugh 400 times a day and adults only laugh 15 times a day?[6] Obviously, the children aren't smiling and laughing about their great status or impressive accomplishments. They find joy and happiness in the simple things—and in simply being. They aren't so worried about impressing others or climbing the ladder of success. What is *your* definition of happiness? We would all do well to check where we've set our sights. What a shame to find at the end of a long life that we've chased the wrong dreams.

> *Success is getting what you want; happiness*
> *is wanting what you get.*
> —DALE CARNEGIE

Here are just some of the ways your life is enhanced when you are happy:

- You perceive the world as safer.
- You are more open with your feelings.
- You make quicker decisions.
- You reduce stress, fear, intimidation, embarrassment, and anger.
- You rate people more fairly.
- You experience better relationships.
- You have greater life satisfaction.
- You have a more positive self-image.
- You are friendlier toward others.
- You make more money.
- Your relationships are enhanced.
- You are more skilled at persuasion.

Today, we have more inventions, more ways to save us time

and energy, yet our happiness has decreased. There are two main reasons for this tendency. The first is that we feel tension and unhappiness with our conflicting goals. In other words, we have goals and aspirations in life that conflict with each other, thereby causing incredible tension and personal unhappiness. Simply understanding that you have conflicting goals is half the battle. Most people just get tense, uneasy, and unhappy over such issues and question why.

Victor Frankl, a celebrated psychiatrist who survived the terror and brutality of the Nazi concentration camps, stated in his well-known book *Man's Search for Meaning:* "Happiness is a condition rather than a destination. Happiness cannot be pursued. The more we aim at happiness, the more we miss our aim. If there is a reason for happiness, happiness ensues. It is a side effect of having a purpose and meaning to life."

This is profound wisdom coming from someone who endured the closest thing possible to hell on Earth. What we can learn further from Dr. Frankl's insight is that because happiness and unhappiness are both states of mind, both of them can be habitual. We are back to mental programming. Most unhappiness, when you get right down to it, is simply our own interpretation of influences in our lives as harmful to our mental, emotional, or physical well-being. Recall a time when you were truly happy, when you were eager to rise each morning and start the day. Chances are very good that you felt an inner assurance and security about what you were doing, and where you were going. Happiness very often includes the constant progress toward an exciting goal or objective. Regardless of the external factors in your life—where you live, what car you drive, how much money you make, etc.—you will feel happiness when you feel a sense of purpose and direction.

TAPPING THE POWER OF
YOUR MIND

In this chapter, we have discussed several of the keys great persuaders use to unlock the power of mental programming in their lives. As you work to implement these new ideas and strategies, you will notice a broad shift in your thinking, attitude, behaviors, and income. You may even find that some of your goals and desires shift. The use of mental programming will sharpen your focus, make your investments of time and energy more productive, and increase your effectiveness all around. Never, ever forget: You won't achieve it unless you can see it. You won't be it until your mind believes it! Want to know where you mentally rank with millionaires. Do you want to know your strengths and weaknesses? Take your millionaire IQ at www.millionaireiq.com. Remember success and wealth is an open book test. If you want financial independence you need to think, act and do what millionaires do.

The Fox and the Grapes: A Fable

One hot summer's day, a fox was strolling through an orchard when he came upon a bunch of grapes. The tempting fruits were just ripening high on a vine, which was hanging over a lofty branch. "Just the thing to quench my thirst and appetite," said the fox. Backing up a few paces, he took a run and a jump, and missed the grapes. Turning round again with a "One, two, three," he jumped up, but with no greater success. Again and again, he tried after the tempting grapes, but at last had to give it up. He walked away with his nose in the air, saying "I'm sure those grapes are sour anyway."

Meaning: You may not achieve your dream right away, but don't give up, or even worse, decide it was never worth pursuing in the first place. Keep trying. Find new ways to go after what you want.

CHAPTER FOUR

PQ Skill #2

Understanding How Your
Audience Thinks

G reat persuaders instinctively sense and know what other
people are thinking and feeling. Imagine if you could get
inside your audience's mind. How do they really feel about
you? Wouldn't it help immensely if you knew the questions and
concerns brewing in their minds? What if you knew their key moti-
vators, their true feelings? Are they telling the truth? Are they lying
to you?

This "sixth sense" takes time to develop. Even the most seasoned persuader needs to take a second look at this skill. Why?
We've found that less than 8 percent of persuaders have mastered,
use, or even understand its importance. They tend to guess and
assume what everyone needs and wants. They might be right part
the time, but of course that means they are wrong most the time.

Understanding human nature is essential to maximizing your

greatest persuasion potential. Have you ever wondered how the mind works? Why do we do what we do? Why do many people do the opposite of what is best for them? Great persuaders can find patterns in human nature and customize their ability to persuade accordingly. Human behavior can be predictable; there are certain triggers or knee-jerk reactions we all have. Great persuaders understand both the decision-making process and consumer psychology. When you go to buy shampoo, there are so many options that you have to develop shortcuts in your decision-making process. Do you decide based on color, smell, recommendation, price, or even ingredients? Typically, you follow your instincts instead of weighing all options. When you ask someone why they bought something, I can guarantee that their answer and the real reason will usually be two different things.

Most persuasion operates below the level of conscious thought. Therefore, understanding persuasion involves understanding the human psyche. Such knowledge empowers you to improve your persuasive abilities. A great persuader can help someone see the inconsistency of his present state and what he needs to do to get to his desired state. This magnifies your effectiveness in relationships, improves your parenting skills, enhances your leadership ability, and helps you sell yourself and your ideas. In short, it maximizes your influence.

Be patient with yourself as you work to implement the principles and techniques I outline in this chapter. Remember, it is not about getting a few more quick-fix gimmicks under your belt. I want you to master these skills to such a degree that they are become natural part of you. I want you to own them. Master these skills and people will feel comfortable around you and you will become more persuasive. You will be able to read them and understand their needs and concerns in a natural, nonthreatening way. People won't even sense that you're trying to persuade them. They'll feel like they're just having a natural conversation with someone who is their advocate.

It sounds too easy, doesn't it? How is it possible that great persuaders can bypass all the scrutiny, skepticism, cynicism, and distrust that people have today? And how can they do so in a non-aggressive, compassionate manner? This is the secret: There are two paths to persuasion—the conscious and the subconscious. Both paths can persuade others to your way of thinking, but each path uses very different means of processing information. With the conscious path, your audience makes a conscious and active effort to understand, define, and process an argument. This type of person is an intellectual decision-maker. She just wants the facts, and she doesn't need the "warm fuzzies." It is best to be direct and not resist this person's desire to cut to the chase. If you try to dress it up, you will annoy, frustrate, and ultimately lose your persuasiveness with her.

With the subconscious path, on the other hand, the listener spends little or no time processing the information. These people respond more to gut instincts, intuition, and other emotionally based triggers. They just want to feel right about things. They are emotional decision-makers. The key to great persuasion is understanding how to balance the use of both logic and emotion.

LOGICAL MIND VS. EMOTIONAL INSTINCT

What are some of your subconscious triggers?

- A smell that brings up a childhood memory.

- Music that increases your adrenaline level.

- Something that disgusts you without your knowing why.

- A color that makes you hungry.

- A word that makes you tense.

- Liking someone you have just met for no apparent reason.

- Certain words, phrases, or gestures that subconsciously make you uneasy.

- The tone of someone's voice that is an instant turn-on (or turn-off).

One of the biggest challenges we face is that we think, and our audience thinks, we are logical creatures. But most of the time, we don't know why we do what we do. In fact, up to 95 percent[1] of persuasion and influence involves a subconscious trigger. This tendency means that inclinations like "It just feels right," "I trust this person," or "I don't like this person" are all based on subconscious emotional reactions. This 95 percent of thought and emotional knowledge occurs in the unconscious mind, without our awareness. What's more, our conscious awareness of reality is the result of the neurons in our brain processing all the information around us in unconscious ways.[2]

The truth is, there is a little bit of both sides—logic and emotion—in all of us. We may be more dominant on one side of the fence than the other, but they are both there. Top persuaders know optimal persuasion appeals to both logic and instinct. For the overwhelming majority of people, emotion is the more powerful motivator, but across the board, the logic component is still critical. Why? Because after the emotional energy of the moment fades, your audience needs something concrete (logic) to fall back on. The elation of the moment is temporary and does you little effect in the long run. The logical component of your approach gives you a way to sustain the momentum long after the persuasive encounter has passed. Emotion inspires us to take action, but logic then justifies those actions.

So how does this concept tie into the conscious versus the subconscious path to persuasion? For most people, the emotional side has the strongest pull. Even the most analytical and intellectual among us have the emotional pendulum that can swing just far enough to sway us. Great persuaders integrate both sides of the equation to best serve the personality type at hand. How do they do this? The Persuasion Institute sought out and researched the input of top persuaders to discover how they achieved this balance and what resources they used. We found that successful persuaders made regular use of the all of the following (regardless of their logic vs. emotional orientation) when attempting to persuade others:

Emotional	Logical
Testimonials	Evidence
Stories	Statistics
Analogies	Studies
Pictures	Graphs
Metaphors	Charts

EMOTIONS WILL ALWAYS
RULE THE DAY

If you would persuade, you must appeal to interest rather than intellect.
—BENJAMIN FRANKLIN

I want to show you some examples of when all the sound, logical reasoning in the world was still no match for people's emotions. Did you know that 80 percent of all new products fail or don't even come close to projected forecasts?[3] Large corporations spend billions on focus groups to see if their product or service is viable. Then, even after focus group participants are sold on the idea, follow-up shows that only a small minority actually buy the product. Logic made it sound like a good idea to focus group participants, but on the actual sales floor, the product or service failed to inspire action.

Let's look at some specific business flops. Did you ever notice that the videophone concept never really took off? Logically, it made sense to be able to see your loved ones as you talked with them. Emotionally, we were not ready to have people see us in the morning, to have them witness that we were not paying full attention to them, or to have them catch us making faces at them.

What about the "see-through fridge" that was going to save everyone loads of money on energy costs? This was a great idea—a transparent refrigerator door that allowed you to see what you wanted before grabbing it, without having the door hanging open while you mulled it over. Logically it made sense, but emotionally the see-through refrigerator made us feel a little vulnerable. Who knew the refrigerator could be just as personal as the medicine cabinet? We simply don't want others to see the rotting lettuce we still haven't thrown out, the juice that spilled three months ago that we never wiped up, or the seven cartons of Ben and Jerry's ice cream that are still in the freezer, even after we proclaimed that we were going to lose twenty pounds by the new year.

And what about when Intel introduced a faulty chip? Statistically, it would only matter in 0.00001 of all computers. Logically, consumers should not have worried about it, but emotionally, the chance of having a faulty chip in a new computer was more than they could bear.

My all-time favorite example is when Coca-Cola launched its new Coke flavor in the 1980s. In the past, Coke was very comfortable at the top of the cola market. Up to that point, Pepsi was not even in the running. Then something strange happened in the 1980s—and Coca-Cola saw their market share suddenly decline. During this time, Pepsi had come within one percentage point of Coca-Cola's market share, even though Coke had spent $100 million more in annual advertising than Pepsi had. Pepsi came out with the "Pepsi Challenge," which in head-to-head blind taste tests against Coke showed that consumers preferred Pepsi by 57 percent. Coca-Cola concluded that it must be because Pepsi was sweeter, so they decided to alter Coke's formula to make it sweeter. Coke tested this new soft drink and found in their own blind taste tests that it consistently beat "old Coke." Given such a response, it seemed like a sure thing. Well, the rest is history. Consumers went berserk and demanded that Coca-Cola bring back the old flavor—even those who had preferred "new Coke" over "old Coke" in blind taste tests!

Coca-Cola COO, Donald Keough, said:

> There is a twist to this story which will please every humanist and probably keep Harvard professors puzzled for years. The simple fact is that all the time and money and skill poured into consumer research on the new Coca-Cola could not measure or reveal the deep and abiding emotional attachment to original Coca-Cola felt by so many people.
>
> The passion for original Coca-Cola—and that is the word for it, passion—was something that caught us by surprise . . . . It is a wonderful American mystery, a lovely American enigma, and you cannot measure it any more than you can measure love, pride, or patriotism.

The bottom line is that people's emotional attachments ran deep, even though they predicted the sweeter-tasting cola to hold the day.

WHY EMOTION—*NOT* LOGIC— DOMINATES OUR DECISION-MAKING

People don't ask for facts in making up their minds.
They would rather have one good, soul-satisfying
emotion than a dozen facts.
—ROBERT KEITH LEAVITT

Acknowledging up front that there are exceptions to any rule, I want to talk a little bit more about why we are primarily emotion-driven creatures. Why is this so? After all, we do have the most sophisticated reasoning powers of all the animal kingdom. What are the main reasons we choose not to think?

First of all, the amount of available information is so overwhelming that we don't attempt to digest any of it. Have you ever heard the saying: "A confused mind says no"? Marketers very deliberately make sure their advertising is clear, direct, and succinct. If there is too much information, or if it takes more than a few seconds to process, the ole brain pretty much just reads it as clutter and tunes it out.

Another reason we don't take the time to think things through is because most of our decisions simply aren't weighty enough to warrant the effort. Both consciously and subconsciously, we selectively choose what we will acknowledge and what we will ignore. This built-in filtering system has been called selective attention or selective avoidance.

People also may ignore certain information when it goes against what they want to believe. The human mind has a great need to always be right. People will tune out conflicting arguments or ignore voices that oppose their ideas or values. Many people will even distort information that goes against what they are looking for. On the flip side, when you find agreement, you have your audience's full attention, support, and interest. In one study, twenty-one students prepared speeches that were written from either a logical or an emotional standpoint. The speeches were presented, recorded, and then evaluated by other college students. Interestingly, there was no real consistency in the findings except that speeches bearing a message that the evaluator agreed with were rated as more rational (even if they were intended to be emotional), while those the evaluator did not agree with were considered to be more emotional (even though some of those were intended to be logical). It seemed that whether a speech was considered logical or emotional depended on the listener. Researchers also concluded that, as a general rule, people seem unable to consistently distinguish between logical and emotional appeals.[4]

So whether we realize it or not, we love shortcuts to thinking. Think about a time when you bought an item, but you didn't take much time to research the product or read the latest consumer guide's ratings. Most of us do it all the time. Instead, we might rely on the persuader's advice, or we might just buy the most popular brand, or we might bring a friend along for his or her opinion. Although we would never admit it, we sometimes even buy an item just because of its color or packaging.

We take mental shortcuts in other situations, too, not just when we're looking to buy. When we decide we like someone, we don't run off and do background checks. If we thoroughly considered every single decision, we would constantly be overwhelmed and never get anything done. Businesses are well aware of this fact. They capitalize on the fact that we are all busy and preoccupied with other things. Great persuaders use this to their advantage as well.

INSIDE THE WORLD OF OBJECTIONS AND CONCERNS

When you become a great persuader, you will view objections differently than most people do. You will even welcome objections and enjoy handling them. Why? You will realize that when people voice objections, it indicates that they are both mentally interested and emotionally involved in whatever it is you are proposing, even if they are skeptical. Interested and involved—what more could a persuader want from their audience? It may be surprising, but when there are no objections during the persuasion process, the persuader's success rate actually drops dramatically.[5] It is much better to get objections out in the open than to let them fester.

Top persuaders do not consider objections or audience concerns as opposition. Rather, they view them as part of the persuasion game. Your audience will naturally delay as long as possible the moment of decision—the moment they need to say yes or no. This stalling can be used to your benefit. Dialogue and exchange of ideas can create a long-term follower, client, or customer. Great persuaders may even solve objections before they are voiced. No matter how good you get, objections will be raised, and the truth is that well-handled objections help you persuade.

Your persuasiveness depends a lot on how you handle objections and concerns, and you can handle them best if you know what the most common objections are. There are thousands of excuses. You'll hear them all, too. But the reality is, there are only seven true obstacles.

Obstacles

All excuses and objections can be boiled down one or more of these seven potential objections:

1. *Fear of Failure*—"Can I do this?" (They don't have confidence in their abilities, fear what others will think if they do not succeed, etc.)

2. *Lack of Support*—Spouse, parents, or friends are unsupportive or condescending. (They hear: You can't do it; it's a scam; it won't work.)

3. *Can't Make the Commitment*—They don't have time/have conflicts with existing obligations (e.g., childcare concerns/want more information).

4. *Motivation*—The discomfort of the prospect's current situation is not great enough to inspire change (e.g., lose weight later; fix it tomorrow).

5. *Functional Concerns*—"Will this really work? Will this solve my problem? Is there something better? Will it fulfill my needs?" (e.g., Is there a better product out there? Will it solve my problem?)

6. *Psychological Trigger*—"It just doesn't feel right. Can I trust this person? My intuition tells me to run." (The persuader did or said something wrong.)

7. *Financial Concerns*—They fear that they can't afford it or will be extremely economically stretched by trying to do so. "Is it worth the investment?" (Is the risk greater than the reward?)

Once you understand that all objections stem from one or more of these seven key areas, you will have a much easier time identifying the root of your audience's discomfort. You will then be able to address their objections in a professional, caring, and non-threatening way. Many persuaders (without realizing it) show tension, uneasiness, or irritation when someone brings up an objection. Usually this unrealized conduct occurs because objection stirs up the persuader's own insecurities (often fear of failure or fear of rejection). The persuader thinks to him or herself, "Didn't I go over that already? I'm doing a good job explaining things! Why is this person still not convinced? Why am I bombing this persuasive encounter? Do I sound like an idiot?" As understandable as this reaction is, it will only makes things worse. Your audience will sense your uneasiness and feel even more uncomfortable. Don't set off more alarm bells than are already ringing!

A calm, natural demeanor opens the door to persuasion and will keep it open in the face of objections. Remember: your audience cannot feel at ease if you don't. They cannot feel relaxed if you aren't. They won't be enthusiastic if you aren't showing enthusiasm yourself. In a very real way, you must create what you want them to feel.

Now we know where objections stem from, let's talk about the optimal time to handle them. You can curb a lot of negative energy when you know your audience is "well-qualified." What do I mean by this? Qualifying your audience is when you define at the outset exactly how you are going to spend your time together and what you want to accomplish. You delineate very clearly what you hope to get out of the meeting. In essence, you are "qualifying" your time together and how it will be spent. Great persuaders are great qualifiers. They don't waste time. Qualification is an excellent approach because it disarms your audience. You've told them exactly what to expect, so they can relax. They won't be caught off guard when you begin to ask questions because they'll understand why you're asking them.

The better you become at handling objections, the more persuasive you will be. The key to great persuasion is anticipating all objections, problems, or concerns before you hear them. Great persuaders are always able to accomplish three critical objectives during the objection process:

1. They can distinguish between a real objection and a knee-jerk reaction. Our studies show that most objections should not be taken at face value, because there are other issues involved.

2. They listen intently to the entire objection before attempting to solve it. They stay calm. Tests have proven that calmly stated facts are more effective in getting people to change their minds than becoming emotional.

3. Great persuaders are never arrogant or condescending. They give their audience room to save face. People will often change their minds and agree with you later, if they have the room to do so.

Another great way to handle objections is to address each of the seven main areas during your presentation, before they become big issues in the mind of your audience. That way, you've stopped any potential resistance before it happens. As a result, there aren't any main objections left for them to bring up. Studies demonstrate that persuaders were four times more successful when they handled objections during the persuasion process, instead of waiting until the end.[6] Also, nothing de-energizes persuasive efforts more than lingering doubts and concerns that remain unresolved in your audience's mind.

What about any concerns your audience voices after your presentation? There are three challenges at work in this scenario. First of all, if you find yourself in this situation, you probably did not "qualify" them sufficiently—your audience was not properly prepared for how their time with you would be spent. Secondly, you probably did not gather enough information from them to accurately anticipate their concerns at the earliest stage. Great persuaders address concerns while they are still seeds, and they will never grow to be rooted plants in your audience's mind. Thirdly, if your audience begins questioning you extensively, you are at risk of being put on the defensive. Such defending of your position flips your roles and weakens your persuasive stance. Worse, if you do project even a hint of defensiveness, it can breed more doubt in your audience's mind than the original concern ever did.

The Man, the Boy, and the Donkey: A Fable

A man and his son were once going with their donkey to the city. As they were walking along by the animal's side, a farmer passed them and said, "You fools, what is a donkey for but to ride on?"

So the man put the boy on the donkey and they went on their way. But soon, they passed a group of men. One said, "See that lazy boy; he lets his father walk while he rides the donkey."

So the man told his boy to get off, and then he got on himself. But they hadn't gone far when they passed three women. One said to the other, "Shame on that lazy man to let his poor little son walk."

Well, the man wasn't sure what to do, but both he and his son began to ride the donkey together. By this time, they had come to the town, and the people began to holler and point at them. The man stopped and asked what they were yelling at. The men said, "Aren't you ashamed of yourself for overloading that poor donkey?"

The man and boy got off the pack animal and tried to think what to do. They thought and they thought. They cut down a pole, tied the donkey's feet to it, and raised both the pole and the donkey to their shoulders. They then walked along in the middle of the laughter of all who met them. Finally, they came to a bridge. That's when the donkey, getting one of his feet loose, kicked and caused the boy to drop his end of the pole. In the struggle, the donkey accidentally fell over the bridge, and because his feet were tied together, the donkey drowned.

Meaning: Try to please everyone and you will please no one. Learn to understand what people mean, not what they say.

PRICING AND THE PERCEPTION OF VALUE

Did you notice on the earlier list of seven potential objections that financial concerns come last? Cost is often the first objection raised, but usually it's not the true reason for rejecting a product or service. Whether you're selling an actual physical product to consumers or an idea to your stubborn teenager, there is always a price involved. It may be financial, an emotional price, or a time commitment. In this section, I'm going use the term "price" in a financial way, but be aware that these principles can be universally applied. I spoke earlier about how we constantly take mental shortcuts. One of the ways we do this is to make comparisons. Instead of taking the time and energy to think everything out, we'll do a quick "side-by-side" price comparison to see how two similar products stack up. The basic formula your audience is always looking for is "How do I get the most for the least?" We all do this. It's human nature. This tendency is critical to keep in mind because as a persuader, you have a lot of control over where your audience sets their benchmarks.

Remember, there is a cost/value relationship. It's not just about offering the lowest price. Many persuaders have a tendency to fight on price, incorrectly thinking that the lowest price or the most economical bid will always seal the deal. The fact is that price is rarely the main factor behind a buying decision. In fact, 68 percent of respondents surveyed by the Persuasion Institute admitted that cost was not the deciding factor, and conversely, when asked what the most important factors were, less than 10 percent cited concerns relating to price. The bottom line is that people want to see value. What seems expensive in one context is economical in another. For example, $200 is nothing if you're getting a $500 value in return. The deal then becomes a no-brainer. If you think about it, it doesn't make sense to buy something just because the price is good, anyway. What if it's not something desirable, useful, or necessary? Would you buy it just because of its price and no other reason? When you do a good job of helping people see how your product will improve their lives and you help move them from their current condition to their desired situation, price is usually the least of their concerns.

THE POWER OF QUESTIONS

One of the major distinctions between mediocre persuaders and highly successful persuaders is the amount of talking they do and the number of questions they ask. We have found that great persuaders ask 2.7 more questions of their audience than average persuaders do. Think about that statistic. An average persuader will ask six questions; a great persuader will ask sixteen. And surprising as it may sound, the highly successful persuaders actually do *less* talking than their not-so-successful colleagues. Why is this? Top persuaders ask lots of questions and then let their audience do the talking. The person asking the questions has control; the person doing all the talking does not. You can control and guide the discussion through questions. As soon as your audience starts grilling you, the tables have turned. You've then lost control.

Consider the following three question-and-answer scenarios and you'll see clearly that the individual asking the questions has control, while, perhaps surprisingly, the one doing all the talking does not have control: (1) An employer interviewing for a job opening; (2) a doctor in the process of diagnosing a patient; and (3) an attorney questioning a witness. Note that in each of these examples, the individual asking the questions is in some sort of authoritative or advisory role. It is not so different when someone comes to you looking for a particular product or service to fit his or her needs. When you are the "interviewer," you glean all the information you need to best guide your audience while still maintaining control over the course the conversation takes. Most importantly, you lead to the final, sought-after conclusion, where your audience jumps on board. And they'll love you for it because they will have done all the talking. Therefore, they will have basically persuaded themselves. You were simply a great listener, sounding board, and concerned advocate!

Another reason the use of questions is effective is because it helps subdue the natural tendency many persuaders have to talk too much. I discussed in Chapter 2 how talking too much is one of the biggest persuasive blunders ever. Nothing kills your persuasive ability more than your inability to stop yakking. Your audience came to get a good deal or solve a problem; they didn't come to hear your discourse on the entire product line. They may listen politely, but as you monopolize the conversation, spouting off about all kinds of sparkles and pizzazz that have nothing to do with their needs and wants, their minds are wandering to where they're headed next. Then, all hope of successful persuasion is lost before you've even asked for it. Information overload just overwhelms your audience.

A final reason questions are so useful in the persuasion process is that they engage your audience. Great persuaders stimulate thinking and get us involved. Anytime we hear a question, we instinctively start seeking an answer. It's an automatic response. Even if we don't actually voice the answer, we think about it in our minds. As you apply this principle in your persuasive encounters, always engage your audience with "easy" questions first. Let general questions precede specific ones. You want your audience to feel comfortable and relaxed, and people are encouraged by answers that they know are right, that don't put them on the spot, and that don't arouse anxiety.

When someone comes looking for advice or input, to buy something, or to make a change in their life, it is all in an effort to improve or enhance their existing situation. The core issue is an emotional need. The actual product itself is just a means to an end; it is not in and of itself the solution. The emotional satisfaction that the product provides, however, is. This is why asking questions is so critical. It is foolish to make a judgment call about your audience's intentions before you've had a chance to ask them questions and to uncover their hot buttons (i.e., what's really driving them). The potential buyer might want your product, but why does he or she want it? That information is really what you need to know to persuade.

Great persuaders know that when someone is evaluating their product or service, they are looking for every reason why they should not purchase. It's a natural defense mechanism. But once they mentally and emotionally commit to the idea that it's the right decision, they start looking for every reason why they *should* go through with it. When we've invested a lot of time and energy into making a commitment, we want to feel validated in our decision. How does this apply to you as a persuader? Once you've helped your audience see the imbalance between their current state and their desired state, and once they feel motivated to act, you must be swift to get them committed. They'll search for positive reinforcement to feel secure in the new balance they feel. If you don't maintain that momentum, their enthusiasm and energy will wane, doubts about their decision will creep in, and they'll drift back to their comfortable state.

Great persuaders use open-ended questions. These questions allow your audience to express their feelings and concerns. Your audience wants to feel that you have their best interests at heart. Open-ended questions also reveal more information. Questions that can be answered with a simple yes or no don't give you much to go on. Remember, you're gathering information so you know best how to suggest the alternative that meets the needs and wants of both parties. You need as much information as possible in order to present a win–win situation. Here are some good examples of open-ended questions great persuaders use to help involve their audience:

- When did you start . . . ?
- Where did you find . . . ?
- What do you think about . . . ?
- Have you ever thought about . . . ?
- How do you feel about . . . ?

HOW MOODS CAN AFFECT PERSUASION

Moods affect our thinking, our judgment, and our willingness to say yes. When the person you are trying to persuade is in a good mood, they are more likely to accept your offer. The opposite is also true. If they're not in a good mood, chances are much higher they won't bite. This is a huge advantage to you when it comes to persuasion. Great persuaders create the right mood. Great persuaders actually put people in a happy state. When we are feeling happy, we tend to think happy thoughts and to retrieve happy ideas and experiences from memory. Conversely, when we are in a negative mood, we tend to think unhappy thoughts and to retrieve negative information from memory.

If you can influence the mood, you minimize the likelihood of objections and resistance. How do you influence mood? The most important thing is to make sure you are in a good mood yourself. Even if your audience is in a good mood initially, a bad mood on your part will quickly dampen their spirits (even if you are trying to hide it). Then, your chances at successful persuasion decrease significantly.

One particular study demonstrated just how much the moods and attitudes of those around us influence our responses. Three individuals sat down to a meal together—two who were in on the study, and one who was unknowingly being evaluated on whether or not his companions altered his opinion of the food. The two conducted themselves in a very disagreeable manner and were unpleasant and contentious. On another occasion, this same individual was brought back to the same place and offered the same food. The only difference was he was given different table companions. This time around, the company was fun, interesting, and enjoyable. How do you think his evaluations of the food differed? You guessed it—the first evaluation was negative, while the second was positive, even though the food itself was identical from the one situation to the next.[7]

There is evidence across the board that mood is a major factor in persuasion. Even simple mood-boosting methods like eating a good snack or listening to pleasant music have been shown to make people easier to persuade.[8] An interviewer who is in a good mood tends to assign higher ratings to job applicants.[9] Happy moods also increase creativity, which is critical for great persuaders.[10] Consumers who are in a good mood will be more aware of positive qualities in products or experiences they encounter.[11] And as any kid has already figured out, parents who are in good moods tend to be more lenient.

Just to reinforce the point, I will highlight one other study. The study was conducted in a hotel room that did not have a window or any other means by which the occupant could know what the weather was like. When the guest ordered room service, the server would describe the weather as cold and rainy, cold and sunny, warm and rainy, or warm and sunny. How do you think these pleasant or not-so-pleasant reports affected the amount of the server's tip? Interestingly, it did not seem to make much difference whether it was warm or cold, but when the weather was reported to be sunny, tips increased by 26.65 percent![12]

KNOWING HOW TO CLOSE THE RIGHT WAY

Persuaders can learn a few things from the world of sales. (Remember, we are *all* in sales.) In the previous chapter, I mentioned that closing skills were not the cure-all for persuasion. But the ability to close is a skill that can be learned to be used in the right way and the right time. For the most part, persuaders use closing or call-to-action skills incorrectly. This lack of proper implementation creates uneasiness and tension between a persuader and her audience. The idea of closing has long been regarded as applying pressure to get a person to buy. This definition of closing is complete nonsense, and there is no place for it in today's business environment. In fact, if you show me a person who uses aggressive, high-pressure tactics to close sales, I'll show you a person whose ability to persuade is so poor that she has no choice but to resort to such measures as a substitute for professional skill.

Most of the time, closing is overused and used in the wrong way. When it is used right and sparingly, it can have a powerful effect by helping others make a decision in a timely manner. The key is to use closing in the right way in any aspect of persuasion. This is where you get the yes. It is not a time to beat around the bush or hesitate. I have noticed with many persuaders that it is like watching them ask a beautiful person for a date. They will do anything, talk about anything, instead of getting right to the point. An interesting note is that 95 percent of audiences say that all the small talk and not getting directly to the point during the close bothers them.[13]

Great persuaders know how to read and interpret their audience's buying signals. It is like the gauges in your car. You need to learn how to read the gauges and know what they mean. Similarly, your audience will tell you when and where to ask for their business. Most persuaders are so captivated with their knowledge of their product or service that they become unable to see any buying signals. When you've mastered the art of persuasion, however, you can tell by your audience's body language, their questions, and their eyes when they are ready to buy. When you miss these signals and shoot past the window of opportunity, your audience's eyes glaze over and you've lost the ability to persuade. Instead of a win–win, you've set up a lose–lose situation. In essence, you have talked them right out of the sale.

STICK WITH IT

Most research shows that a sale is made, on average, after five attempts. This tendency is why great persuaders have thick skins.

They must shake off the rejection and forge ahead with great persistence if they are to stay on track. Studies show that most persuaders usually give up after one or two attempts. Great persuaders know when to keep contacting—and when to part as friends. But you would be surprised by how many sales come through because a persuader approaches the prospect *one more time*. In light of this tendency, it is more surprising that over 80 percent of salespeople still don't approach their prospects again after the initial rejection.

When we get that initial no, we just accept it because we assume the person has thought it through and come to an educated conclusion. Well, the truth is, he or she often hasn't. People forget or they get distracted. That's why repetition and persistence are worthwhile in a persuasion scenario. It's often not that people are putting you off as much as they just haven't taken the time to really sort it all through.

In the sales industry, even among the most seasoned professionals, a 20-percent close rate is considered very successful. The question is: Are most people persistent enough to make ten calls to get two winners? Or if they're not yet seasoned in the art of sales and persuasion, are they persistent enough to make one hundred calls to get one winner? The answer is no, most people are not. Their first person falls through, and they are distraught. That just isn't how the game works, however. So the first part of persistence is just realizing how many no's you have to go through before getting a yes.

THE TWELVE LAWS OF PERSUASION

Great persuaders know and understand consumer mindset and objection psychology. They know that the majority of persuasion involves a subconscious trigger. I have identified twelve laws of persuasion that work below the radar. Knowing these laws is your final step in being prepared to handle whatever objections may come your way. When you understand these laws, then you will understand human nature, and when you understand human nature, you will then understand why your audience is objecting. You will understand what the real issues are behind the surface-level objection, and you will know how to respond in a positive, caring, and helpful way. Grasping these subconscious laws and being able to see how they dictate human behavior will help you be more persuasive. Their mastery is critical to anyone desiring to be a skilled persuader. For an overview of the twelve laws of persuasion from my book *Maximum Influence* go to www.persuasioniq.com.

CHAPTER FIVE

PQ Skill #3

Instant Rapport and Social
Synchronization

We've all been told, "Never judge a book by its cover." Yeah, right. Everyone is judging everyone else. Intentionally or not, people are constantly judging and categorizing others, compartmentalizing them into boxes. There are many boxes—sharp, strange, weird, intelligent, dense, geeky, powerful, annoying, and more. But here's what my research has shown: When you create a positive perception, you have an 85 percent chance of persuasion. With a negative perception, you have only a 15 percent chance.

A great persuader can connect with anyone in thirty seconds or less. First impressions take only seconds to form, but they last a lifetime. This is a critical skill to develop because the cement dries fast. How do you ensure that you're making those early seconds really count? That first judgment or opinion about you is vital to your success. In this fast-paced world, you probably won't get a second chance—you have to make it happen the first time.

Have you ever met a perfect stranger and just hit it off? You had plenty to talk about, and you almost felt as if you'd met before. It just felt right. You were so comfortable with this person that you were able to talk about anything. You probably even lost track of time. Everything just clicked between the two of you. You felt your ideas were in sync and you enjoyed your time with each other. This is rapport.

Rapport is equivalent to being on the same wavelength with the other person. Rapport is the key to mutual trust. With rapport, we can differ in our opinions with someone else yet still feel a strong bond. Rapport can even exist between two people with little in common.

Many persuaders can't tell if they're connecting. They think that they're doing everything right, that they're doing all the stereo-typical rapport-building things: being friendly, enthusiastic, or fun. But the reality is that in most cases, they are not building rapport

© Randy Glasbergen.
www.glasbergen.com

"If you want to be a top salesman like me, you need charm, charisma, and a natural ability to make other people like you. Why can't you get that through your thick skull, you idiot?!"

and are failing to connect with their audience. Studies show that not only do 75 percent of people not like all the "gushy, chit-chatty stuff," but 99 percent of them won't even bother to stop you when they're annoyed.[1] The proverbial bad salesman comes to mind here. He acts too chummy and tells stupid jokes, all the while thinking everyone loves him. You've probably met him. What did you do when you met this person? If you're like most people, you politely endured the encounter, made up some excuse to get him off your back, and then swore to yourself that'd you'd never get stuck talking to him again. Reality check: This annoying person could be you.

The Rabbit with Many Friends: A Fable

A rabbit was very popular with the other animals—all claimed to be her friend. One day, she heard the hounds approaching and hoped to escape them with the aid of her many friends. She went to the horse, and asked him to carry her away from the hounds on his back. But he declined, stating that he had important work to do for his master. "I am sure," he said, "that all your other friends will come to your assistance." The rabbit then asked the bull, hoping he would scare the hounds with his sharp horns. The bull replied, "I am very sorry, but I have an appointment. I am sure, however, that our friend the goat will do what you want." The goat feared he could get hurt. The ram, the rabbit felt sure, was the right friend to ask. So she went to the ram and told him the story. The ram replied, "Another time, my friend. I do not like to interfere, the hounds have been known to eat sheep as well as rabbits." The rabbit then asked, as a last hope, to the pig, who regretted that he was unable to help her. He did not want to take the responsibility upon himself. By this time, the hounds were getting close, and the rabbit decided to run. Luckily, she escaped from the hounds.

Meaning: Everyone will act like your friend until you need help. Everyone will act like they like you until you ask for their business.

94   Persuasion IQ

BUILDING INSTANT RAPPORT

Old-school persuaders have a tendency to walk into an office and look for things on the wall or a desk to make small talk about. They then use this small talk to try to bond with a potential client. There was a time this technique worked. However, we live in a different world today than we did decades ago. Time is now of the essence. Because your audience is pressed for time, you have to get right to the point. Most people don't appreciate useless dribble-drabble. Research tells us that the majority of people do not appreciate unsolicited small talk, and many find it offensive. People buy from those who understand their wants and needs. As I was doing research for this book, I had a couple of managers tell me that they had removed items from their office (trophies, golf clubs, pictures, fish) so that annoying salespeople wouldn't force them into talking about it—one more time.

How do you make sure you're really connecting? You want to be friendly, but not fake. You aim to be engaging, but not annoying. You're enthusiastic, but not overbearing. If you can harness the power of your "rapport radar," you'll be able to read nonverbal cues, detect unspoken messages, and decipher the true feelings behind facial expressions, body language, and attitude. Instead of taking them through a rigid, preformulated routine, your radar will enable you to monitor their receptivity as you go. Great persuaders customize each presentation. Bringing individuality to each exchange provides the critical vitality to the relationship and dramatically increases the likelihood that your audience will feel a connection with you. Any time we are in need of someone else's input, whether it's for a new product, or just because we need advice on a personal issue, we place ourselves in a vulnerable position. In doing so, we acknowledge that we need help. When in this state, we can usually tell whether the person trying to persuade us has our best interests at heart or not.

It is not your customer's job to remember you. It is your obligation and responsibility to make sure they don't have the chance to forget you.
—PATRICIA FRIPP

We know that when we meet someone for the first time, we are being judged by our past history, communicated expectations (what have people said about us?), our body language, our tone of voice, and our word choices. Being aware of how you come across to others, therefore, is crucial to your success. We are very good at categorizing people when deciding whether they deserve our trust or our business. To demonstrate, a study was done with students in which they were shown a two-second video clip of a professor. A survey was then given to the class that had just finished the semester with the professor and those who only knew him from the two-second video clip. The evaluations of effectiveness were very similar between the two groups.[2] In other words, the two-second group made the same judgments as the whole-semester group.

We tend to judge rapidly, and that snap judgment is usually correct. When you meet someone for the first time, he will tend to categorize you like someone he already knows.[3] The positive or negative characteristics of the person you resemble tend to be transferred to you (fair or not). The bottom line is that your audience is pretty good at sizing you up in the first seconds of your meeting. Great persuaders know how to create magic in those first few seconds, and those feelings will last a lifetime.

The old-school approach to persuasion put a lot of the emphasis on the final outcome: clinching the deal, closing the sale. Back then, it was a lot more about getting the sale than having a true and lasting relationship with an actual person. The problem with being so closing-oriented is that a persuasive encounter is not a static, one-sided arrangement. The "persuadee" is not some brainless lump who will unquestioningly accept everything you say. They are living, breathing human beings, which means the exchange is two-sided. You have to establish rapport very early on, making a good and lasting first impression, *and* you have to keep the rapport going.

Many persuaders don't know how to maintain rapport throughout the entire exchange. They're good at breaking the ice and helping their audience feel comfortable, but when it comes to "getting down to business," all of a sudden their demeanor changes. Their light-hearted, jovial manner may turn into intense seriousness as they launch into "the bottom line." When this transformation takes place, what is the audience supposed to think? The person they were joking around with for the past ten minutes has now completely morphed into someone else. Which one is the real person?

There is an interesting correlation between lawsuits and the likeability of a doctor. Malpractice lawsuit statistics show that patients who feel rushed, treated poorly, or ignored (all blows to their esteem) are the ones who are most likely to sue their doctors.[4] Evidence shows that people *don't* sue doctors they like. This correlation also holds true for you, for your products, your services, and your long-term customer care.

Great persuaders don't focus on their persuasive encounters in terms of initial "kick-off" and final "closing." They maintain rapport and connection by keeping the exchange emotionally and logically on the same plane. Think of your audience as a friend you will see and do business with again. Do not allow yourself any abrupt mood changes; be flexible and willing to adjust to the many moods and emotions your audience may go through.

It can help to know some of the things your audience may feel. Consider the following emotions that are commonly felt during a persuasive encounter, and understand that you can maintain rapport by being supportive, empathetic, and understanding:

- Indifference
- Suspicion
- Skepticism
- Inquisitiveness

- Distrust
- Fear
- Nervousness
- Interest
- Curiosity
- Enthusiasm

- Surprise
- Eagerness
- Concern
- Confusion
- Fickleness
- Excitement

THE NECESSITY OF LISTENING

To listen is to learn, and to understand is to inspire.
—**CHINESE PROVERB**

One of the very best ways to establish and maintain rapport is to be a good listener. Most of us hear—but don't know how to listen. Listening is one of those skills that gets a lot of lip service, but we still stink at it. (That same old Wobegon Effect at work!) We think we know all about it, and therefore are already good at it. Unfortunately, nothing could be further from the truth. Studies show that poor listening skills still account for 60 percent of all misunderstandings.[5] Even persuasion professionals—perhaps the most likely of all to trumpet themselves as listening experts—show dismal ratings on their listening skills. When corporate buyers were asked to assess the representatives of other companies, over 50 percent felt that the reps talked way too much, and that they were not in tune with the buyer. And when they did ask questions, they didn't ask the right ones. When it came down to the bottom line—were they persuasive or not—only one percent of the respondents answered affirmatively.[6]

Another common misconception is that great persuaders are people persons or extroverts. Wrong! The latest research shows that the introverts out-persuade the extroverts. Why? Because they

We know there is a positive relationship between effective listening and being able to adapt to your audience and persuade them. Great listeners are great persuaders. Listening mastery:

- Allows for better audience participation.

- Adds impact to the message.

- Helps the audience feel understood.

- Helps the audience understand the message.

- Provides valuable feedback for adjusting the presentation.

listen more, they ask more questions, and they find out what their audience needs. Most extroverts, on the other hand, tend to overwhelm their audience with an endless list of features and benefits and hope one of them will do the trick. Introverts are simply better equipped to sense the wants and needs of their audience. Extroverts come across as old-school salespeople while introverts come across as desirable consultants.

Why are we so bad at listening? A big part of the problem is just that we talk too much. We think we're being helpful by offering lengthy, in-depth explanations. This may be appropriate on some occasions, but for the most part, your audience's emotional side begins to tune out. Let's face it: we are self-centered, self-interested, and self-absorbed. So we talk too much because we like to feel important, knowledgeable, and helpful, but it is still a subconscious focus on ourselves. Meanwhile, the attention and focus of the encounter is not on the audience, and they start to drift.

Now consider the opposite: If you talk less and invest all of your energy and attention into making your audience feel good, important, and understood—if they can feel in that moment that your world truly does revolve around them—then, my friend, you will have rock-solid rapport and lifetime loyalty. Remember, they don't need information overload. They need to feel like they are your top priority. They want to feel confidence in your ability to find the solution to their challenge, the missing puzzle piece. You can't provide that elusive puzzle piece unless you know what it is, and you won't know what it is if you aren't listening. It's been said that "we never learn anything with our mouth open."

> *Take a habit of dominating the listening and let the customer dominate the talking.*
> —BRIAN TRACY

So how do we sharpen our listening skills? For one, consider listening a whole-being experience—listen not just with your ears, but also with your heart, your mind, your eyes. What is this person really telling you? Take it all in. Not just their words, but the whole package—their tone and body language, their hopes and fears.

Studies conducted by the Persuasion Institute have found critical distinctions between the listening skills of great persuaders and those of average persuaders. Compare and contrast the following and see which ways you can improve.

Great Persuader	Average Persuader
Patient.	Anxious to move on to next topic.
Lets the audience speak for him.	Jumps to conclusions, makes assumptions.
Makes sure the audience understands.	Agrees too hastily.
Asks clarifying questions.	Moves on without seeking clarification.
Lets audience finish thoughts, sentences.	Interrupts, cuts audience off.

Great Persuader	Average Persuader
■ Listens carefully.	■ Anticipates—incorrectly—what audience will say next.
■ Cooperative, two-sided effort.	■ Offers a predetermined, one-sided solution.
■ Listens to everything.	■ Listens selectively.
■ Resists distractions.	■ Mind wanders, easily distracted.
■ Takes notes.	■ Shows no interest in long-term relationship.
■ Offers verbal and nonverbal support.	■ Makes no attempts to show support.
■ Senses concern, frustration.	■ Not in tune with audience.
■ Does not become emotional, remains calm.	■ Allows personal emotions to cloud judgment.
■ Offers silence.	■ Talks too much.
■ Nonjudgmental.	■ Judgmental.
■ Knowledgeable in a helpful way	■ Knowledgeable in an arrogant way.

*The inability to listen accurately and effectively
cost this country billions and billions or dollars annually.*
—DAN KENNEDY

I have facilitated exercises, seminars, and training to monitor effective listening. I present persuaders with a win–win situation. We begin with a very easy role play with a very easy solution. To reach this win–win scenario, all my audience members have to do is listen and ask questions. Yet 95 percent of these people start to get angry, confrontational, and tense with each other. The answer is so obvious it could have bit them in the butt, but none of them saw it because they did not listen. They were so concerned with themselves and with winning that they missed the big picture. Listening is a skill we can all work on.

HOW YOU CAN TELL IF YOU'RE REALLY CONNECTING

I've talked about common rapport-building obstacles and how you can know for sure that you're *not* connecting. But how do you know that you *are* connecting, especially when your audience is not going to tell you? One of the most obvious signs of a good connection is that the initial defensiveness and skepticism begins to dissipate. The mood relaxes and your audience begins to relax. They begin to voluntarily offer personal thoughts and feelings without your having to pull it out of them. Openness increases, and resistance decreases. There is more eye contact and more open body language. It could best be summed up by saying things start to "feel right." The exchange is natural, sincere, positive, and upbeat. You could compare it to how you feel when talking to a good friend.

One of the myths about having rapport with people is that you have to agree with each other on every point. Rapport and agreement are not the same. When you have good rapport you will no doubt agree on many things, but this is incidental and not essential. Your ability to connect with people cannot be conditional. To be a powerful persuader, your persuasiveness cannot have any contingencies. You must be persuasive no matter who comes to your table, and that means accepting people as they are and still respecting them, listening to them, and caring about them. Some may think I go too far in saying agreement is incidental. Is it possible to have rapport with someone with whom you agree on nothing? Think of your friends and family. You can probably think of someone you like and connect with very well even though you don't agree on financial, political, or religious matters.

HOW TO CONNECT WITH PEOPLE

Now let's talk about how great persuaders connect with people—what they actually do. Research at the Persuasion Institute sheds light on critical factors that are present when the audience feels the greatest connection with their persuader. Review the list below and see if you can add any of these items to your persuasion repertoire.

- You hold no preconceived judgments or expectations.
- You are positive and upbeat, both up front and throughout the encounter.
- It is clear that you are there to serve, assist, and help.
- You are respectful.
- Your body language is open and friendly (eye contact, gestures, smile, etc.).
- Your tone of voice is warm and friendly.
- Your use of language and word choice is thoughtful.
- You speak in a natural, relaxed manner but still maintain energy and enthusiasm.
- You instill in your audience both hope and optimism.
- Your demeanor is always comfortable and genuine; it's never artificial.

There is a lot of talk about body language and other nonverbal communication. Does it really make a difference? It absolutely does. Every single gesture you make either attracts or repels your audience. Nothing is neutral. If there is a way to enhance your persuasiveness and help your audience feel more comfortable connecting to you, why not use it? Albert Mehrabian, an expert in the understanding of communication, delineates three different ways in which we are perceived:

1. Visually—body language, appearance—55 percent.

2. Vocally—the tone in which our words are delivered—38 percent.

3. Verbally—the actual spoken words themselves—7 percent.[8]

As you can see, our visual self-representation, including body language, is a big player in determining how we will be perceived by others. Most studies show that the majority of our communication is nonverbal, and that people often place more stock in our nonverbal communication than in our words (hence the saying, "Actions speak louder than words"). Most of us are simply unaware of the potency of our nonverbal communication. We don't realize the treasure trove of possibilities it offers. Did you know that the facial muscles can produce over 250,000 different expressions?[9] And even if we did realize these things, knowing how to utilize the information is another story entirely.

Have you ever seen yourself on video and found it to be an unpleasant experience? Most persuaders are unaware of their nonverbal behavior. A powerful way to raise your awareness is to practice in front of a mirror, or better yet, record yourself. Stepping into the audience's shoes and watching yourself from the other side of the fence will teach you far more than any other method.

Being well versed in body language is not only important to how you come across as a persuader, but it also helps you detect when your audience is lying. That's because it's very difficult for someone to control all their nonverbal communication when they are being deceitful. A brief list of some deceptive red flags includes the following:

- Forced eye contact
- Irregular eye contact
- Hesitation
- Irregular speech
- Touching the face
- Increased vocal fillers

Accomplished persuaders understand nonverbal behavior. This understanding will help you make sense of your audience's interest or buying signals. Are they ready to go or are they still resisting you and your message? The studies show, and great persuaders know, that facial expressions, increased mirroring, changes in the eyes, and specific questions asked all dictate that your audience is being persuaded or ready to buy. Spend the time to master the skill of recognizing these signals. This is critical to great persuasion. Your audience is telling you they are ready to go. Are you listening or still droning on?

You will best connect, and therefore best persuade, when you can effectively identify the feelings and emotions of your audience. We carry our psychology in and on our bodies; whether we like it or not, our bodies reflect what's going on inside of us. Being able to discern the psychological and emotional state of your audience by observation helps you know what to say and do next. Their nonverbal communication helps you know how to adjust, monitor, and enhance the persuasive cycle.

The simple act of shaking someone's hand is paramount. Sometimes this is your only physical contact with your audience, and it is a common sign of respect. It can communicate strength, weakness, indifference, warmth, concern, or even disrespect. Your audience will pick up on and judge all aspects of your handshake. They are judging you on:

- Amount of eye contact
- Grip firmness
- Duration of grip
- Type of grip
- Degree of wetness/dryness of hands
- Depth of interlock
- Posture
- Use of other hand[10]

We can decode a nonverbal message at great speed with incredible accuracy. Nonverbal communication is decoded in our brain's limbic system, where genuine emotional expressions and responses are controlled. These activities are all part of our subconscious mind. As such, our nonverbal communication communicates our emotional state, our feelings, and even our tension. Remember that 95 percent of all persuasion is subconscious. We just feel it. The same tendency holds true for nonverbal communication: it is just something we sense.

How do we pick up trust, tension, uneasiness, or even fear? Our feelings and reactions to nonverbal communication usually fall below the radar, and they typically take place in an instant. Microexpressions cross your face in a fleeting instant, lasting less than a few tenths of a second. These expressions appear instantaneously in response to an emotionally provoking event and are next to impossible to suppress. They reveal one's true emotion or feeling.[11] It is also interesting to note that if you can get someone to mimic or configure their faces to resemble a specific emotion, they will experience that feeling. Studies show that these changes in facial expressions also correspond with precise changes in physiological activity resembling the real emotion or feeling.[12]

RECOGNIZING PERSONALITY TYPES

A big part of connecting with people and building rapport is simply discerning what personality types you're dealing with. For personality types like your own, you will probably find that connection and rapport come fairly quickly and easily. What about personalities that totally clash with yours? We talked about this before—to be a master persuader, you must be able to adapt to every individual, no matter where he or she is coming from. Whether you click with someone or not, you're trying to influence him and help make his decision easier. You do this by "harmonizing" with his personality. If you can present a style he'll be comfortable with, you'll be more persuasive. If he's not comfortable, you could say everything right, do everything "by the book," and he still won't budge. I'm sure you can think of a time you didn't buy because you just didn't like the persuader and for no other reason. We are emotional creatures, and we want to like the person who is persuading us. The goal is to persuade others the way they want to be persuaded, not the way you like to be persuaded.

I have learned from great persuaders that the art of adapting to the people you're working with is getting a feel for *their* style. Get used to their style, preferences, desires, and expectations before attempting to persuade. This can be done by observation when you first meet and as you visit and get to know each other.

There are many different classifications psychologists and other social scientists have developed to assess and analyze personalities. If you have a feel for some of the general personality types, it can give you some clues as to how to get inside the person you're working with. Below are some samples of how various schools of social science categorize the four personality types:

Group 1 Yellow	Group 2 White	Group 3 Blue	Group 4 Red[13]
Supportive	Reflective	Emotive	Director[14]
Turtle	Squirrel	Hare	Owl[15]
Amiable	Analytical	Expressive	Driver[16]
Supportive/ Giving	Conserving/ Holding	Adapting/ Dealing	Controlling/ Taking[17]
Relater	Thinker	Socializer	Director[18]
Perceiver	Feeler	Sensor	Judger[19]
Steady	Conscientious	Influencing	Dominance[20]
Amiable	Systematic	Social	Assertive[21]
Sanguine	Melancholic	Phlegmatic	Choleric[22]

As much as we may hate to be categorized, we all belong to a distinct personality type, or at the very least, a personality *direction*—the way we lean most of the time in terms of how we act and react to the majority of stimuli. This means that we are pretty predictable creatures. For the master persuader, it is essential to become a student of human nature so as to be able to predict their personality direction.

Always be on the lookout for attitudes, traits, and behaviors within each style. A great persuader knows there is a great difference between the following:

- Expressive vs. passive
- Friend vs. foe
- Superiority vs. inferiority
- Assertive vs. receptive
- Controlling vs. submissive
- Decisive vs. indecisive
- Casual vs. professional

- Animated vs. lifeless
- Results vs. relationship
- Manipulative vs. sincere
- Approachable vs. standoffish
- Exciting vs. boring
- Impatient vs. tolerant
- Devious vs. honest

HUMOR CAN HELP YOU CONNECT WITH JUST ABOUT ANYONE

Actor John Cleese once said, "If I can get you to laugh with me, you like me better, which makes you more open to my ideas. And if I can persuade you to laugh at the particular point I make, by laughing at it you acknowledge its truth." Understanding the value of humor in a persuasive context gives you tremendous leverage. Your task is not only to realize humor's profound influence, but also to develop the necessary skills to be able to use it in a powerful and ethical way. As you become more and more skilled at incorporating humor into your presentations, you will discover that humor almost always has a place.

Great persuaders naturally develop rapport while using humor. I have always known that humor had some effect on rapport but

Research shows that humor can have all of the following effects:

- Creates a positive environment.
- Increases audience attention and involvement.
- Makes presentations more memorable.
- Entertains and empowers.
- Makes persuaders more likeable.
- Helps establish rapport and connection with the audience.
- Increases audience receptivity.
- Makes the audience more trusting.
- Disarms negativity, skepticism, and resistance.
- Distracts the audience from overanalyzing.

my research is showing that the effect extends beyond anything I ever expected. Ultimately, your goal as a persuader is to give your audience the motivation they need to take the next step. You want them to come away with a fresh perspective that inspires them and makes them hopeful. Think of your humor as having a therapeutic effect that will give your audience the fortification they need to confront their challenges. Dwight D. Eisenhower said, "Laughter can relieve tension, soothe the pain of disappointment, and strengthen the spirit for the formidable tasks that always lie ahead." It is very unlikely that your audience will feel angry, depressed, anxious, guilty, or resentful while enjoying your humor. Your humor can have a domino effect of goodwill and of instilling positive emotions in your audience. If you can help your audience members to feel happier, you will in turn open the locked doors of persuasion and influence. Humor also increases energy and productivity, which will feed your audience's positive emotions even more.

Humor must be deployed cautiously, however. If used inappropriately, it can be offensive and may cause your audience to turn against you. Humor should only be used as a pleasant, but moderate interruption. An important rule of thumb: if you are generally not good at telling jokes, don't attempt to crack them when you are in a persuasive situation. Be sure that you have good material. Non-funny humor is not only ineffective, but it's also irritating. Modify your humor so that it is appropriate for your audience. Once your audience feels comfortable with you, they will be more in tune to your message and more likely to remain attentive. Don't despair if everyone does not laugh. In fact, many people won't laugh, but they will still be smiling on the inside. If your audience is smiling, either physically or mentally, you've done a great deal toward increasing your ability to persuade them.

This vital humor for persuaders not only connects you to your audience but also increases people's attention to you and your message.[23] Humor can enhance or detract from your message. What has been found is that humor that is relevant to your message works (based on a good delivery), but when it is irrelevant, it will disrupt your message.[24]

Humor puts your audience in a good frame of mind. When your audience is in a good disposition, they are less likely to disagree with you.[25] When you develop rapport with your audience, they will like you more.[26] Humor also increases trust.[27]

The skill of using humor can be learned and mastered, but only with consistent practice. Sometimes you may fail, but keep at it until you have harnessed the power to make others laugh. Then others will always feel good when they are in your presence. They will also take what you have to say more seriously. Humor will give you the power to motivate and influence others in a productive, positive way. Humor is rapport. For example, you have noticed I used Randy Glasbergen's cartoons in every chapter to generate a smile. His cartoons are so easy to use and can create that instant connection in your presentations. See www.glasbergen.com for more information about their use—and for more cartoons.

MIRRORING AND MATCHING: SCIENCE OF SYNCHRONIZATION

It is human nature to mirror and match, or to "synchronize" with, the people we connect with.[28] We don't even think about it. It happens so quickly and so subconsciously that without a replay, one is unlikely to even notice it.[29] What if you were aware of it? Could it be used to help you be even more persuasive? Research says definitely yes. When you mirror your audience, you build rapport with them.

Mirroring operates at a subconscious level and demonstrates that the parties are starting to synchronize and get into rapport. People are inclined to follow and obey those they perceive as similar to themselves. If they shift in their posture, you should eventually do so, too. If they cross their legs, you should cross your legs as well. If they smile, you smile, too. When you mirror them, they will subconsciously feel that you have much more in common with them than may actually be the case. Why is this so? He likes you because you are like him. He perceives you the same way he perceives himself. When using mirroring and matching, you want your audience to subconsciously say, "It feels like I have known you for years." Mirroring speeds up the process of connecting and effectively communicating with anyone.

You can develop rapport by mirroring your audience in the following areas:

- Emotional state
- Energy level
- Language
- Breathing rate
- Voice patterns and inflections
- Mood

Obviously, it is imperative that mirroring and matching come across as natural. Great persuaders know how to mirror or reflect their audience's actions, not to imitate them. If people think you are imitating them, they may feel mocked and become offended. They will see you as phony, and they will no longer trust you. Instead of directly imitating, just mirror or match the overall tone and demeanor of your prospect. You can safely mirror things such as language, posture, gestures, and mood. The reality is that mirroring is the best predictor of rapport.[30]

PEOPLE SKILLS: YOUR KEY TO ROCK-SOLID RAPPORT

This principle may seem overly obvious, but it's another one of those skill areas that we think we've mastered when we definitely have not. We found that a full 96 percent of those surveyed rate themselves as much better in their people skills than they actually are. Remember, more jobs are lost due to an inability to work well with others than any other factor. Conversely, the numerous studies show that only 15 percent of employment and management success is due to intelligence or technical training, while the other 85 percent is due to the ability to deal with people successfully. Roger Ailes, public relations advisor to Presidents Ronald Reagan and George H. W. Bush, had this to say on the matter: "If you could master one element of personal communication that is more powerful than anything . . . it is the quality of being likeable. I call it the magic bullet, because if your audience likes you, they'll forgive just about everything else you do wrong. If they don't like you, you can hit every rule right on target and it doesn't matter."

Whole books have been dedicated to this topic, so here I'd like to focus on just a few of the essentials mastered by great persuaders.

1. *Show concern.* Showing concern means exhibiting genuine friendliness and goodwill for the other person's best interest. It means acting with consideration, politeness, and civility. It is the foundation for all interactions and it creates a mood of concern in return.

2. *Be positive.* People want to be around those who are positive and optimistic. Focus on the positive and bring hope to your audience. Hopeful messages bring out the best in people and create a positive image about you and your position.

3. *Remember names.* One of the quickest ways to form an immediate bond with people is by remembering their names. Try to use your audience's name within the first ten seconds of the conversation. Using his or her name tells your audience that you care and value him or her as a person. Research also shows that it increases your persuasiveness.

5. *Smile.* A smile helps make a great first impression and demonstrates happiness, acceptance, and confidence. Your smile shows that you are pleased to be right where you are, meeting this person. As a result, your audience in turn becomes more interested in meeting you.

6. *Build respect.* The more your audience respects you, the more persuasive you will be. Building respect often takes time, but there are things you can do to facilitate it. Remember that how someone feels about you is often influenced by how you make her feel about herself.

HOW APPEARANCE STRENGTHENS OR WEAKENS RAPPORT

Whether we like it or not, appearance definitely affects our ability to gain and maintain rapport. Your physical appearance, your clothing, your office accessories, and your personal accessories are all part of your appearance. Appearance lies in the simple things that many people overlook, like being in shape and watching your weight, picking nice clothes to wear, paying attention to your accessories (i.e., jewelry, glasses, earrings, etc.) or having well-groomed hair. A study at the University of Pittsburgh shows that there is also a direct correlation between good appearance and higher incomes.[31] The bottom line is that attractive people are more persuasive than less attractive individuals.[32]

Appearance can be considered in the following areas:

- Hairstyle
- Clothing
- Weight
- Shoes
- Face

- Strange hairs
- Hands
- Nail care
- Jewelry
- Accessories

Physical attractiveness can trigger greater:

- Confidence
- Strength
- Assertiveness
- Candidness
- Warmth
- Kindness
- Friendliness
- Sensitivity

- Poise
- Excitement
- Nurturance
- Happy relationships
- Social and professional success
- Prestige
- Life fulfillment[33]

As you can see, being "attractive" is more than just looking beautiful or handsome. It deals with the whole person, inside and out. When we come in contact with someone of the opposite sex, the attractiveness concept is magnified. Attractive females can persuade men more easily than unattractive ones, and attractive males can persuade females more easily than unattractive males can. This type of attraction works because it creates a positive association trigger, it captures attentions, and it builds esteem.[34] When a persuader is likable and optimistic, these traits increase attractiveness.[35]

HOW SIMILARITY AND FAMILIARITY STRENGTHEN RAPPORT

Similarity theory states that we like familiar objects more than less familiar ones. The same holds true with people: we like people who are similar to us. This theory seems to hold true whether the commonality is in the area of opinions, personality traits, backgrounds, or lifestyles. If you watch people at a party, you will see them gravitate toward those who are similar to themselves. As a persuader, you can increase your ability to connect with your audience if they feel that they have a lot in common with you.

Here are some ways great persuaders try to find common ground:

- Values
- Goals
- Interests
- Past history, experience
- Point of view
- Attitude
- Morality
- Appearance
- Socioeconomic background
- From same geographical region

Here are some ideas (from great persuaders) for specific things you can do to help find your similarities:

- Share experiences and personal background.

■ Exhibit a pleasant personality.

■ Present a professional and well-groomed appearance.

■ Focus on the positives.

■ Share knowledge and information.

■ Be an active listener.

■ Engage in appropriate humor.

■ Be a good conversationalist.

People hate to be treated like children. Insulting questions, condescending attitudes, or pure arrogance are included in this category. As great persuaders find similar attitudes between them and their audience, the attraction toward these great persuaders becomes more positive.[36] People associate and interact with those they view as similar to themselves. Cliques are often based on such commonalities as friends, gender, age, school, educational background, professional interests, neighborhood, hobbies, and ethnic background. Great persuaders are able to find agreement in as many areas as possible.

PROXEMICS: THE SCIENCE OF SPACE

The anthropologist Edward T. Hall created the science of proxemics, which studies how people use, react to, configure, and occupy the space around them. We all want our own space, and we feel uncomfortable when people violate our personal territory. While it may sound overly obvious, research shows that many persuaders get too familiar, too fast. Disrespect for your audience's personal space—especially when you are first meeting them—will definitely not build rapport. Many persuaders don't even know that they are violating their audience's space. They may think, for example, that by reaching out and touching their audience members on the arm, they will be seen as warm and extending. Such as gesture may really be a turnoff, though. What does it feel like? Imagine that you go to a movie theatre and there are 150 seats but only ten people watching the movie. Social custom calls for everyone to spread out. Let's say you take your seat and the nearest person is twenty feet away. How would you feel if a stranger came and sat down right next to you in this theatre of empty seats? That would be a violation of your personal space.

Understanding proxemics requires an understanding of territory and the role of dominance. The bigger office, the armrest on the airplane, the larger chair, sitting at the head of the conference table, getting into someone's face—all these things have hidden meanings. It could be unwanted touching or jumping into a conversation that damages likeability and rapport. Be observant. How is your use of space perceived by your audience? Always err on the side of giving extra space, instead of too little.

Does the science of proxemics really matter? The distance you keep or don't keep when persuading someone communicates a message. Great persuaders understand rapport and interpersonal communication, and they respect personal space. You will find that the amount of space between a person and a persuader affects the way they are able to interact with each other and what message their interaction sends. When we sit at a table or across from a desk, we each draw invisible lines of our perceived personal space. When these invisible territorial lines are violated, tension is created. We all have regions or areas where we permit others to enter or prevent others from entering. Great persuaders recognize when an invitation to enter their audience's private zone is being extended.

Your audience's intimate area is not to be violated by you, the persuader. In North America, that area extends from your audience's face out to about twenty-four inches. Most social interaction takes place between four and twelve feet of distance. This personal space preference not only varies by individual but also by culture. For example, in the Middle East or Latin America, it is reduced by almost 50 percent.[37] In Germany, on the other hand, the space is larger. It is comedic to watch two people from two different cultures trying to communicate. One is violating the other's personal space, while the other is backing up in an attempt to regain his personal space. The two are in some sort of dance to maintain and regain comfortable communication space.

PUTTING IT ALL TOGETHER

Once you pour the water out of the bucket,
it's hard to get it back in.
—CHINESE PROVERB

Your first impression is critical. It does not matter how fast your car is, or how it will perform, if it is rusted and unpainted. That first impression of a rusted, dirty car will inhibit your ability to convince someone that it is a great car. The ability to create and establish a relationship is critical to your success as a persuader.

Learning to establish an instant connection and to develop long-term rapport will enhance your ability to persuade. Fine-tune your radar to understand how to best respond to the person you are persuading. Remember, first impressions last a long time, and they're hard to change. Applying these principles will ensure that your first encounters go smoothly. Once you've made that initial connection, you can focus on maintaining a genuine, lasting rapport. You will know when you've connected and established rapport. Your audience will be at ease. They will be happy, relaxed, and personable. Your exchanges will flow and feel very natural, like you're talking to an old friend.

So, do you attract or repel people? Of course you answer in the affirmative, but it is not what *you* think, but what your audience thinks that matters. Do you really want to know? Go to www.persuasioniq.com and find out the ten things that you may be doing to repel your audience (and you don't even know it).

CHAPTER SIX

PQ Skill #4

Establishing Automatic Trust

Trust is critical in persuasion. Unfortunately, we live in a day and age when people are more skeptical and mistrustful than ever before. Twenty years ago, the mindset was: "I trust you; give me a reason *not* to." Now the mindset is: "I don't trust you; give me a reason why I *should*." You could say trust is at an all-time low and still falling. Gone are the days when there was a baseline of trust, no matter where you were coming from. A Gallup poll found that the majority of people feel you can't be too careful when dealing with others.[1] Another study found that only 4 percent of respondents felt complete trust in any of the persuaders they had conducted business with in the last twenty-four months.[2]

What does this mean for you as a persuader? It means you cannot assume that people trust you. This assumption is one of the most common persuasion mistakes. Many persuaders think that because they are friendly or good at helping people feel comfortable, they will automatically be trusted. Studies show that nothing could be further from the truth. One study conducted by the Persuasion Institute monitored persuasive situations and then asked both the prospects and persuaders how much trust was established between the two. Only 12 percent of the prospects trusted their persuaders, while 88 percent of the persuaders felt they had established trust with their audience. It is safer to assume that your audience lumps you in with the rest of the world that they don't trust. Don't take for granted that trust exists. You must work to earn and develop a trust that is instant, genuine, and lasting. The bottom line is great persuaders establish instant trust.

It's no use carrying an umbrella if your shoes are leaking.
—Irish proverb

You can have the greatest product in the world, but if there is no trust, there is no persuasion. Trust can be an ambiguous concept, but certain things are quite clear: 1) You can't get others to trust you unless you first trust yourself; and 2) your message will not be convincing to others unless it's convincing to you.

Whenever someone tries to influence us, in our minds we ask ourselves, "Can I trust this person? Do I believe him? Is she really concerned about me?" We are less likely to be influenced if we sense that the person trying to persuade us is driven solely by self-interest. Trust is the glue that holds the entire persuasion process together. Trust is created when you put your audience's interests and wants before your own. Many times trust comes when your audience feels you are predictable. For some people, trust is a leap of faith; they simply want and need to believe in the persuader's intentions. Research shows that, deep down, people want to trust others.

If you can't assume that your audience automatically trusts you, then your next focus should be on how to acquire this sense of trust as early on in the persuasion process as possible. To do this, it's helpful to understand how trust works. Most people can't explain why they trust certain people more or less than others. Usually there is not a lot of rational thought behind it; more often, it is an instinct or feeling about the particular person. Your audience will feel you out, trying to discern whether or not they can trust you and how much. Remember it is a sliding scale. This means that you want to be perceived as trustworthy right away, before your audience members even know you (because, fair or not, they're already making judgment calls about you at this point). Then, you can demonstrate that this trustworthiness is genuine through your correspondence and interactions. Gaining and keeping trust for both the short term and the long term is vital to your success as a persuader.

There are some instances in which the importance of trust is magnified even more. Being aware of these situations can help you devote more effective attention and energy to establishing and developing trust. Consider the following situations:

- It is the first time you have met someone.

- There is misunderstanding or misconception about your industry.

- Your audience has never heard of your product.

- Your company is unknown to your audience.

- Your audience considers the purchase price to be expensive.

- You or your company makes the first contact.

- The company you represent has a poor history.

Trust is also magnified or diminished based on your occupation or profession. For example, medical professionals enjoy higher trust levels than lawyers do. An individual's general trust of a certain industry or profession is dictated not only by experience, but also largely by rumor and reputation (especially if they have had no direct experience with that industry).The Persuasion Institute conducted various polls in which the general trust levels of different professions were surveyed. In a five-year time period, we saw that the trust level generally fell across the board by 5.6 percent. Trust levels in some fields stayed the same, while a few actually experienced small gains.

Here are the Persuasion Institute's most recent findings on profession-based trust levels. Remember it does not matter if these numbers are fair, we deal with reality. The scores are based on a 100-point scale.

Occupation	Trust Level	Occupation	Trust Level
Firefighters	65%	Business executives	34%
Nurses	58%	Computer salesmen	33%
Schoolteachers	57%	Real estate agents	32%
Engineers	56%	Home repairmen	31%
Accountants	55%	Building contractors	30%
Pharmacists	54%	Jewelers	29%
Professors	53%	Auto mechanics	28%
Dentists	52%	Labor union leaders	27%
Veterinarians	51%	State governors	26%
Police	50%	Lawyers	25%
Clergy	49%	Journalists	24%
Small business owners	48%	Large corporations	23%
Medical doctors	47%	Television news	22%
Chiropractors	46%	Gun salesmen	21%
Judges	43%	Insurance salesmen	20%
Daycare providers	42%	Advertisers	19%
Military officers	41%	Stockbrokers	18%
Funeral directors	38%	Network marketers	17%
Bankers	37%	Members of Congress	15%
Nursing home operators	36%	Car salesmen	7%
Real estate investors	35%	Telemarketers	6%

*All things being equal, people will do business with, and
refer business to, those people they know, like, and trust.*
—BOB BURG

THE FIVE CS OF TRUST: NO TRUST—NO PERSUASION

We have already established that we cannot assume we are trusted as persuaders. If we want to master persuasion, we have to proactively ensure that trust is established not only in our initial contacts, but that it remains intact for the long term. Now I want to give you the five essential keys to building instant, genuine, lasting trust. I call these the Five Cs of Trust: Character, Competence, Confidence, Credibility, and Congruence. If any one of the five Cs is missing, you diminish your ability to gain trust, which ultimately means you will not have lasting persuasion. Let's examine each of the Five Cs of Trust that great persuaders have mastered.

Character

Character is the combination of qualities that distinguishes one person from another. These qualities make up who you are on the inside—not the external front you may sometimes put up. Who are you, really? What do you do when no one is watching, when there is no one to impress? How do you treat people when you don't need something from them? Character is also made up of such qualities as integrity, honesty, sincerity, and predictability. I consider solid character to be at the very foundation of one's ability to succeed. No success is going to be profound or lasting in its effects if it stems from questionable ethics, motives, or behaviors. In his best-selling book *The Seven Habits of Highly Effective People*, Stephen Covey offers a powerful explanation for how character is crucial to one's ultimate success:

If I try to use human influence strategies and tactics of how to get other people to do what I want, to work better, to be more motivated, to like me and each other—while my character is fundamentally flawed, marked by duplicity or insincerity—then, in the long run, I cannot be successful. My duplicity will breed distrust, and everything I do—even using so-called good human relations techniques—will be perceived as manipulative. It simply makes no difference how good the rhetoric is or even how good the intentions are; if there is little or no trust, there is no foundation for permanent success.[3]

Newsweek magazine published its findings about character in the workplace. I was surprised to read from the report that today's workers are more tolerant of deception. Many workers feel that lying and cheating are acceptable.[4] *Newsweek's* findings do not stand alone. Another survey found that nearly half of the workers surveyed engage in unethical or illegal acts.[5] I've even found in my personal training of persuaders that many will openly admit that they wish their integrity were better.

What is my point? This disregard for honesty and sincerity is prevalent, but it always catches up with you. People can sense falsehood, deception, or insincerity. Even if they don't pick up on it right away, time will tell. The Latin root of the word "sincerity" is *sincerus,* which means "without wax." Pillar sculptors sometimes used wax to hide their mistakes so they could still pass their work off as unflawed. Years of weathering, however, eventually revealed their deception. As a result, a sincere person was considered to be one without wax or camouflage. It is the same with people. Deception that we may deem as harmless may get us short-term results, but it will not give us the long-term lasting results. It will also taint others' opinions of us.

The worst thing for a persuader is that your audience members probably won't ever confront you about your dishonesty or deception. They are not going to tell you that they think you are lying.

They'll just never work with you again and they'll then tell all their family and friends about the bad experience they had with you behind your back.

Character cannot be developed in ease and quiet.
Only through experience of trial and suffering
can the soul be strengthened, vision cleared,
ambition inspired, and success achieved.
—Helen Keller

Even if you're an honest person of admirable character, it is human nature for people to cast sweeping judgments and formulate opinions without all the facts. So, if you want genuine trust and lasting persuasion, you must avoid even the slightest appearance of anything that might be considered dishonest. If you never place yourself in a situation where one might be misled about you or your integrity, then your good, hard-earned reputation will never be compromised. Phillips Brooks, a nineteenth-century clergyman, taught: "Character is made in the small moments in our lives." Remember in those small moments to be caring, honest, and forthcoming. Don't embellish the story to make it sound better; don't omit certain information to cover your own skin. Put the interests of others ahead of your own and keep your priorities straight. In all things, exercise self-discipline, self-control, and self-mastery. Character is knowing what is right, desiring to do right, and then doing what is right.

Clear conscience never fears midnight knocking.
—Chinese proverb

Abraham Lincoln stands as a worthy role model for anyone who wants to develop character. He once said, "When I lay down the reins of this administration, I want to have one friend left. And that friend is inside myself." This statement is particularly poignant given that Lincoln was criticized so viciously while he was in office. Nevertheless, he always remained true to what he believed in his heart was right and just.

Competence

Competence is your knowledge and ability in a particular subject area. True competence comes from lifelong learning and experience. Competency exists on many levels. When we are observing someone from a distance, or when we are meeting them for the first time and our experience with them is very limited, we subconsciously perceive and assign them a certain competency level. These assumptions are usually based on external things, such as their title, their position, their height, how they dress, their demeanor, which kind of car they're driving, the décor of their home or office, how they talk, their tone of voice, how they carry themselves or even things like what kinds of electronic devices they use. These initial impressions are important, because they can influence whether or not someone will pursue working with you. But then you have to be sure you possess true competence— not just perceived competence. Can you really do what you say you can do? Can you deliver? Does your audience think you have the skills, the knowledge, and the resources? Whether or not you have this deeper level of competence becomes glaringly obvious as people interact and work with you.

One of the key ways to keep your competency on track is to be a lifetime learner. We consider others to be competent when we see them continually learning and advancing their training and education. I can remember going to buy computer products and discovering that I knew more about the product than the sales reps did (and I didn't know much). In an attempt to cover up their lack of knowledge, these ill-informed salespeople tried to bluff their way through my questions. If they had kept themselves educated about the product, the field, and the industry, then they would not have lost my trust in them as competent professionals—and they would not have lost a customer. Learn to become the best in your field. Demonstrate you know your area of expertise. You should know more about your subject than 99 percent of the population.

The following are some specific ways you can gain and strengthen your competence, both actual and perceived:

- Degree(s)
- Professional standing
- Affiliations with respected organizations
- Publications
- Referrals

- Endorsements
- Reputation
- External surroundings
- Definite opinions
- Testimonials
- Passion

Confidence

According to Jay Conrad Levinson of *Guerrilla Marketing* fame, confidence is the number-one reason people are persuaded to buy. Confidence triggers trust. Demonstrating confidence in everything you do increases others' abilities to place their trust in you. I've seen plenty of people of only average to mediocre ability persuade and influence more effectively than others who were more naturally gifted simply because they exuded greater confidence. The people we admire and look up to the most are usually the type of people who know what they want and how to get it. Can you think of a time when you went to buy something and your sales rep seemed uneasy? I'm sure you felt less eager to buy, even if you originally fully intended on making the purchase.

People who lack confidence will always struggle to effectively influence others. If you're perceived as doubtful or underconfi-dent, your audience will feel that way, too—about your product,

People who lack confidence:

- React defensively to criticism.

- Are not honest about their own abilities/limits.

- Shun the advice/input of others.

- Tend not to learn from their mistakes.

- Set unrealistic goals, and have unrealistic expectations.

- Use problems as an excuse not to try.

- Blame others for things that go wrong.

- Avoid new challenges and play it safe.

- Repeat self-defeating habits over and over again.

- Expect the worst, and often get it.[6]

about your idea, or about anything else you might ever try to present to them. Don't panic if you don't feel full confidence 100 percent of the time. Complete confidence in oneself takes experience, time, practice, and patience.

Since confidence is so critical, it is important to understand what hinders it. This can be summed up in one word: fear. All doubts, questions, concerns, insecurities—can ultimately be traced back to fear in one form or another, whether it's deeply hidden or right out on the surface. You need to make sure that your confidence and your commitment to success are bigger than your fears. What does your audience sense? Are you afraid to pick up the phone and talk to people? The desire to overcome your fear needs to be bigger than the fear itself. When you are afraid, that fear will breed doubt and suck the energy right out of you. While it is okay to have fear, you must be able to handle and manage that fear. Consider the following factors that inhibit our confidence and feed our fears:

- Lack of belief
- Replaying failures
- Negative attitude
- Indecision

- ■ Destructive thoughts
- ■ Hesitation
- ■ Worry
- ■ Mood

You may be wondering, "If a persuader seems overly confident, can't that also hurt the ability to persuade?" The answer is a resounding yes. It is important that you do not come across as cocky or arrogant. How can you tell the difference? It's all about the intention. Confidence is motivated by a sincere desire to serve—you can help make a difference, and you know you can do a great job. You know that you have the tools, resources, ability, and inclination to do the job that's required of you. In contrast, cockiness is driven by a need to serve yourself, instead of serving others. Deep down, cockiness actually reveals insecurity—the very opposite of confidence. The distinguishing feature seems to be intent. Cocky individuals seek approval, recognition, and honor from all the wrong sources, in all the wrong ways, and for all the

"Nine out of 10 people disagree with my idea, which sends a very clear message — nine out of 10 people are idiots!"

Cocky or arrogant behavior usually elicits these types of complaints:

- He acted like he owned the place.

- She treated me like a child.

- She did not listen to what I wanted.

- He didn't ask permission to . . .

- He blamed others.

- She did not own up to her mistake.

- He never answered my question.

- She always has to be right.

- He is arrogant and condescending.

wrong reasons. They are really looking for pats on their own back. Cockiness is self-centered, whereas confidence is people-centered. Cockiness is about the persuader and confidence is about the customer.

If your audience senses any pride or superiority, the game is over, just the same as if you were not confident enough. It simply doesn't matter if you say and do all the right things. If you turn people off, it's a lost cause. If they don't like you, they will not allow themselves to be persuaded by you. Here are some additional ways you can avoid the trap of seeming overly confident:

- Always be genuinely open to feedback or criticism.

- Be willing to listen—don't always be the one talking.

- Admit when you're wrong.

- Be honest about the strengths and weaknesses of your product and competing products.

- Never interrupt.

- Ask questions to demonstrate care and concern *and* to be sure you clearly understand your audience's needs and wants.

- Use external credibility (testimonials, endorsements, referrals, etc.) instead of "tooting your own horn."

Credibility

When the Persuasion Institute polled respondents to see which one of the Five Cs they thought was most important, 44 percent said credibility. And interestingly, despite its importance, respondents felt it was established only 11.4 percent of the time. Why the dismal rating? It's harder to gain credibility nowadays than it ever was in the past. Most consumers are fairly sophisticated and have grown cynical with all the exaggerated and unsubstantiated hype that is thrown at them. People who have been burned in the past develop thick skins against almost every persuasive message they are exposed to.

How do you overcome this lack of credibility? Here are several ideas great persuaders use to boost their credibility:

1. In this very skeptical world your prospect is looking for a weakness. If you don't give them some type of weakness (personal or product), they will assign a weakness for you. Great persuaders increase credibility by revealing an apparent weakness and turning that perceived weakness into a desired benefit.

2. Credibility is enhanced by every minute of preparation. Great persuaders never "wing it" or leave anything to chance. If your audience ever feels you should know the answer but don't, you have lost credibility. Plan, rehearse and polish your presentation. Always research your audience.

3. Your audience is going to judge you in the first thirty seconds. How do you really look? How are you really coming across? Can you maintain eye contact? Is your appearance professional, polished, and what your audience expects?

4. When you enter a low-credibility situation or when you audience does not know you, borrow the credibility from someone else. Who can endorse or recommend you? Who

can introduce you that already has credibility with your audience? Learn to always ask and get testimonials from happy current clients.

5. One of the quickest ways to lose your credibility is to bad-mouth the competition. You don't have to resort to pulling down others to enhance your own product or service. If you can't persuade based on the quality of your product or service, it is time to change careers. If the consumer needs to be legitimately warned about the competition, provide ways for them to find out for themselves.

6. Pepper your presentation with credible facts, figures, statistics, or studies to reinforce your message. Never assume your audience thinks you are credible without using outside resources. Always remember to cite your sources. Your audience will always believe someone else before they will start to believe you.

7. Find ways to reveal your qualifications without coming across as a braggart. You need to reveal (or display) your expertise, qualifications, education, and experience so you will come across as the expert. The moment your audience accepts you as the expert, you have their undivided attention. Reveal to your audience why you are the expert and why you have earned the right to persuade about your product, service or idea.

You have to be careful in how you explain and exhibit your credibility. If you launch into a laundry list of your accomplishments or of your education and titles, you might be perceived as a self-centered. Take advantage of less direct or less self-proclaiming ways to show your audience how competent you are. For example, you can hang your degrees on the wall, have someone else give a brief bio, or have someone else offer his recommendation of you. You can borrow credibility from others using a testimonial or statement from them. Credibility can also be defined as "having expertise, trustworthiness, goodwill, dynamism, extroversion, sociability, composure, or expertise."[7]

Trust builds with dependability. Do you have a track record? Are you a person of your word? When you make an appointment, are you there on time? When you commit to doing something for someone, does it get done as promised? Do you think they will forget? Well they don't. They usually just won't bring it up. When you make a promise, do you make sure it is kept, or are you full of excuses and alibis? Be reliable and follow through with all your promises. Credibility is "the single biggest variable under the speaker's control during the presentation."[8]

Another way to boost your credibility is to present yourself in a calm, organized, and authoritative manner. Being overly emotional or flustered throws your credibility out the window. Consider the most highly successful attorneys or CEOs. No matter how rushed or pressured they are, you don't ever see them running into the room, slamming their stuff down on the table, and throwing themselves into their chairs. No! They are absolutely composed at all times. That's because they must always convey an air of authority and control. Jury studies show that lawyers who appear well organized are thought of as being more thorough and better prepared than their disorganized counterparts, which of course increases their credibility.[9]

Another way to boost credibility is to be honest about your product's weaknesses and how it compares with the competition. Your audience is looking for a weakness, so give them one. If

If your prospects are doing any of the following, check your credibility:

- Calling to complain
- Failing to give you repeat business
- Exhibiting no loyalty
- Needing outside testimonials
- Needing references
- Not returning calls
- Canceling appointments

you don't give them a weakness, they will assign one to you or your product. Or your audience might think what you have to offer is too good to be true. Revealing a weakness tends to make people view you as more honest and trustworthy than those who try to cover up a product's faults. Great persuaders can even turn weaknesses into selling points. Think of the following examples:

Avis™—We are #2 and we try harder.

Listerine™—The taste you hate twice a day.

7-UP™—The Un-cola.

L'Oreal™—Because I'm worth it.

VW™ Bug—VW will stay ugly longer.

Dr. Pepper—Not a cola.

Heinz Ketchup—So thick it pours slowly.

Smucker's—With a name like Smucker's, it has to be good.

When you're able to turn weaknesses into positives, your audience is going to appreciate that you have been open and frank. You never want to appear defensive or to be avoiding your audience or the issue. Let them understand your thinking process. I am not saying you need to disclose everything about your product or service. What I am saying is that you need to provide a reason why you are doing what you are doing. Be willing to share the information your audience needs and wants.

Trustworthiness increases when we are big enough to own up to our mistakes and weaknesses. People can forgive weakness, but they won't be as quick to forgive cover-ups. Oftentimes, if a persuader is open about a weakness or a drawback in a particular product, he still seals the deal. Frequently your honesty will be the characteristic that wins people over. In the end, it is better to risk rejection than to hide something your audience will later find out on their own. If your audience is only hearing positive angles from you, you could lose credibility. At the Persuasion Institute, I have analyzed thousands of client offers. One common theme among many of the deals that were not selling is that they appeared too good to be true. While the offers may have been legit, the audience just did not buy into them. When we weakened such offers, sales often increased.

Lying decreases your credibility. Most persuaders think that only when they are *caught* in a lie that it decreases their credibility—and they have been caught, more often than they know. We have found that most people will not call you on a lie. They will sense it, mentally record it, and simply won't come back. You thought you would get away with it, but they still sense it. Whatever you want to call it—lying, fibbing, untruthfulness, creative license, fabrication, or deception—it still decreases your overall trustworthiness.

As you already know, a confused mind says no. A related danger is that when you don't provide any additional forms of credibility, the audience will base all their opinions of credibility on you, the communicator.[10] And the more involved your audience is, emotionally or financially, in the topic you're going to present to them, the harder it will be to establish credibility. (High involvement increases skepticism, and it is credibility that will decrease that skepticism.) An audience with low involvement (not a big issue) in a particular issue is more likely to defer to other sources (including you) because it requires less mental strain or emotional investment than trying to figure it out for themselves.

Congruence

Great persuaders are congrooent, but what is congrooence? When things match, we don't notice, but if something seems off, it grabs our attention either consciously or subconsciously. Just like the misspellings in the first sentence of this paragraph. You noticed it and your mind told you something was wrong with that word.

Congruence is when your words match your actions. Agreement and harmony between what you say and what you do are paramount to instilling trust in those you work with. The more consistent and congruent you are in every aspect of your life, the more honest and genuine you're perceived to be. If you believe in your message, you'll practice what you preach. If you practice what you preach, you'll be more authentic, and the door of trust will then swing wide open for you. When you possess congruency, there's no need to manipulate or camouflage your behavior.

An interesting study was conducted with dentists, whereby an ad was put in the newspaper asking for people to participate in a painful dental procedure.[11] The first amazing thing about it was that people actually showed up. During the first part of the study, the dentists were told that they would only pretend to use a painkiller on their patients. A placebo would actually be given. The dentists were instructed to do everything just as they would normally do during the procedure. Most of the patients in this half of the study felt pain during their dental procedure. During the second half of the study, the dentists were told to perform the exact same procedure, except this time they would be administering a real painkiller to their patients. When told that the dentist was going to numb their mouths, most of these patients did *not* feel pain. The reality was, however, that unbeknownst to dentist or patient, a placebo had again been administered again in place of the painkiller. Even though in the dentists' minds they had performed the exact same procedure with both sets of patients, the first group of patients picked up on incongruities in the dentists' behavior. Consciously or subconsciously, they knew that something was wrong and thus felt pain.

Are you congruent with your history, your last interaction, and your reputation? Does your nonverbal behavior match your actions? Are your emotions congruent with your message? What are your audience's expectations of you and your message? When your past history and your message don't match, flags of incon-

What are some nonverbal behaviors that will trigger incongruence and a sense of deception?

- Forced eye contact
- Shifting back in chair
- Rubbing lips
- Scratching your face
- Dilated pupils
- Yawning
- Pitch of voice rising

gruity will wave in your audience's face. Suspicion will be roused and your audience will start to look for things that are wrong with you or your message. This inconsistency will decrease your ability to gain influence and trust. That's because humans are natural lie detectors. When we attempt to fake congruence, we must also spend our time and energy trying to fake our message.

YOU NEED ALL FIVE Cs FOR POWERFUL, LASTING TRUST

We've looked at trust and its role in the persuasion process in depth, including at the five critical components that we call the Five Cs of Trust: Character, Competence, Confidence, Credibility, and Congruence. For powerful, lasting trust, all five Cs are essential. Gaining trust is like having a car that is finely tuned. The engine and all the components work together harmoniously. None of the five Cs will carry you where you need to go without the others. Let me use a story to illustrate how these elements work together. Imagine you're experiencing extreme tooth pain. You've put off going to the dentist as long as possible, but now nature is telling you that your time has run out. You've recently relocated, so your previous dentist is 1,400 miles away and no longer an option. You ask your new friends and neighbors about their dentists and you get the following five responses:

1. "My dentist has great character. He belongs to my church group. He is one of the most honest people I know. He's not very *competent*, though. I heard he's famous for sticking the needle completely through your cheek."

   —Would you go to this dentist?

2. "My dentist went to one of the top dental schools in the country, and he's one of the top dentists in the state. He's extremely competent, but has no *character*. In fact, you will have to wait two months before you can see him because he's in prison for insurance fraud."

   —Would you go to this dentist?

3. "My dentist is a really great guy. He's a goodhearted person, and he always does exactly what he says he's going to do. But he doesn't have much *confidence* in his work. One time he said to me, 'I've never been very good at reading X-rays. I'm not sure whether I should give you a root canal or just leave the tooth alone.'"

   —Would you go to this dentist?

4. "I'm not sure if my dentist is licensed. I didn't see any degree or diplomas on his wall, and no one seems to know where he went to school. His office doesn't have the latest equipment. He doesn't take insurance and I always have to pay cash instead of writing a check. Everything lacks *credibility*."

   —Would you go to this dentist?

5. "My dentist is a nice guy, but he doesn't keep his stories straight. There is something about what he says and how he acts that doesn't seem right. He seems to lack *congruence*. He tells me one thing and I feel something else. I don't think I am getting the whole truth. It just doesn't feel right. He tells you one thing one time, and

another thing the next time. You never know which one is right."

—Would you go to this dentist?

I'm sure you would spend more time trying to find a dentist who met all five criteria before you'd resort to one who lacked even one of the Five Cs of Trust. If a person is lacking in just one of these areas, every aspect of his or her ability to build, gain, and maintain trust will be affected. As a persuader, never assume that people trust you. Always show your audience that you are someone to be trusted, no matter the circumstances.

WHERE CAN YOU IMPROVE?

*A man who doesn't trust himself can never
really trust anyone else.*
—CARDINAL DE RETZ

In closing, review the following behaviors that are harmful to building trust. Can you improve in any of these areas?

- Ignoring promises
- Being unreliable
- Overpromising and underdelivering
- Covering up failures and weaknesses
- Blaming others
- Using emotion without logic
- Shifting responsibility
- Exhibiting apathy for others
- Being inaccessible

- Never apologizing

- Gossiping and telling half-truths

- Hiding mistakes

- Assuming people completely trust you

- Presenting an offer that is too good to be true

- Embellishing to make your point

- Being emotional and unpredictable

The Fox Who Lost His Tail: A Fable

It happened one day that a fox caught his tail in a trap, and in the struggle to free himself, he lost his tail, leaving behind an ugly stump. At first, he was ashamed to show himself to his fellow foxes. But at last, he wanted to put on a better face upon his bad luck and called all the foxes to a meeting to consider a new proposal. When they had gathered together, the fox proposed that they should all cut off their tails. He pointed out how inconvenient a tail was when being pursued by enemies. He also mentioned how much a tail got in the way when they wanted to sit down. He failed to see any advantage in carrying about such a useless thing. "That is all very well," said one of the wiser foxes, "but I do not think you would have recommended us to dispense with our chief ornament if you had not happened to lose it yourself."

Meaning: Your audience is always wondering what is in it for you. Can they trust you? Why are you dispensing advice? Should they trust you? Would you do what you are asking them to do?

How trustworthy are you? Do you have the credibility to gain the trust of your audience? Go to www.persuationiq.com to take your credibility evaluation.

CHAPTER SEVEN

PQ Skill #5

Command Attention with Power and Authority

G reat persuaders know and understand how to use different forms of power, but if you're like most people, you just cringed at the word "power." Is power something we're really allowed to talk about? Is it good or bad? Can we have power over our audience?

The answers to these questions depend on what form of power it is, how it is used, and what the user's intentions are. We all possess different forms of power in different situations. It is human nature to respect and follow power and expertise, and power certainly has legitimate, ethical, and necessary uses. Of course, we know that power can also be used unethically to manipulate and control. When your audience trusts your power, you will be very persuasive in moving them to action. What causes them to trust your power or authority? What causes them to trust your expertise? They trust your expertise and authority when you can help them access something they need or desire. This could be a product or service, rewards, freedom, or information.

Power is different from force. It is all about your intent. Power creates trust, it strengthens, and it empowers. Force must always be maintained, enforced, and warranted. Force sucks the energy and life out of people. True power encourages, revitalizes, and creates unity and synergy. Power causes us to listen and obey. Force causes us to be skeptical and run. David R. Hawkins said it best: "Power gives life and energy—force takes these away. We notice that power is associated with compassion and makes us feel positively about ourselves. Force is associated with judgment and makes us feel poorly about ourselves."[1]

Note that power or force does not have to be exerted to be effective. A bank robber holds power as he stands menacingly with a gun, yet he doesn't have to actually shoot anyone to exert this power. A police officer wields power just sitting in her car, even if she's not following you with her siren and lights on. The same is true for a doctor wearing a white coat. We also see it with the knowledge of a college professor. Knowing your boss can fire you, even if she hasn't made any threats, still gives her a position of power over you. Similarly, when you know more about whatever it is your audience needs or wants, it automatically places you in the position of greater power, expertise, or authority.

It is a natural human tendency to seek power. The whole world runs on the concept of power. There would be no order without it. The legal system has the right and the power to interpret laws. The military and police have the power to enforce laws. A manager has the power to fire a dishonest employee. Parents have the power to discipline children. Power is ingrained in our psyches, our culture, and our society. Dr. Floyd Allport, a social psychologist, talks about this instinctive characteristic in his book *Social Psychology*.[2] He believes that deep inside each person there is a desire to incite reactions in others. He further asserts that as we age, these desires grow more strongly into a yearning for control.

Why is power so seductive? When we possess power and control over our environment, we feel strong, invincible, and often exhilarated. As Abraham Lincoln said, "Nearly all men can stand adversity, but if you want to test a man's character, give him power."

The question remains then: What makes the exercise of power good or bad? Power tends to make us nervous—and with good reason. We have all seen great abuses of power—tragic, deadly abuses. We also feel that power inhibits our personal freedoms and our ability to control our own lives. We have all been forced to do things against our will, and we have all experienced someone who threw his power around in the wrong way. These past experiences are why the pursuit of power makes us feel uncertain. Many people think that power is all about using dominance, coercion, force, strength, or even control. Sure, these actions can be used as power, but not for genuine, long-term persuasion. Great persuaders don't get stuck on power trips or feel the need to exert themselves on others. They understand that the proper and ethical use of power opens their audience to persuasion. Most average persuaders use power in the wrong way—too much, too soon, and too obvious.

> *Do not remove a fly from your friend's forehead*
> *with a hatchet.*
> **—CHINESE PROVERB**

The truth is that power is a neutral force. It can be used for great good—to inspire and to uplift—as well as for coercion. The good or bad quality comes from the person who is exercising it. If a police officer uses his power to stop a murderer, he is bringing good to the world. However, he could use that same power to help drug dealers. The power is the same, but the intentions of the person behind it are different. If you know you will use good judgment and wield your power to benefit, serve, and protect others, the pursuit of power shouldn't intimidate you.

THREE DIFFERENT RESPONSES TO POWER

Research shows that there are three general human responses to power. First, there is an *automatic response*: following instructions without thought or questions. Second, there is a *manual response*: You understand that the person has power over you, you have second thoughts about doing what he requests, but you comply anyway because of his greater power position. Third, there is *resistance*: You know the person has power over you, but you do everything within your personal power to resist. Great persuaders need to be able to interpret individual reactions to power. That's because each reaction requires a different response.

Great persuaders have the ability to use power to put their audience at ease. Power has impact on the choices and actions of the people you deal with. Great persuaders can also sense when to use or not use certain forms of power. We know that power that is used in the wrong way has a repelling effect, the exact opposite of the persuader's intention. When you have the ability to customize your power with your audience, they are more likely to accept your advice. Understand that when we are unsure or have doubts, we always look to an authority figure or expert to help us make a decision.

Power, if used improperly, can make people feel controlled or manipulated. By wielding the wrong power, you may get the immediate results you're looking for, but they're not going to last. What's more, you're not going to have people's respect or friendship when all is said and done. Ultimately, this kind of manipulation will destroy cooperation and breed resistance. It will kill enthusiasm and stir up animosity. Great persuaders know how people handle the different types of power.

I would rather try to persuade a man to go along, because once I have persuaded him he will stick. If I scare him, he will stay just as long as he is scared, and then he is gone.
—**General Dwight David Eisenhower**

USING AND RESPONDING TO POWER

There are many different forms of power, but I want to focus on four in particular. They are not negative or unethical forms. Rather, they are positive and ethical forms that boost and enhance your ability to persuade. They are authority, respect, knowledge, and reward power. Great persuaders know and use all these different forms of power.

Authority Power

The main source of a persuader's power is her authority. You know what you are talking about, what you are doing, and how you can solve your audience's challenges. Authority power is based on how other people perceive your expertise. You have authority over others when they believe you have greater clout or strength than they do. Authority allows those in a power position to persuade others to comply with them because of their status, position, background, or rank. CEOs of large corporations carry this form of power. Police officers are another excellent example of this type of power holder: you feel compelled to comply with police based on their position of authority.

We can't be blamed for our natural urge to follow authority. We have been taught since childhood to believe and follow proper authority. It started when our parents taught us that disobedience to authority is wrong and has consequences. We are taught to listen to our teachers, our parents, or political figures. Often, we submit to authority figures in an effort to avoid pain and punishment. Disobedience can lead to stiff penalties.

Exercising authority power does not mean being arrogant or condescending. Your audience has certain expectations that you have the ability to help, serve, and advise them. Your audience has a need, and they want it fulfilled. They want to be led in the right direction by a competent and knowledgeable person. Think of a time when you were faced with an important buying decision. Do you think that an apologetic and insecure persuader, one who was constantly wringing his hands, would have made you feel more positive and confident about your purchase? Probably not. In fact, you probably would have found his behavior annoying, maybe even disturbing. Have confidence and demonstrate your expertise.

Great persuaders look at the persuader–persuadee relationship as a student–teacher relationship. Think of yourself as a consultant or an advisor; you are the teacher. When you look at the persuasion process this way, you are practically under obligation to conduct yourself as an authority figure. When you can demonstrate that you are proficient, skilled, and capable, you gain additional authority power. People value and admire those who know their job and thus they submit to your input, suggestions, and counsel.

Authority power can be further subdivided into the following categories: authority by position, uniform, title, public opinion, or external characteristics. You will see with the following examples that authority power can have a very persuasive influence on an individual.

Authority by Position   Those who have authority based on the position they hold within the community have positional authority. Such authority figures include a boss, the U.S. President, or a judge. A landmark study conducted by Stanley Milgram at Yale University illustrates just how powerful positional authority can be. Milgram had some participants pose as "teachers," while others portrayed the "learners." The teachers were told that they were going to help the researcher test the learners' learning levels by giving the learners progressively more intense shocks each time they answered memory questions incorrectly.

Of course, no real shock was administered, but the teachers did not know this, and the learners were instructed to act as though the pain were real. The purpose of the study was to see how far the teachers would go in obeying the head researcher's authority, even if it meant inflicting great pain on another human being. Many of the labels on the switches warned "Danger: Severe Shock." The results were astounding. Two-thirds of the subjects delivered as much pain as they could (450 volts), pulling all thirty of the shock switches, even when the acting learners pleaded, begged, and even screamed for them to stop the experiment.[3]

This experiment strikingly demonstrates several key points concerning positional authority. First of all, the teachers were noticeably uncomfortable with what they were doing. In fact, they hated it. Many of them asked the researcher to please end the experiment. But when he refused, they continued on, trembling, perspiring, and sometimes even laughing nervously. In spite of their extreme discomfort, almost all of the teachers continued to obey the head researcher until the experiment was over. When the teacher left the room and started to give the instructions by phone, however, only 23 percent went on to deliver the maximum shock. This result demonstrates the importance of the face-to-face component of positional authority.

The converse is also revealing. When the scripts were reversed and it was the learners who were ordering the teachers to deliver more shocks while the researcher protested, not even one single person obeyed! In this scenario, 100 percent of the teachers refused to obey the learners over the researcher. After obtaining the shocking results of this experiment, Milgram wrote, "It is the extreme willingness of adults to go to almost any lengths on the command of an authority that constitutes the chief finding of the study."[4]

When someone has more authority than you do, you may automatically assume that whatever that person says must be true. An FAA study illustrates this point. It found that many errors by flight captains were not challenged or corrected by other members of the crew. This blind obedience to position and authority resulted in catastrophes. One airline, concerned about this evidence, tested their own flight crews via flight simulators. Specifically, they created conditions that would lead to mental overload and emotional stimulation. The captains often made fatal mistakes at a critical moment. The airline was shocked to find that 25 percent of the flights would have crashed because the subordinates did not take corrective action and challenge the position of the plane's captain.[5]

Authority by Uniform Does it matter how you dress? Do great persuaders actually think about what they wear? Do clothes really "make the person?" In most instances, the answer is yes. When you wear a uniform to play a certain role, that uniform evokes authority and prestige. Now, when I say uniform, I am including business attire in that definition. Business attire is considered the uniform of power persuaders. People create vital impressions of power with what they wear. When you wear the right clothes for the situation, you can persuade without even speaking.

Think of what a police uniform says. Imagine a police officer trying to clear a riot situation in street clothes. The uniformed officer will get our immediate attention because we respond and respect uniforms. Now what about negotiating a big deal in jeans and a faded T-shirt? Even clergy who wear their robes command more respect and are able to persuade and influence better than they can when wearing street clothes. We see a doctor in a white coat and automatically assume he is a medical professional who knows exactly what to prescribe. Likewise, when a businessman shows up in a $1,500 suit and polished shoes, we automatically assume he is in charge or is the decision-maker.

In one experiment, a man would stop pedestrians in New York City. The experimenter would point to another man nearly fifty feet away, telling them that "the man had "overparked and didn't have change to put in the parking meter." He would then tell them to go give the man the necessary change. Researchers watched to see how many people complied with the experimenter's request when he was dressed in normal street clothes versus when he was dressed as a security guard. After giving the command, the experimenter would turn a corner so he was out of the pedestrian's sight. Incredibly, almost all of the pedestrians obeyed when he was dressed in uniform, even after he was gone! When he was dressed in street clothes, however, less than half of the pedestrians complied with his request.[6]

In another study, Lawrence and Watson found that individuals asking for contributions to law enforcement and healthcare campaigns gathered more donations when wearing sheriffs' and nurses' uniforms than when they just dressed normally.[7] The experimental conclusions prove that dressing the part increases your power and authority over others.

Authority by Title   We are all suckers for titles because they create power. For example, the titles "president," "CEO," "esquire," "manager," or even "boss" create certain expectations of authority and respect. When we hear "doctor" in front of a name, it automatically registers in our mind that this person is important, powerful, or intelligent. We don't even ask if he or she graduated at the top of his or her class. In the medical profession, the doctor is the head decision-maker. We love to hear "two out of three doctors recommend . . ." or "nine out ten dentists use . . ." Our tendency to follow such recommendations is all based on title authority power.

In one particular case, researchers wanted to test to see if the power of authority by title won out over established rules and regulations. They were looking to determine whether nurses would administer an unauthorized drug to a patient when requested to do so by a doctor they didn't know. A researcher would call a nurse on the phone and tell her he was a doctor and that he wanted a 20 mg dose of a particular drug to be administered to a certain patient. He instructed her to do it as soon as possible so the drug would have time to take effect by the time he arrived. He further stated that he would sign the prescription upon his arrival.

The experiment intentionally violated four rules: first, the hospital forbade prescriptions to be made over the phone; second, the drug was an unauthorized one; third, the dosage was dangerously excessive—in fact, double the amount specified on the label; and fourth, the order was given by a doctor whom the nurse had never met or even heard of. In spite of these red flags, a whopping 95 percent of the nurses headed straight for the medicine cabinet and on to the patient's room. Of course, researchers intervened before they actually administered the drug.[8] A subsequent study asked nurses to remember a time when they had obeyed a doctor's order that they felt was potentially harmful to the patient. When asked why they had complied anyway, 46 percent said the doctor was the expert and authority figure in the matter.

Your title is important. When you hold a title that projects power, respect and attention are directed toward you, and your ability to persuade others is strengthened. Think about it—when you are upset with a company or a persuader, you want to talk to the boss, the manager, or even the president. I was amazed when I was hired to do sales for a local company and my business card read "regional sales manager." Although I was just a rookie, I did notice that the title on the card garnered respect. Find a title that is appropriate for you and your work. For example, "vice president," "senior partner," "managing director," or "account executive" might work for you.

Authority by Public Opinion   Authority by public opinion occurs when a person has power or authority not directly because of experience or expertise, but simply because of his or her reputation. An example of this type of power can be seen in scholarly journals, which are more likely to publish articles written by people who are established and renowned within their respective fields versus people who are virtually unknown. What has your audience heard about you, your product, and your company? What is the public perception about you? Very often, public opinion carries more weight than facts.

Here is another great example of public opinion authority. An error in Intel's Pentium chip was detected in 1994. News spread quickly about the flaw, and public outcry exploded as Intel tried to downplay the issue. Reality was the average user would never be affected by this flaw. There was only a one in a nine billion chance of getting an inaccurate result.[9] It wasn't long before Intel was flooded with e-mails and phone calls requesting a no-questions-asked return policy on the microprocessor. In the heat of the whole mess, complaints peaked at 25,000 in one day! In spite of the huge public outcry, Intel refused to offer the requested return policy. Not surprisingly, the press got hold of the story, and Intel's stock dropped dramatically. Finally, Intel was forced to adopt a new return policy. What was the result of resisting public opinion for as long as they had? A mere $475 million write-off.[10] In just a matter of weeks, public opinion had influenced the value of the entire company, and ignoring public opinion proved a very costly mistake indeed.

Authority by External Characteristics   Great persuaders command authority. Like it or not, some people view others as powerful simply because of their physical characteristics. For example, being tall can emit authority over another, even before you've spoken to that person. If you look back through history, presidential elections in the United States have been won by the taller candidate twenty out of twenty-three elections since 1900.[11] Height also scores points in the battle for affection. Research suggests that women are significantly more responsive to a man's published personal ad when he describes himself as tall.[12] Another example of how physical characteristics portray authority is exhibited in our response to someone who has a deeper speaking voice. We subconsciously respond to deeper voices as more commanding and authoritative.

**"I read someplace that tall employees
get better pay and faster promotions."**

Recognize that many of the physical characteristics we possess (or strive to possess) serve as status symbols. The more positive physical attributes we have, the more we tend to be perceived as "rich and powerful." One study conducted in the San Francisco Bay Area showed that people driving expensive cars received better treatment from other drivers than those driving more modestly priced cars. For example, motorists waited significantly longer before honking at a new luxury car that was lingering at a green traffic light than at an older economy model doing the same thing. What's more, nearly all the motorists honked their horns impatiently more than one time at the cheaper car. In the case of the luxury car, 50 percent waited respectfully, never honking at all.[13]

Another determinant of external authority is our surroundings. In one study, the appearance of a professor's office changed the way a student perceived that professor. The students were shown pictures of different professor's offices. Some were clean and some were cluttered and disorganized. Researchers found that the photographs of the office had a dramatic influence on the students' overall perceptions of the professor. In particular, the students who saw the cluttered and disorganized office rated the professor as less conscientious, less agreeable, less competent, and not as friendly.[14]

Appearance affects your authority. External objects and environment also affect perceptions of power. It is therefore wise for all of us to check out our appearance and surroundings to make sure we're sending the right message.

Respect Power

Respect commands itself and it can neither
be given nor withheld when it is due.
—**ELDRIDGE CLEAVER**

Respect power is the hardest of all power types to gain. This power comes naturally to great persuaders. It must be earned one drop at a time, but it is also the longest lasting. It has a sustained influence on the audience long beyond the persuader's actual physical presence has departed.

Respect is based on the sum total of how you have conducted yourself in your professional and personal affairs. If you have shown respect, integrity, and character in all your dealings, people will know it. People will sense it. Respect power is the type of power an individual has when he is placed in special regard because of his honorable character. As a result of being honorable, other people trust and respect these individuals and willingly follow them. Parents and religious leaders often possess this type of power. Because of respect for these individuals' overall conduct, people are influenced on the spot, without needing to analyze the persuader or the persuasive situation.

Respect

Respect is enhanced when there is:

- Integrity

- Character

- Dependability

- Mutual respect

- Unspotted history

- Long-term stability

- Proven track record

- Unquestionable reputation

Knowledge Power

Francis Bacon once said, "Knowledge itself is power." Knowledge power is based on proficiency in a certain subject, procedure, or situation. Remember that you are the expert. People can be persuaded if they think you have more knowledge or expertise than they do. For example, lawyers, mechanics, and doctors possess knowledge power. People rely on these professionals' opinions, believe what they say, and trust implicitly what they do because of the extent of schooling or experience they have. We accept the arguments and data of people we assume have knowledge, whether it's real or perceived. In addition to coming from formal education and training, knowledge power also comes from life experience and innate intelligence and aptitude.

Great persuaders use three different types of knowledge power: informational, resource, and expertise.

1. *Informational Power.* When you know something others need to know, you hold power over them. Informational

power is exercised when someone needs, wants, or desires the information, facts, or data you possess. As Aristotle Onassis said, "The secret of business is to know something that no one else knows."

2. *Resource Power.* If you have access to key persons, commodities, goods, or services that are valued by others, you hold some power over them. As the saying goes, "It's not what you know; it's who you know." Are you perceived as having the right affiliations? What connections do you have?

3. *Expertise Power.* When you have special skill sets, expertise, or knowledge that others believe is relevant to their needs *and* which exceeds their own, they will do what you say or listen to your opinions. Why are you the expert?

Check yourself against the following list to be sure you're up on all that you could be in your field. Do you have:

- Product knowledge?
- Competition facts?
- Industry information?
- Important affiliations?
- Access to useful information?
- Economic forecasts?
- Specific expertise?
- Awareness of your audience's needs and wants?

You have to keep yourself aware of and on top of new industry improvements, changes, and updates, so that you always possess cutting-edge information. You will very quickly lose your persuasive power if your audience detects that they have a more sound or current knowledge base than you do.

The bottom line is that the persuader who has done the research and has the most knowledge is the one who comes out ahead. Always try to stay ahead of the pack.

Reward Power

Reward power refers to delivering rewards or benefits to influence others. These rewards can be financial, material, or psychological in nature. Reward power is the fastest way to persuade. You have to be careful, though, because the danger is that such rewards can come to be expected. Once you condition your audience to expect something for their compliance, they will always seek external rewards for their behavior. This strategy may well cause them to do your bidding only for the reward and not for any other reason. In that case, even if the person were willing to exhibit the desired behavior *without* the reward, once the reward has been given, the subject will rarely perform the desired behavior without the reward.

One experiment proved this concept. Subjects sitting together at a table worked on a puzzle for half an hour. Some were being paid to be research subjects and some were not. After the half hour was up, the experimenter told the subjects that the solving session was over and that they had to leave the room. The experimenters then began to monitor the behavior of the subjects when they went into the waiting room.[15] What would they do during their free time? Would they play with the puzzles? Would they choose other activities? The study found that those subjects who were paid to do the puzzles were far less likely to play with them for fun during their free time in the waiting room. On the contrary, those who did not receive an external reward for their efforts were far more likely to play with the puzzles during their free time in the waiting room.

Persuaders know that a behavior that is chosen out of free will last longer than a behavior that is selected in expectation of external reward.

Reward power is based on utility—on an understanding that in every transaction the potential for exchange exists. Basically, reward power recognizes that there is always something I want and something you want. We can meet each other's needs by swapping what we have for what the other wants. Other examples of reward power include sales bonuses, paychecks, incentive clauses on contracts, bonus miles on airlines, and bonus points on credit cards.

It is important to understand that some incentives will work well with one person but not with another. For some people, money is the optimal reward. For others, it is recognition. As a persuader, you need to find the reward that will most inspire each person you work with. In other words, you must understand the desires of the person or group you are attempting to persuade. Reward power is extremely effective in changing human behavior and in increasing your ability to persuade. You can get what you want with minimal effort.

However, there are several inefficiencies to note when using rewards. For one, "diminishing returns" quickly takes over when you employ this type of power. Diminishing return means that the more you use the reward, the less powerful it becomes. When people become accustomed to an incentive, they can also become bored with it. As we discussed earlier, they will then either expect more of the reward, or drop performance standards if it is removed. One example is the common practice of offering elementary school children rewards for reading. They win pizza or other prizes after they have read a certain number of books. These incentives often backfire, though, because many of the children think they need a reward to read.

Reward power ultimately leads to the desired outcome, but the incentive generally has to be repeated each time to get that desired outcome. The reward is only effective as long as the person doesn't see a "better deal." It is important to recognize that your incentive will always be compared to the next person's offer. Rewards reinforce behavior, but so as long as you are employing them, also expect your audience to keep demanding them.

USING POWER TO PERSUADE

The ability to use power is like having a turbo charger on your car. It increases your speed by enhancing your power. Your ability to harness these forms of power will enhance your ability to persuade and influence. Great persuaders understand and appropriately use different forms of power to gain huge persuasion advantages. Remember that power is neutral—it can be used for good or for bad—so use it wisely. If you want genuine, long-term persuasion, you will always use power to benefit and motivate others for good.

The Shepherd's Boy: A Fable

There was once a young shepherd boy who tended his sheep at the foot of a large mountain near a forest. It was very lonely for him all day long, so he devised a way in which he could get a little company and some excitement. He ran down toward the village calling out "Wolf, wolf!" and the villagers came out to help him. Some of them even talked with him for a significant amount of time. This attention pleased the boy so much that a few days later he tried the same trick, and again the villagers came to his aid. But the next week, a wolf actually did come out from the forest and began to attack the sheep. The boy of course cried out "Wolf, wolf!" louder than before, but this time nobody came. That's because the villagers had been fooled twice before and thought the boy was deceiving them yet again. As a result, the wolf made a good meal of the boy's flock.

Meaning: When power (position of authority as the flock's guardian) is abused, it will lose the ability to persuade and influence.

What is the dark side of power? What are the underhanded, manipulative and condescending things some people might try on you? Do you want to know the top ten dark tactics of unethical people? Warning: These are not for you to use. There are for your understanding and preparation only. When you are prepared for these dark tactics you will be prepared to handle them in an honorable and ethical fashion. Go to www.persuasioniq.com to learn about the ten dark forms of power.

CHAPTER EIGHT

PQ Skill #6

The Ability to Influence Other People

Influence is the highest form of persuasion. Why? With influence, people take action because they are inspired by your overall makeup, rather than by your external actions. Persuasion is what you do or say (i.e., techniques, people skills, laws of persuasion), but influence is who you *are*. How do you gain influence? How do you develop yourself to the point that people will act simply because an idea came from you? How do you ensure that your influence continues to compel people even when you're not around? In my studies, I have found that great persuaders possess most (if not all) of seven essential characteristics of the ability to influence others:

Charisma	Empathy
Passion	Vision

Optimism   Self-Esteem

Attitude

CHARISMA

Great persuaders have charisma. We can all think of charismatic people. They have a certain presence and charm about them; they are captivating. They command our attention; we hang onto every word out of their mouths. Their energy prods us, motivates us, and inspires us. We feel better for having met them, seen them, been persuaded by them, and interacted with them. So what exactly is charisma? It can be a mysterious attribute. It's not leadership, assertiveness, or enthusiasm, nor is it personality or being a "people person," although all of these things seem to be a part of the package in one way or another. Attorney Gerry Spence has perhaps summed up the concept of charisma best:

> Charisma is energy from the heart zone. If the speaker has no
> feeling, there is nothing to transfer. Charisma occurs when the
> speaker's feelings are transferred in the purest form to another.
> Charisma is not a diluted feeling. It is not disguised. It is a raw
> feeling. Charisma is the passing of our pure energy, our pure
> passion, to the other.[1]

It may seem that people either have charisma or they don't. If you're not one of those people who "has charisma," can it be learned? The answer is yes. How is this possible? First, you must know the traits and attributes of charismatic leaders.

Professor Jay Conger has identified four general characteristics of charismatic leaders:

1. They have a strong and clear vision, and they know how to present it so it best fits the context of their audience's needs.

2. They know how to present their vision so that the weaknesses of the present condition are apparent and the recommended changes are seen as not only justifiable, but also desirable and necessary.

3. They have a history of success, expertise, and vision to make educated departures from old traditions that may be less effective.

4. They possess the behavior they encourage others to have. They model the results of change themselves and thus help their audience feel motivated and empowered to do likewise.[2]

Once you know the characteristics of charismatic leaders, you must take steps to acquire these traits for yourself. Here are eight specific ways great persuaders augment their charisma:

1. *Develop confidence in yourself and in your message.* Don't show nervousness or discomfort. If you do feel these negative emotions, work through what is causing them so that they can be resolved. Confidence must permeate every thought, word, and deed.

2. *Show a lighter side.* Find your sense of humor and happiness and have fun. Don't take life too seriously. Learn to laugh at yourself.

3. *Have great presence and energy.* Project the Five Cs of Trust: character, competence, confidence, credibility, and congruence.

4. *Be knowledgeable about your subject matter* and make sure that knowledge is based on a solid foundation. Gain an understanding of where your audience stands in relation to your subject and what background, knowledge, and experience they may bring to the table.

5. *Have a pleasant, professional appearance.* Make sure your clothes, hair, shoes, and accessories, are appropriate for the message and the setting. Dress the part.

6. *Be sensitive to people and their needs.* Develop rapport with your audience by connecting with them and being a good listener.

7. *Make sure your message is clear and easy to follow.* Make sure there is a good flow from one point to the next. Don't jumble the message with too much information; stick to the pertinent points and keep it concise. This way you will not only hold their attention better, but they will be much more likely to remember your message later.

8. *Make sure you are exciting and engaging to listen to.* Tell spellbinding stories. Make sure the things you talk about are interesting.

PASSION

More than anything else, passion recruits the hearts and minds of your audience. Great persuaders radiate heartfelt passion. When the audience can sense your passion and genuine conviction for your cause or product, they will emotionally jump on board. We all love people who are excited and filled with believable zeal for their subject. Passion is critical to influencing others, yet less than half of all persuaders interviewed have a passion for their product or service.

When you have passion for something, you want to share it with the world. You want to convert as many people to your cause as possible, and you're not swayed by the opinions of others. When you possess passion, you have a sense of mission that drives you, stimulates your imagination, and motivates you to higher levels of achievement. Passion alone can be effective in influencing others to support your product, service, or cause.

There is a difference between charisma and passion, however. Charisma is a characteristic, while passion is an emotion. Your ability to transfer your passion about what you do, your product, or your service is a required skill if you are to excel in the world of persuasion. As I monitor great persuaders and their Persuasion IQ scores, I have noticed the essential role of passion. I can monitor two persuaders who possess roughly the same scores in persuasion knowledge and application, but their success is not identical. Passion is often the differentiating factor. Ask yourself if you have passion or if you are simply going through the motions. Are you singing the song and really feeling it, or are you just singing the words (going through the motions)? Think about it.

Enthusiasm falls under the umbrella of passion, but you can be enthusiastic without having passion. Passion, however, always includes enthusiasm. Enthusiasm is described as a strong excitement or feeling on behalf of a cause or a subject. In Greek, the word enthusiasm means "to be inspired by a god." Enthusiasm is contagious. Enthusiasm infects people so much that they tangibly feel your energy and excitement. Ralph Waldo Emerson said, "Nothing great was ever achieved without enthusiasm."

People are persuaded more by the depth of
your conviction than the height of your logic;
more by your enthusiasm than any proof you can offer.
—DAVID A. PEOPLES

You have probably seen persuaders who radiate enthusiasm. It is in their faces—they are undeniably motivated—and it creates sparks of interest in their audience. Enthusiasm not only reduces fear, but it also creates self-acceptance, great confidence, compassion, and harmony between you and your audience. It assists in generating interest in strangers and in motivating them to want to get involved.

Great Persuaders increase their enthusiasm by gaining insight and knowledge about their product or subject. They have developed a true belief. Believe in yourself and your message, tap into your emotions, and learn how to express them. On the flip side, fake enthusiasm, unrealistic hype, and false energy:

Lower credibility.

Project phoniness.

Repel people.

Are experienced as deceit.

Are viewed as arrogance.

In the past at my persuasion workshops, I have my students give a two-minute speech about their personal passion. Many times, their passion is contagious, and they've influenced even me. Over the years, I've had students get me excited about ice cream, get me more committed to recycling, and make me want to start rock climbing. Passion springs from a combination of belief, enthusiasm, and emotion.

What is your passion? What are you wildly enthusiastic about? Tap into the things in your life about which you are passionate, and you'll find a new driving force in your life that will keep you going until the goal is reached. Norman Vincent Peale said, "When one gets enthusiastic, the entire personality lights up. The mind becomes sharper, more intuitive; the entire life force and creative ability are enhanced. Such a person is motivated and will certainly make an impact." Enthusiasm can be learned. Great persuaders enhance their enthusiasm by increasing their knowledge, having a sincere interest, and tapping into their purpose.

OPTIMISM

Optimistic persuaders outpersuade pessimistic persuaders every time. Not only is optimism essential to influencing others, but is also a critical for success in *life*. Optimism is more than a positive mental attitude. It is not constantly saying positive things to your-self and then hoping they will come true. Rather, true optimism is a state of mind that dictates how you look at the world. An optimistic view of life and the world around you can inspire hope and courage in others. We all want to feel inspired and encouraged. When a persuader can deliver this type of message, we want to follow that person. This tendency is how optimism helps you in influencing others.

Pessimism on the other hand is always taking the negative view. Others will consider a pessimist as irritable and always looking for the negative in every situation. Pessimists are the ones who will be the first to complain and tell everyone else that nothing goes right. As a result, they never get the success or recognition they deserve.

Countless studies have shown that optimists do better in school, persuade better, have more friends, perform better in their careers, and live longer than pessimists. Pessimists, on the other hand, frequently battle depression, have fewer friends, find it difficult to persuade, and give up faster and more easily. To illustrate this point, in one study, those who sold insurance were monitored on their optimistic or pessimistic outlook in relation to setbacks. The optimistic persuaders sold more policies and were half as likely to quit.[3]

No pessimist ever discovered the secrets
of the stars, or sailed to an uncharted land,
or opened a new heaven to the human spirit.
—HELEN KELLER

Great persuaders have what we call "influential optimism." This means that they see the positive in all situations. Rather than focusing on disappointment, cynicism, or negative feelings, they look for ways to move forward. People want to be persuaded by individuals who have a positive view on life. As an optimist, you see the world as a series of exciting challenges. You inspire positive feelings about everything you stand for. People want to be around you because they live in a very pessimistic world. The optimistic mindset is contagious and helps to empower other people to believe in you and in themselves. As an optimist, you help others see failure or setback as temporary. You have no doubt that success will happen.

To achieve true optimism, you have to learn to control your pessimistic voice. We all have both an optimistic and a pessimistic voice inside of us. Which one do you listen to?

Can you be overly optimistic? It depends on the situation. You can have too much false cheer—taking optimism to nausea-ism—but I think it is rare to have too much realistic optimism. The only time optimism will backfire is when you are persuading a diehard pessimist. If you start off with too much optimism, you will clash with your audience. If, on the other hand, you gradually offer small doses of optimism, you can turn even the pessimist around. Great persuaders find that it is essential to mirror their audience's reality and to gradually raise their audience's optimism level.

Work on refining your educated optimism—that is, the ability to see around corners, to anticipate challenges, and to still maintain a positive outlook, while preparing for bumps in the road.

ATTITUDE

Great persuaders know that maintaining a healthy attitude is an ongoing commitment to excellence. Most people don't spend time thinking about their attitudes, and yet they allow their attitudes to control them throughout the day. Rather than attending to their own attitudes, most absorb the attitudes of others and react accordingly. Most of our attitude starts in neutral and is altered by what we decide to think and feel, then we are well on our way to controlling it. The moment we decide how to respond to circumstances, we then determine the degree of our success. We don't have control over everything that's going to happen, but we do have 100 percent control over our own attitudes. Psychiatrist Viktor Frankl said, "Everything can be taken from a man but . . . the last of the human freedoms—to choose one's attitude in any given set of circumstances, to choose one's own way."[4] Once we realize that attitude is a choice, we must remind ourselves that it is a choice we must make daily—even moment by moment.

Attitude is a habit, and it arises from our expectations—what we expect of ourselves and of others. Great persuaders create, enhance, and maintain expectations with themselves and their audience. Frustration is normally just the result of an unmet expectation or a contradiction between reality and attitude. Great attitude, understanding frustration, and expectation management are part of joining top persuaders.

At the Persuasion Institute, we found that only 14.2 percent of people polled felt they had great attitudes on a daily basis. How can you consistently improve your attitude? One of the biggest factors is in how we talk to ourselves. Remember, we all have a positive voice and a negative voice inside of us. Which voice do you give more power? It is essential that you master the skill of quieting the negative voice. I have noticed with great persuaders that any time negative thoughts arise, they have a plan to disarm them and replace them with positive thoughts. Whatever goes on in your mind is exactly what will come out in performance. It is in this way that we actually have much greater control over our lives than most people realize. William James, psychologist and philosopher, said, "The greatest discovery of my generation is that human beings can alter their lives by altering their attitudes of the mind."

Why is having a positive attitude so critical in influencing others? Our attitudes will be reflected back by those we seek to influence. If you don't feel positively about whatever position it is you're trying to advance, then how can your audience feel positively about it? Whatever attitude you want your audience to possess, you must possess it first. Only then will you be influential.

Attitude

You can often tell where a person's attitude is simply by examining his words. Do you ever catch yourself saying any of the following?

"I'll just sit this one out."

"It takes too much effort."

"That's just human nature."

"I'm helpless in this situation."

"Price is the only thing that matters."

"It's the industry; it is out of my hands."

"They already have a supplier they are happy with."

"It doesn't matter what I do; it won't change anything."

"That's how employees are. What do you expect me to do?"

Even when it is true that circumstances are not under your control, you must be very careful that you don't adopt a defeatist attitude. Instead of brushing it off as "out of my hands," "nothing I can do about it," or other such dismissive and reactive attitude, seize the opportunity to focus on what you *do* have control over and let your attitude positively center around that.

EMPATHY

The word "empathy" has both Latin and Greek roots. The two parts of the word mean "to see through" and "the eye of the other." The ability to see through the eye of another creates long-term influence. When people know that you can see what they see, feel what they feel, and hurt the way they hurt, then they will be willing to be influenced by you. Great persuaders have mastered and understand the use of empathy.

Empathy is identifying with and understanding someone else's situation, feelings, and concerns in a realistic way. It is having the ability to put yourself in their shoes and then genuinely appreciating where they're at and what they're dealing with. When people sense that you sincerely empathize with them, they will be significantly more open to your influence. In a world that is full of people who are always trying to get us to do things for their reasons, without any regard for how we may feel about it, it is refreshing to have a truly empathetic person come along.

Empathy helps you feel better, too. Contrary to the messages that we are constantly bombarded with, we actually feel happier when we put others first. As Zig Ziglar wisely said, "The best way to get what you want out of life is to help others get what they want." Empathy has also been shown to increase productivity and personal satisfaction, which again is just more proof that in helping others you are also helping yourself. It is interesting to note that studies show that those who are able to show and demonstrate empathy had an above-average self-esteem and felt more socially responsible.[5]

Despite all the evidence of the importance and usefulness of empathy in persuasion, our studies show that while the majority of persuaders feel they are showing empathy toward their audience, the majority of their audience members feel their persuaders are just going through the motions. Empathy is next to impossible to fake. Even if you feel your audience has bought your empathy, think again. They just haven't called you on it.

When you can understand how your audience feels, persuasion and influence become easy. You have walked in your audience's shoes, and they know you feel what they feel. It takes talent to come across as empathic, even when you have true empathy. We live in a self-absorbed world and being empathic is contrary to almost everything you've learned from the world. We learn as children to be demanding, self-centered, and egocentric. Great per-

© Randy Glasbergen.
www.glasbergen.com

**"The number one rule of selling is: find out what the customer
wants. The customer wanted me to shut up and go away."**

suaders forget themselves in the persuasion process, find out what
their audience needs, and connect through empathy. It works, and
I know this technique is one you can fine-tune. Empathy even creates a close relationship between two strangers.

Unfortunately, the rush of modern life doesn't seem to cultivate
a mindset of pausing to help others. If you want to master empathy, you must look for—or even create—the opportunities yourself.
If you need to find ways to develop greater empathy, ask yourself
the following questions:

"How would I feel if I were that person?"

"Why is that person feeling this way?"

"How can I help?"

"How would I feel if that happened to me?"

Basically, even when assessing situations individually, you will
never go wrong by always regarding the universal psychological
and emotional needs of the human family: approval, attention,

encouragement, and understanding. When you accept the whole person unconditionally, you create empathy. You accept his strengths and triumphs along with his weaknesses, failures, doubts, and fears.

VISION

Great persuaders have and can instill a commanding view of the future with their audience. When you want to influence others, it is essential that you have a strong and clear vision. People come on board when they can see that there is a vivid, solid vision in place that they can touch, taste, feel, or see. No one wants to buy stock in a sinking ship. People want to know: What's the plan? Where are we going? What are we aiming for? In other words—what is the vision? Your job is to powerfully present how your vision is the solution to their problems. Your vision must bridge the gap between their present situation and their *desired* situation—where they are, and where they wish they could be.

A common vision pulls people together toward the same goals and objectives. Influential people have clearly defined visions that are forward looking and filled with great excitement and anticipation. Remember more than anything else in life, vision—whether it's yours or somebody else's—dictates our daily decisions.

Vision is a powerful tool in helping others see the big picture. No matter your persuasive role, whether it is as a parent, a spouse, a teacher, a coach, a friend, a sales rep, or an employee, turning your audience on to your vision is a powerful way to increase your influence.

Vision is such a powerful force because it keeps us focused on the future. Vision gives a sense of directional purpose to people, most of whom don't have a clearly articulated purpose or direction in their lives. Stephen Covey said, "To begin with the end in mind means to start with a clear understanding of your destination. It means to know where you're going so that you better understand where you are now and so that the steps you take are always in the right direction."[6] All human beings yearn for direction. That's why someone with a vision is so alluring to us. When you craft your vision, you must think big. Walt Disney advised:

> Make no little plans; they have no magic to stir men's blood and probably themselves will not be realized. Make big plans; aim high in hope and work, remembering that a noble, logical diagram once recorded will never die, but long after we are gone will be a living thing, asserting itself with ever-growing insistency.

True vision affects your audience, even when you're not around, because a contagious vision influences our thoughts and imagination twenty-four hours a day.

SELF-ESTEEM

Influential persuaders have healthy self-esteem. Self-esteem is how much we like ourselves. It is how confident we are, and how satisfied we are with how we are. Great persuaders with great self-esteem are comfortable with themselves. High self-esteem causes people to be more generous, upbeat, open-minded, and more influential. People who possess self-esteem are strong and secure, meaning they can admit when they are wrong. They are not unraveled by criticism. As you can imagine, their self-confidence permeates into all aspects of their lives: jobs, education and relationships. Great persuaders with their high self-esteem have the ability to raise the self-esteem of their audience, making them more open to your persuasion and influence.

All human beings need and want praise, recognition, and acceptance. To know and be assured of our worth is perhaps our deepest craving. We want praise and recognition so that we can feel admired and respected. If you communicate and work with individuals in a manner that enhances their self-esteem, you increase your influence with them. The proper use of esteem building and giving sincere compliments can change and enhance behavior. The individual receiving the praise now has a reputation to live up to and an opportunity to prove and fulfill the compliment's validity.

Great persuaders do not become a threat to someone's self-esteem. They are sure that their audience feels capable of what they are asking them to do. If you are offering to help someone, and they perceive that they should know how to help themselves, it is a blow to their esteem. If receiving help sparks a negative self-message, recipients are likely to feel threatened and respond negatively.[7] We are quicker to believe flattering descriptions of ourselves than unflattering ones.[8]

Low self-esteem also affects our thinking and our actions. Here are several ways low self-esteem dictates what we say and do:

> We remember and justify our past actions in self-enhancing ways.

> We exhibit an inflated degree of confidence in our beliefs and judgments.

> We exhibit group pride (for example, we tend to see our personal group as superior, whether it be our religion, where we went to school, or the country we're from).

> We overestimate how much others support our opinions and share our shortcomings.

> We continuously compare ourselves to others.

> We feel strength and esteem based on our status or possessions.

> We tend to tear others down to enhance our own feelings about ourselves.

The studies at the Persuasion Institute indicate that most of our communication is construed as negative, regardless of the intention. Even when you say something positive, there are those people who will turn it around and take it as something negative. When you find yourself in a persuasive situation, it is essential that you seek to enhance your audience's ego in a sincere way. Too often, we present ourselves in a manner that instills feelings of threat, competition, jealousy, and mistrust in our audience. Be sure your praise is sincere and genuine.

You can't ever go wrong offering sincere praise. It's only going to make people feel better, happier, more energetic, and more productive. You've probably experienced this yourself. When you receive sincere praise, you get a smile on your face and your spirits soar. Don't wait for a good reason or for something big to happen. Be generous with your praise. Make it a habit to give sincere praise every day and you will be well on your way to increasing your potential to positively influence others.

In a culture that grows increasingly cynical, you may worry about whether or not your praise will be taken as sincere. Consider the following three points to help ensure that your praise is accepted:

> Find something positive to praise.
>
> Praise the specific act, not the person.
>
> Be sincere and genuine.

People will be much more open to your input and suggestions when you help them feel good about themselves, their work, and their accomplishments. This only works if you have a high self-esteem yourself. Top persuaders know that there is a direct correlation between their self-esteem and their ability to raise their audience's self-esteem. When you make your audience feel that their contributions are essential, it will not be long before they become your willing supporters.

INFLUENTIAL PRESENCE

A bit of fragrance clings to the hand that gives flowers.
—CHINESE PROVERB

Influence is the cruise control on your car of success. Once established or set, you don't need facts and figures to persuade someone. You can influence them because of who you are. It will take seconds instead of hours to influence. Great persuaders know how to develop both short-term and long-term influence. Development of your influential presence will enable you to build, motivate, and empower others to take action. When you master and utilize all of the essential elements of influence—charisma, passion, optimism, attitude, empathy, vision, and self-esteem—you will be giving yourself the energy and presence you need to get results.

The Blue Jay and the Peacock: A Fable

A blue jay ventured into a meadow where peacocks lived. There, he found a number of feathers that had fallen from the peacocks when they were molting. He tied the feathers to his tail and strutted down toward the peacocks. As he neared, they discovered his deceit and began to peck at his head and pluck away at his borrowed feathers. So, the blue jay had to go back to the other blue jays, who had watched his behavior from a distance. They, however, were equally upset and annoyed with him.

Meaning: Not only will deception and deceit fail to influence your enemies but it will also destroy your friendships.

Do you have charisma? You might think so, but what do others really think about you? Do you attract people and do they want to be influenced by you? Do you repel people and don't even know it? Do you posses the ten traits of charismatic people. Go to www.persuasioniq.com and find out.

CHAPTER NINE

PQ Skill #7

*How to Motivate Yourself and
Others Every Time*

Winning isn't everything, but wanting to win is.
—VINCE LOMBARDI

Motivation is everything to a great persuader. Motivation is critical not only for achieving the big, milestone steps toward your objectives, but also for making all the little steps in between. If you're not driven or motivated, then not only will nothing be accomplished, but you probably won't even get started. Motivation takes on a dual role in the world of persuasion mastery. Motivation is first and foremost about keeping yourself motivated. Then, once you are a consistently self-motivated person, your focus turns to inspiring and motivating others to take action. Since great persuaders have mastered each of these skills, this chapter is about mastering both of them.

Notice that I said, "once you are a *consistently* a self-motivated person." Consistency is the key. You can probably think of countless examples of times when you've gotten really excited about something and felt gung-ho about it, ready to take on the world—and then what happened? After a little while, your enthusiasm, excitement, and commitment wore off. Great persuaders stay consistently and predictably motivated.

We have to understand human nature and the psychology of why we do what we do. Sometimes we're super-motivated, and sometimes we can't get out of bed in the morning. Why is this? So often, we don't have a system or understanding in place to keep the motivation going after the initial spark. Motivation doesn't serve us when it comes exclusively in sporadic bursts. The initial spark is important, but then we need to make sure there's a way to keep the flame going. Motivation is another one of those key success skills that are not taught in school.

Part of keeping motivation constant is being honest with ourselves and realizing that our emotions, our circumstances, and our discipline will all fluctuate every hour and every day. It is inevitable that we're all going to have some bad days. You have to be prepared with a motivation safety net. You've got to have a system. When your energy, excitement, and motivation are high, think through the ways you're going to keep the motivation alive on a consistent, daily basis. Envision it as a steady stream rather than a big wave that hits all at once. This concept may sound simple—and it is—but it is its very simplicity that makes it one of the most commonly overlooked persuasion tools. Studies through the Persuasion Institute found that when persuaders were asked about their ability to motivate and energize themselves on a daily basis, over 50 percent felt it was a problem. I believe this statistic is as high as it is because people just don't realize that motivation must be maintained day by day, sometimes even moment by moment.

A lot of our motivation challenges would be remedied if we treated them like physical nourishment. We never say, "Well, I've had a big meal. That should do me for the rest of the month."

Obviously, our bodies need nourishment day in and day out. Motivation is the same. Our greatest successes will always occur when they have been accompanied by clear and steady motivation.

We live in a world where we want everything *now*. We want a quick fix. We want instant gratification and quick results. Not only do we want instant gratification, but we also want it with minimal effort. For example, if you were to ask a random group of people off the street if they wanted to be financially independent, to lose weight, or to have better relationships, most everyone would say yes. But how many of them would then be able to outline a detailed action plan they are actually following to make those things happen? Few, if any, I'd bet. This lack of follow-through is just uneducated human nature. When encouraged, most of us feel the sparks, but we don't ever actually get the fire started. Or if we do, we don't have a plan for keeping the fire alive.

MOTIVATION INHIBITORS

All too often, the path to success, initially so clearly defined, begins to get blurry again. What is it that blurs the path or inhibits our motivation? We could all name hundreds of little things that get in the way. But lack of long-term success goes much deeper than daily setbacks, hassles, and frustrations. Take time to examine where all the detours come from: the self-doubt, the self-sabotage, the nagging, the negative inner voice, the inability to stick to the things you know you should be doing. Sometimes, our lack of persistence stems from the fact that the required behavior is not part of our customary pattern. Other times, it's because we're not doing it for the right reasons or in the right way. Sometimes, it's because we're trying to treat the surface problem or behavior rather than an underlying issue. That is, we're treating the symptoms instead of the disease.

Great persuaders, along with maintaining a positive outlook

themselves, surround themselves with people who are just as successful (or even more so) as they are. One of the big reasons we don't stay motivated is because we unintentionally sabotage our own efforts or we let others sabotage us. Sometimes we don't even realize this is happening. It's like we stand around dumping buckets of water on our fire, or letting others dump buckets of water on our fire, and then we scratch our heads wondering why the fire won't burn.

Two of the big motivation inhibitors are mindset and the people we associate with. Take a look around you. Are the people in your life pulling you up or pulling you down? Are they encouraging you or discouraging you? How do they view your goals, dreams, and aspirations? Many times, we give up simply because we don't have support or encouragement from those we respect and love. This lack of support may be because they are being protective, or they don't fully understand the situation. Or they may understand the situation and all its implications, but they just don't buy into it. Or it may simply be jealousy and resentment; they didn't pursue their dreams, so why should you get to pursue yours? However, for all those who discourage you, don't understand or believe in your plans, or who see their lives going down the tubes and want to take you with them, there are also those who are successfully pursuing their dreams. These people will encourage you to do likewise. Surround yourself by inspired and motivated people.

Another strain on your ability to motivate yourself is your mindset. In many cases, our dreams have become lifeless, or we've given up dreaming altogether. But when our capacity to dream is lost, part of us dies. If you ever find yourself in this situation, you must revise and rekindle the dream. Be honest with yourself: Do you ever make up excuses for why you can't do it, shouldn't do it, or don't have time to do it? This is called "self-handicapping."[1] We sabotage our own efforts and desires by finding excuses and anticipating future failure. Deep down, we may feel this mentality is the safer route. The idea of success can be scary—it may mean sacrificing the old and familiar and embracing the new and unfamiliar. It will mean new commitments, change, and a few adjustments.

You have probably heard the example of keeping a baby elephant chained up to a stake. The baby elephant tries to get away, but the stake is too deep. When the elephant reaches adulthood, it could easily pull out the stake, but it has long since given up. It no longer even tries. Dr. Martin Seligman, founder of Positive Psychology, calls this concept "learned helplessness."[2] When we don't take accountability for our learned helplessness, Dr Seligman says it could trigger the following negative results:

- Disrupts the ability to learn from the situation.

- Inhibits the ability to be creative.

- Lowers the expectation for future successes.

- Produces emotional disturbances, i.e., anxiety, hostility, fear, and depression.

- Reduces the body's immune system.

- Limits earning capacity and decreases job security.[3]

When we are honest with ourselves, we may find that there are areas where learned helplessness prevails. To overcome this tendency, you need to dream, and dream big. You've got to feel inspired to break those shackles. Remember, your inhibitions have only as much power as you give them. Like the baby elephant that has grown to maturity, the chain and stake are not a real obstacle. What's holding you back? What are the chains and stakes in your life? What would it take to make you want to leap out of bed each morning? If you have dull dreams, it is difficult to stay motivated.

Great persuaders take full ownership of their success, their failures, and their life. If you tried hard enough, I am sure you could come up with twenty reasons why you might fail. But these don't matter, because all you need is one good reason to be successful. We could spend all day and night finding excuses. In fact, here are some of the excuses I hear all the time in the persuasion world.

- "I can't cold call."
- "They just got lucky."
- "I have a bad territory."
- "The economy is down."
- "They set me up to fail."
- "The employees hate me."
- "I tried and it didn't work."
- "The marketing is outdated."
- "I'm not good on the phone."
- "The competition is everywhere."
- "The product needs improvements."
- "I'd be successful if I had that account."
- "How do they expect me to compete with . . . ?"
- "The company doesn't generate enough leads."

Whatever form the discouragement comes in, you must fortify yourself and forge ahead. Think what would have happened if Abraham Lincoln had listened to his critics, or if Thomas Edison had paid attention to everyone who said his inventions were impossible. What if Bill Gates had listened to his counselors while he studied at Harvard and stayed in school? What if Mark Victor Hansen and Jack Canfield had listened to the over one hundred publishers that turned them down for *Chicken Soup for the Soul* (which ended up selling millions of copies)? There are volumes of similar stories. What is your story? Are *you* going to write it—or is somebody else going to write it? The main thing to take from these experiences is that you cannot allow others to suck the energy and motivation out of you.

Let's get past our learned helplessness, our pre-excuse for fail-ure, and decide on victory.

COMMITMENT

The men who have succeeded are men who
have chosen one line and stuck to it.
—ANDREW CARNEGIE

Commitment has a lot to do with perspective. When you consider your personal perspective, do you see the big picture, or are you swept up by the whims of the moment? You have to make sure your perspective is rock solid; otherwise, your commitments will be flimsy. We all know that when someone says, "I'll try," it will never happen. "I'll *try*" versus "I *will*" are two different attitudes. With one, you are committing. With the other, you're leaving your-self room for a way out. Make sure the commitments you make in a moment of excitement have the sustaining motivation to take you to the next level. Great persuaders make their commitments stronger than their moods.

One of the key ways to make sure our commitment remains strong is to develop willpower and the ability to delay gratifica-tion. Walter Mischel, a psychologist at Stanford University, per-formed a study that has come to be called the "marshmallow test." He invited groups of four-year-olds into a room and gave each of them a marshmallow. He told them they could eat their marsh-mallow now or they could wait fifteen to twenty minutes and be rewarded with a second marshmallow when he came back. Many of the children were able to hold out, but there were some who couldn't wait. After the study was over, Mischel followed all the children to see how they performed in life. The results were star-tling. He found that the kids who were able to delay gratification were twice as likely to be successful academically, socially, and emotionally than those who could not wait. While in high school, the kids who had exhibited willpower had better grades and scored 210 points higher on their SATs than those who had not.[4]

Even for the strongest individuals, their commitment level or willpower is not always constant. Willpower is like a battery. As you exercise your willpower throughout the day, the battery power starts to decline. What drains your battery? Fatigue, negative emotions, low blood sugar, suppression of emotions, and even peer pressure will drain your willpower battery faster than anything else.

An interesting study gives more credibility to this idea that willpower may actually be made stronger if given periods of recess. Researchers had college students arrive to participate in an experiment regarding taste perception (or so the students thought). The students were instructed to come to the study hungry by abstaining from foods for three hours prior to their arrival. When they entered the room, they were greeted by the scent of freshly baked chocolate cookies, which were piled high on a side table, next to a bowl of freshly washed and trimmed radishes. As they entered the room, they were divided into two groups. One group was told they could only eat the chocolate chip cookies and the other only eat the radishes. They were then left alone to walk around the room as they waited for the researchers. Obviously, the radish group of students had to exercise their willpower to refrain from eating the chocolate chip cookies and only eat the plain radishes. After five minutes, the students were told that they needed to wait for their sensory perception of the food to fade before performing a new task. This next, unrelated assignment (or so they thought) was to solve a puzzle. Unbeknownst to the students, the puzzles were unsolvable. The researchers just wanted to see how fast the subjects would give up on the puzzles.[5]

Remember that the researchers were suggesting that willpower and self-discipline would weaken after doing sequential tasks, much like an overused muscle that has been strained to fatigue or a battery that has lost its charge. In looking at the two groups—one

You need to able to know when your willpower battery is low. Here are some things you can do to recharge:

- Take a nap.

- Have a snack.

- Talk to a positive person.

- Review your goals.

- Do some exercise.

- Replay your vision.

- Employ humor.

- Meditate.

- Engage in service.

that ate cookies (requiring no willpower) and one that ate radishes (exercising their willpower against the tantalizing cookie smell)—the results proved interesting. The cookie-eating group worked on the puzzles for 18.54 minutes before they gave up while the radish-eating group worked on the puzzles for only 8.21 minutes before giving up. In other words, the radish group, the one that had exercised willpower, gave up 2.25 times faster than the group that did not exercise any willpower at all. The bottom line is the more we sequentially exercise our willpower, the more we have drained our battery.

THE DESPERATION CYCLE: WHY DOES MOTIVATION FAIL?

Better to light a candle then to curse the darkness.
—CHINESE PROVERB

One of the biggest criticisms of motivation as a persuasion tool is that the results often appear to be temporary. There is some truth to that notion, but only when motivation has not been properly utilized. Motivating or being motivated with the wrong things for the wrong reasons will never work. I call motivating for short-term results the "desperation cycle." The desperation cycle describes our tendency to take the easiest path instead of the best one. We dwell in our comfort zones—places where we don't have to expend much energy in analyzing our surroundings—and in these zones, we live by habit and routine. As a result, we become resistant to change. We are unlikely to stretch ourselves or strive for excellence. Fear of the unknown and fear of making mistakes are also reasons why we stay in our comfort zones. As Mark Twain said, "A cat that steps on a hot stove once will never step on a hot stove again, but neither will it step on a cold one." The comfort zone is safe and familiar, but it keeps us paralyzed by fear and unmotivated to venture out.

Fear, however, will creep into our complacency. At some point, we realize that we haven't accomplished any of the things we needed to do. Suddenly, we fear what we are becoming and where we are going as a result of neglect. As we contemplate our destination, we may panic, working frantically to make up for lost time. This frantic rehabilitation lasts just long enough for us to see exactly how steep the hill really is—how long the marathon will really take—and then our excitement begins to fade. We find ourselves lulled back into our comfort zone, numb to the stark realizations that had us panicked only a little while before. We're then perfectly positioned for it to start all over again. Hence, we find ourselves in the "desperation cycle."

Here's a common scenario. Let's say you have a high school reunion coming up, but for the past decade, you've been enjoying some of life's finer foods (maybe chocolate chip cookies). As a result, your clothes are feeling pretty snug. You don't want to go to your reunion in this ample state. You begin to fear what it's going to be like to show up at your reunion looking this way. Panic hits, and you vow that you will lose weight before the looming event arrives. To that end, you starve yourself. You even start to exercise. The pounds come off and you go to your reunion a slimmer and more confident individual. Then you get home and think that it'd be nice to continue shedding the pounds, but you realize it's harder than you thought. You begin to overindulge again, just a little

**"My boss gave me a motivation tape.
It's a recording of him firing people."**

bit at first then more and more as time goes by. You let your exercise regimen go. The weight returns, and the vicious cycle starts all over again.

MOTIVATING THE UNMOTIVATED—MASLOW'S HIERARCHY OF NEEDS

Great persuaders are able to find and fulfill unmet needs and wants. Two of the major keys to knowing how to motivate others are: (1) discovering their needs and wants, and (2) figuring out how to fulfill them.

Great persuaders know that not everyone can be motivated the same way at the same time. Many of us are familiar with Abraham Maslow's "hierarchy of needs." A renowned researcher and psychologist, Maslow proposed a hierarchy of needs that demonstrates the human needs we are most motivated to satisfy.[6] The base of the motivational order begins with the fundamentals of life. These fundamental, life-sustaining needs must be met before the higher needs can be addressed. When lower needs are not met, the higher needs become less urgent.

As the more basic needs are fulfilled, they lose their motivating power. We then move up the hierarchy and target needs in other areas. For example, if running water is something we take for granted, then the need for a glass of water is unlikely to spur us to action. Conversely, if we can't meet this month's rent, then we most likely are not thinking too much about fulfilling our self-actualization needs. After all, as they say, a man with a toothache cannot fall in love.

To motivate effectively, be sure you address your audience's lowest unmet hierarchical need and then offer opportunities for that need to be met.

Don't make assumptions, either—they are often wrong, as you will see in the tables below. Great persuaders talk to the person directly and take the time to hear and understand their needs and wants firsthand. Below, you can see an example of how what employees want is one thing, while what their managers think they want is another. How much more effective could these managers

What Motivates Employees as Ranked by Managers

1. **Compensation**
2. Job security
3. Growth and promotional opportunities
4. Good working conditions
5. Interesting work
6. Personal loyalty to employees
7. Tactful discipline
8. Appreciation of work done
9. Help with personal problems
10. Being well informed

What Motivates Employees as Ranked by Employees

1. Interesting work
2. Appreciation of work done
3. Being well informed
4. Job security
5. **Compensation**
6. Growth and promotion opportunities
7. Good working conditions
8. Personal loyalty to employees
9. Tactful discipline
10. Help with personal problems[8]

be in motivating their team if they were really in touch with their employees? What we think others want and what they really want are usually two different things. Studies show that only one in ten people are recognized/motivated in ways that are meaningful to them.[7] Great persuaders can consistently find those wants and needs.

INSPIRATION VS. DESPERATION

There are only two things that motivate us in life: inspiration and desperation. We either move toward that which inspires us, or we move away from that which fills us with despair or discomfort.

Most people only use desperation's motivational energy. Any persuader can motivate an audience with desperation, fear, and worry. The problem is that motivation spurred by desperation does not last. People who are moved by desperation or fear are typically so preoccupied with what they're trying to get away from that they can't think of anything else.

If you want personal motivation to last, you need to rely on inspiration, which is rooted in our emotions and vision. The positive results that come from using inspiration as a motivator are obvious. And, inspired people don't need a carrot dangling in front of them to get something accomplished. They are self-motivated and don't wait for external factors to drive them one way or the other. Motivation is not stagnant; we all will require different types of motivation. Every day, every hour we will require a different form of motivation. Great persuaders know when, how, and what type of motivation to use not only as a persuader but also in their personal lives. It is also critical to know which combination of motivation to use in each persuasive situation.

> *Motivation is a fire from within. If someone else*
> *tries to light that fire under you, chances are*
> *it will burn very briefly.*
> —STEPHEN R. COVEY

PERSUASION INSTITUTE'S MOTIVATION SYSTEM

Great persuaders have mastered their ability to motivate different people with different methods. I am going to go deep here to help you understand what exactly motivates people (including yourself). What do great persuaders do to motivate their audience to action, and motivate themselves, even when they don't feel like doing what needs to be done? Let's talk about the science of motivation (see graphic on facing page). Notice that motivation (or desire to change) does not exist in the center of the motivational system. This center point represents our comfort zone, where we experience complacency. How do you persuade yourself or someone to move out of the center?

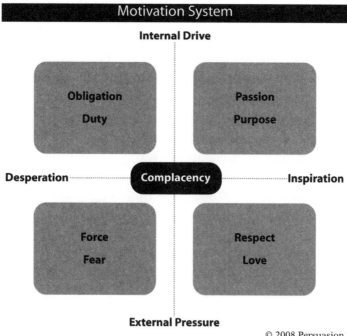

© 2008 Persuasion Institute

Let's start with the lower left quadrant, where we find external desperation. This area can be used for short-term motivation. Anyone can be motivated when she is in this area of the grid. When you are experiencing fear or feel forced to do something, this will trigger desperation. Let's say you hate your job. You don't want to go to work and you only do so because you feel like you have to. This external (pressure) desperation tells you that if you don't go to work, you will lose your job, you'll have no income, or you'll lose your home. This area of the quadrant is where most people reside. That is, they do things because they are forced to or they have to. True fear is four times more motivating than discomfort.⁹ Fear is a powerful tool of persuasion, but it should not be your only tool. There is a time and place for the use of fear in persuasion. Great persuaders have learned how and when to use fear and what amount to use.

Moving to the upper left quadrant, we discover internal desperation. Again, you don't want to go to work, but the internal desperation you feel convinces you that this is what needs to be done, that this is what you are supposed to do. In other words, you feel a duty or an obligation to go to work. You're only going through the motions because you have to. You might feel obligated to show up at work because of a particular project you are working on. You might also feel a sense of duty toward your manager or coworkers to be there and to help out with the workload. You still go, even though you don't want to be there. Your logic wins over your emotions. Watch and you'll find that the people who use desperation to motivate themselves are invariably unhappy. You will never be a true master of your destiny nor will you ever achieve the success you want until you emerge on the other side of the Motivation System.

Next, let's take a look at the lower right quadrant, external inspiration. Here, you feel moved by outside sources that inspire you to do what you need to do. Remember that inspiration is rooted in your emotions. Once you tap into your emotions, you will be able to propel yourself and others toward long-term, permanent motivation. When your logical mind says you can't do it, your emotional mind takes over. In this area of the Persuasion Institute's Motivation System, you do things out of respect or love. That is, you go to work to provide the best for your family. You apply yourself to your job because you want to send your children to the best schools or you wish to buy a new home for your family. You are motivated to go to work by the external things around you.

The best type of long-term motivation is found in the upper right quadrant, internal inspiration. Internal inspiration is what we also know as passion. You have found your purpose in life.

During persuasion, if you can get others to tap into their internal inspiration, then you will bring about pure long-term motivation in them. Using the previous job example, when you are passionate about your career, you are excited to go to work. Rather than seeing your job as a chore, you view it as doing what you love to do. You are changing the world and serving people around you. What's more, you are dedicated with the passion to share your message, product, or service with the world. Great persuaders know how to use motivation. When you are persuading and you use the wrong motivation at the wrong time, it will backfire on you and produce the opposite results from what you intended. Study the PI Motivation System until you understand it well, for it can be adapted to every persuasive situation.

> *The royal road to a man's heart is to talk to him*
> *about the things he treasures most.*
> —DALE CARNEGIE

HOW TO IMPLEMENT MOTIVATION

Great persuaders use every quadrant of the PI Motivation System to persuade and influence. The four different areas of this system can guide you in tapping into the logic and emotions that will motivate yourself and each member of your audience. Some people can only be motivated in the short term, so you have to use desperation with them. When you tap into someone's passion, you have uncovered somebody who will fulfill your long-term call to action and who will willingly do what you ask him to do. He will be excited about your message and will comply with your requests. Great persuaders are able to read vocal inflections, word choice, and body language to see if their audience is in inspiration or desperation.

One study had groups of college students spend about three hours learning complex neurophysiology material. Half the students were told that they would be tested and graded after their study session. The other half were told that they were going to put the material they had learned to use by teaching it to others. After the three study hours were up, the students were surveyed. It turns out that those who believed they were learning so they could help teach others were more internally motivated than those who believed they would be tested.[10] Believing they would be doing good for others allowed them to internalize the desire to perform the task.

> *Motivation is the art of getting people to do*
> *what you want them to do because they want to do it.*
> —DWIGHT D. EISENHOWER

FIND THE MOTIVATOR THAT CREATES HUNGER: PASSION

In order to successfully motivate others or yourself—or to get someone to internalize motivation—you have to create a deep hunger or thirst. On your persuasive journey, you will find that people tend to get motivated for the short-term, that they lose steam, and that they then fall back into the rut they were trying to pull themselves out of in the first place. As a persuader and motivator, you have to understand what pulls people away from action and into inaction. What causes them to lose excitement, vision, and energy? Our research at the Persuasion Institute has found that these are the most common reasons:

- *No Passion.* They are going through life using desperation as a motivator, or they haven't yet found anything that really inspires them.

■ *Poor Attitude.* They have habitual negative attitudes. Their expectations and beliefs are not congruent with their goals.

■ *Diminishing Intent.* They have previously been on the right track but they've now lost their drive. They have forgotten the real reasons why they were motivated in the first place.

■ *Indifference.* They just don't care anymore. They have lost the ability to express concern or to care about making a difference in their own life or in the lives of others.

■ *Creatures of Habit.* They have not replaced their previous bad habits and have fallen back into old ones.

■ *Lack of Persistence.* They have given up too easily and have gotten stalled at the first obstacle.

■ *No Sense of Urgency.* They have set no time frame for achievement. The pain of not changing doesn't hurt badly enough to act right now.

■ *Peer Pressure.* The people around them are more motivating than themselves. They have not found the support they need to resist their friends and peers.

■ *Lack of Vision.* They have sacrificed long-term success for short-term pleasure.

■ *Lack of Knowledge.* They don't know how to make the necessary changes in their lives or they are not making them correctly.

■ *Lack of Confidence.* They don't have the confidence that comes only after action, knowledge, and success have been achieved.

■ *No Game Plan.* They are overwhelmed or waiting for everything to fall into order. They have no action plan.

■ *Don't Really Want It.* They don't want to pay the price.

Their goal is only a dream and nothing more. They are using external desperation as their motivator, or they are living their lives the way others want them to.

MOTIVATION FORMULA: FIND THE SWITCH AND TURN MOTIVATION ON

Great persuaders systematically eliminate or overcome obstacles that stand in the way of their audience. You can apply the Motivation Formulas to learn how it applies to each particular person.

The Motivation Formulas looks like this:

$$\frac{(\text{Want} \times \text{Reward}) + \text{Tools}}{\text{Difficulty} - \text{Time Frame}} = \text{Degree of Inspiration}$$

$$\frac{(\text{Fear} \times \text{Consequences}) + \text{Tools}}{\text{Difficulty} - \text{Time Frame}} = \text{Degree of Desperation}$$

© 2008 Persuasion Institute

How do you maximize the motivation formulas? Look at the first element of the Inspiration Formula: want. This concept is easy to understand. In order to successfully tap in to your audience's motivation, one of the first things you have to understand is what they want. "Want" also includes what they need, what their goals are, what they are trying to accomplish, and where they want to go.

The second part of the Inspiration Formula is reward. In other words, is it worth it to your audience to take action? What is their reward for doing so? What are they going to get from such action?

What's in it for them? Is it something they can fully understand the value of? Can they feel it, touch it, or taste it?

When you look at the first part of the Desperation Formula, it starts with fear. Yes, sometimes fear and desperation are necessary to motivate people. Fear is something they are running away from. What are their concerns, what scares them, or what are they worried about? Panic, anxiety, and what makes them nervous also fall into this category.

The second part of the Desperation Formula is consequences. What is going to happen if there is no movement or motivation? What is the penalty? What is the cost of not changing one's ways? What is going to happen in their lives if they don't take action? As a persuader, you have to make the worst-case scenario come alive in the mind of your audience.

The rest of the formulas are the same for both inspiration and desperation. The next part of the formula involves tools. Does your audience have the necessary tools to perform the task you are asking of them? Do they have the competence to get the task done right? Do they have the knowledge or intelligence to put your call to action into motion? Do they have the necessary resources (for example, transportation, finances, relationships, or self-confidence) to accomplish the task?

Now we move to the bottom half of the formulas, where things get a little tricky. How difficult is the task you are asking of your audience going to be to perform? Or, more importantly, how hard does your audience perceive it to be? Will they perceive it to be more difficult than it's worth? Can they see themselves performing this task you are asking them to do? Is it worth their effort?

The last part of the formulas deals with timeframe. Can your audience fulfill your request in the period of time you are asking them to do it? Will a long timeframe cause them to lose focus and discover more obstacles to justify not completing the task you are asking of them? Do they feel that your deadline provides them with enough time to complete your request? Do they have the drive to stay on task until it is completed?

With these formulas in your persuasion toolbox, you can analyze your audience. When you can understand each aspect of the formulas in regard to your audience's motivational level, you can customize your proposition so they will be motivated to take action every time.

LIFE ALIGNMENT

Another way to enhance your ability to motivate yourself and others is to make sure all things are balanced in your life. Great persuaders lead a balanced life and keep everything in perspective. I call this delicate balance "life alignment." Make sure there is balance in every aspect of your life. Imbalance can undermine motivation and cause inaction and unhappiness. Many times, we quit early because of imbalance, even when we don't realize an imbalance exists. It may be only one area of our life that is out of whack, but it can still have a direct effect on other areas of our life. Just as in a mutual fund, where one bad stock can pull down the fund's overall value, one bad area in your life can also have a disproportionate negative effect.

Ask yourself these questions: Would I invest in my own mutual fund of myself? Would I suggest that my family or friends invest in me? These are hard questions to ask, but the answers to them are necessary as you get your life on track. Take a look at the stocks in which you have invested in your own life. What stock is pulling the rest of your portfolio down? Are you a growing mutual fund or is your mutual fund losing money? Is your fund stagnant? If you won't invest in your personal mutual fund (yourself), who will?

When we look at life, we have to realize that it is not lived in segments, but rather, it is part of a greater whole. Every aspect of your life will either help or hurt the rest of your life. Our aim is to get all aspects working together to create a high-performing fund. Realize, however, that you can invest too much in one aspect of your life. When you do, you can get unbalanced just like a tire on a car. Even too much of a good thing can lead to disaster.

As you invest in yourself, you must make sure you are diversifying in the following six areas:

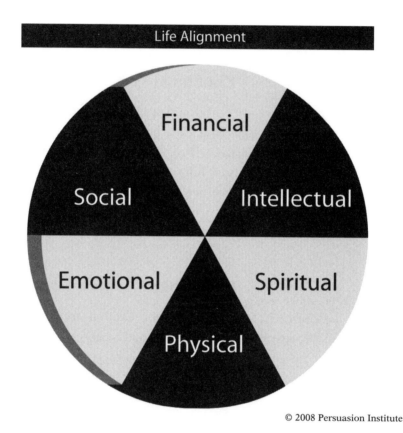

Financial

If you can't take care of your financial needs, then you can't take care of your basic needs. If you neglect your finances, imbalance will ensue. We all know that an inability to pay the bills affects every aspect of our lives. Financial freedom enables us to find true balance in our lives.

Physical

If you don't feel well, you can't even begin to think about the other aspects of your life. You need to have a health plan in place. Do you understand nutrition and exercise? If you don't, your lack of health or energy will drop the value on your own personal mutual fund.

Emotional

By our very nature, we are emotional creatures. Our emotions are like a thermostat or gauges in a car; they tell us when and where to make changes in our lives. You cannot allow emotions like anger, resentment, frustration, hate, and envy to control your life. You are in control. If you are not able to control your emotions, you will be unable to control your actions. Emotional mastery is essential to a balanced personal mutual fund.

Intellectual

Personal development is what keeps you excited, motivated, and enthusiastic. We are at our best when we are continually learning and growing. Personal edification is something we need to achieve every day. That's because a lack of personal development causes us to become negative, cynical, and pessimistic.

Spiritual

You have to be in tune with yourself, with who you are, and with where you are going. We are spiritual beings; we all have a spiritual side. We all define spirituality differently. It could be serving others, religion, meditation, or getting back to nature. You need to take the time to listen to your inner voice and to tap into your spirituality.

Social

We are also social creatures. Our greatest strength and well-being stems from our relationships. As such, relationships are an integral part of your happiness and balance. You have to have a sense of meaning and purpose to lead a fulfilled life. No man is an island in and of himself.

We often spend too much of our time spinning our wheels and investing in stock that has no value or that is diminishing the value of our mutual fund. We get so busy buying the stock society recommends that we forget to examine whether this stock is helping or hurting us. There may also be times when you need to sell a stock (change a habit or belief) because it is not performing. We always need to make sure that we are a growth fund and that we are continually investing the right things in ourselves. If we neglect any one of the life-alignment areas, our overall happiness and success will diminish.

THE UNDERLYING KEY: LONG-TERM MOTIVATION

Motivation begins with a clear, passionate vision. Great persuaders are able to help others believe that they will succeed in what they are being motivated to do. No one likes to lose. The best way to overcome the hurdles of doubt and disbelief is to instill a vision of winning in your audience. Thinking we can win and seeing that victory in our mind's eye stirs our internal motivation. Olympic coach Charles Garfield has said that the highest performers are driven by a sense of mission.

Great persuaders present a winning package to their audience. When people sense victory or accomplishment, they will make sacrifices and become energized to reach their goals. Somehow or other, they will find a way to succeed and win. If they sense defeat, however, they'll exert little personal effort. Instead, they'll come up with lots of excuses, and they'll exhibit a lack of energy for the cause. You can make the excuses sound so compelling, but they are still excuses; they're not results.

> *If you put a silk dress on a goat, he is a goat still.*
> —IRISH PROVERB

Motivation is a true art. When you understand human nature and the role influence plays in it, you will not only be able to motivate, but you will also have earned the right to motivate and inspire others. Can you stay motivated 24/7? Do you have what it takes to achieve your passion and goals? If you want to stay on track, download your motivation system and your will be able to stick to your goals, dreams and passions. Go to www.persuasioniq.com

The Dancing Monkeys: A Fable

A king had some monkeys that were trained to dance and perform. Monkeys are naturally great at impersonating men's actions. The monkeys showed themselves as great students. When dressed in their fine clothes and masks, they danced as well as anyone. The show was often repeated with great applause, until one occasion when a mischievous audience member threw a handful of candy on the stage. At the sight of the candy, the monkeys forgot their training and stopped dancing. They then became (as indeed they were) monkeys instead of actors. Pulling off their masks and tearing off their clothes, they fought with one another for the candy. The dancing show came to an end amidst the audience's laughter and ridicule.

Meaning: Tap in to your own internal motivation. Don't pursue the dreams of society; start learning to own your own dreams. Find out who you really are. Don't let the little candies of life throw you off course.

CHAPTER TEN

PQ Skill #8

*Advanced Presentation and
Communication Skills*

*If all my talents and powers were to be taken from me
by some inscrutable Providence, and I had
my choice of keeping but one, I would unhesitatingly
ask to be allowed to keep the power of speaking,
for through it I would quickly recover all the rest.*
—DANIEL WEBSTER

Have you happened to notice the dramatic changes that have evolved in presentations, communication, and training over the last twenty years? The basic focus used to be on education. Now, the latest research is all about how to grab your audience's attention and then maintain their interest. We can no longer focus simply on educating; we must now entertain. We must keep our audiences mentally engaged.

Great persuaders can maintain the attention of their audience. Research shows that people's attention spans are getting shorter and shorter. You don't have to be a stand-up comedian, but you do have to make sure your audience sticks with you, your words resonate with them, they pay attention, and they understand you. The moment you lose their attention, you can no longer persuade them. You could have a great website, be a sharp dresser, publish a great brochure, or have any manner of impressive credentials. The reality is, however, that the number-one persuasion tool is *you*, and a big part of how you present yourself is through your communication. Long gone are the days of counting on the subject matter to speak compellingly for itself, compensating for your inadequacies as a presenter. Nowadays, you've got to get inside your audience's minds, and you've got to get there fast. It can take only seconds before people's minds start to wander. To combat this tendency, you have to educate, inspire, and entertain with passion, compassion, and purpose.

Great persuaders are great communicators. Well-known motivational speaker and best-selling author Jim Rohn said it best: "When I learned how to effectively persuade and communicate, my income went from six digits to seven digits." Your communication skills are critical for your success, yet this is another set of overlooked skills that are not effectively taught in school. Communication includes phone skills, face-to-face interactions, group presentations, and even email.

Most persuaders feel, incorrectly, that they have above-average communication skills. Are yours "above average" too? Our research shows that 34 percent of persuaders feel they have mastered the ability to effectively communicate. However, by talking to your audience, we know that your presentation and communication mastery was rated at only 11 percent. Great persuaders work on their presentation skills on a continual basis. There is always something to fine-tune and improve.

The studies show that, on average, a persuader communicates

six to eight features of his product or service to his audience, but the average person will only remember one, two, or three of them. In over 40 percent of cases, the person will remember one of the features incorrectly. In 30 percent of cases, the person remembers a feature that was never even mentioned by the persuader. (Ouch!) We also found that 93 percent of persuadees misunderstood some part of a persuader's message. The worst part is that most of them did not ask a question or even try to seek clarification. Remember, a confused mind says no. A "confused mind" has to think about it. A "confused mind" will get back to you. A "confused mind" is hard to persuade and influence.

CAPTURING ATTENTION IMMEDIATELY

What can you do in the first thirty seconds of your encounter to capture your audience's attention? Can you prove to them that you are worth listening to? Think about this: Every time you communicate with someone, they are paying with either time or money. Your audience is rooting for you; they *want* you to succeed. They don't want their time or money wasted any more than you want to waste it. Then why is it getting wasted?

Sometimes when you're approaching something new, figuring out what you should *not* do is just as important as figuring out what *to* do. Let's first take a look at some communication "complaints."

- Speaking in a monotone.

- Avoiding eye contact.

- Fidgeting and other annoying mannerisms.

- Using vocal fillers ("uhm," "uh," etc.).

- Lacking any emotion or conviction.
- Sounding mechanical or rehearsed.
- Rushing through the presentation, speaking too fast.
- Talking down to the audience.
- Not finding common ground.
- Failing to help the audience see value in the presentation.
- Pushing or pressuring the audience.
- Overloading the audience with too much information.
- Being disorganized, jumping from one point to the next without any flow.
- Not checking environment beforehand to limit interruptions and distractions.
- Exhibiting poor listening skills.
- Saying the wrong things at the wrong moments.
- Not adapting to the particular personality or personalities you're working with.
- Displaying nervousness and fear.
- Jumping to conclusions.
- Constantly interrupting.
- Pushing a predetermined, one-sided solution.
- Listening selectively.
- Not being in tune with audience emotions.
- Allowing personal emotions to get involved.
- Being knowledgeable in an arrogant way.

The good news is most of these things are easily remedied once they are pointed out. We just don't realize how often we commit them. Great persuaders have found their presentation weaknesses. They record themselves as they present and talk on the phone. Recording yourself will let you step into your audience's shoes and give you a true-to-life representation that's easy to evaluate. Plus, there won't be any second-guessing—the recording doesn't lie. Sure, it can be a painful exercise, but you will gain invaluable insights that cannot be found in any other way. Remember what they say: "No pain, no gain." Great persuaders will endure a little pain to maintain their high income.

FEAR OF PUBLIC SPEAKING

Given the choice of speaking in public or boiling in oil, most people would choose olive.
—PHILLIS MINDELL

Most of us have been faced with a bad case of laliophobia at one point or another. What is laliophobia? It is the fear of public speaking. As common as this problem is, there is hope in knowing that most all of our fears are not innate but rather are learned (remember, as we learned in Chapter 3, the newborn's fears of falling and of loud noises are the only fears he or she is born with). Why is this good news? It's good news because if you can learn a fear, it also means you can *un*learn it.

In the meantime, it is totally normal to feel some nervousness before you present. We are often tempted to "win over" the audience by being upfront about being nervous, tired, or unprepared (apologizing in advance), but this can backfire. They don't know how you feel or how much you prepared; why would you tell them to start looking for these things?

Great persuaders still get a little nervous, but they take that nervousness and transfer it into energy. Here are some ways in which great persuaders channel or settle some of their nervous energy:

- Performing stretching exercises.

- Listening to soothing music.

- Quietly meditating.

- Walking briskly.

- Engaging in breathing exercises.

- Visualizing success.

- Rehearsing their presentation.

- Leaving the country (just joking).

As you improve this skill, it will rip you out of your comfort zone. There's some definite discomfort at first. After you gain more and more skill and confidence, however, it becomes more comfortable and the results begin to show. When you have mastered these things, you will see your persuasion skill sky rocket to the next level.

Another thing you often have direct control over before your communication has even begun is the physical environment in which you will be presenting. You can choose where you speak, or make adjustments to a facility that has been chosen by someone else. Speakers often overlook these details, even though they make an impact on how well a message is received. Here are some of the environmental factors that are easily adjusted:

■ Lighting	■ Number of attendees
■ Ventilation	■ Entrances/Exits
■ Time of day	■ Audience expectations
■ Chair setup	■ Distractions

PREPARING YOUR MESSAGE

*Think twice before you speak, because
your words and influence will plant the seed of
either success or failure in the mind of another.*
—NAPOLEON HILL

We have addressed the big communication complaints, so we have a long list of don'ts. Now it's time to look at the do's. What are the common factors in great presentations and great communication? Whether you're talking to someone one on one or over the phone, or to a room full of people, great presentations should:

- Be complete.
- Anticipate questions and concerns.
- Avoid distracting mannerisms.
- Be clear and concise.
- Build value.
- Inspire interest.
- Avoid rambling and vocal fillers.
- Suggest the next step to take.
- Have a call to action.
- Capture attention.
- Flow well.
- Contain visual aids.
- Be well-organized.
- Be filled with passion.

Another thing you have direct control over is the crafting of your message so that it will fit and resonate well with your audience. It is critical that you make sure they know you are about to share something that is both meaningful and useful to them. In order to do this, you must clearly communicate the answer to your audience's three most pressing questions:

1. Why should I care?

2. How will this benefit me?

3. Will this fulfill my needs?

Your audience has to have a reason to want to listen to you, and providing them with the answers to these questions gives them a reason to listen. This strategy naturally leads to the next set of questions: What are the needs and wants of this audience, anyway? What do they want to hear about? How can I customize my message to them? Answering these questions, of course, means you must know and understand your audience. Obviously, any large audience is going to represent many different personality types. Try to get a sense of the general feeling and background that is coming from the group. What is the common theme that draws them all together?

AUDIENCE-MEMBER TYPES

Monitoring great persuaders reveals that you must understand how to interact with different people and understand where they are coming from. Here are composites of the most common audience-member types persuaders face:

The Hostile Person

This person openly disagrees with you and may even actively work against you. When faced with a hostile person, use these techniques:

- Find something to agree on.
- Don't start the presentation with an attack on her position.

- Focus on your credibility.

- Show them that you've done your homework.

- Respect their feelings, values and beliefs.

- Hear them out.

The Indifferent Person

This person understands your position but doesn't care about the outcome. The key to dealing with this type of person is to create motivation and energy: In other words, be dynamic. To persuade the indifferent person:

- Spell out the benefits or the "What's in it for me?"

- Use a combination of inspiration and desperation.

- Grab their attention by using a story.

- Get them to feel connected to your issues.

- Avoid complex, hard-to-understand arguments.

- Tap into your passion.

The Uninformed Person

This person lacks the information she needs to be convinced. To persuade the uninformed person, you should employ the following techniques:

- Encourage questions.

- Keep the facts simple and straightforward.

- Keep your message interesting and maintain attention.

- Use examples and simple statistics.

- Quote experts the person respects.

- Make sure they understand what you are saying.

The Supportive Person

A supportive person already agrees with you. As a result, you may think that persuading this type of person will be easy, but remember that your goal is to get him to take action, not necessarily to just agree with you. These techniques should be used with a supportive person:

- Increase their energy and enthusiasm with inspiration.

- Prepare them for future attacks by inoculating.

- Get them to take action and to support your cause.

- Enhance their esteem.

- Use testimonials.

- Get their commitment.

When speaking to a larger audience, you will find a mix of all four of the previous types. When dealing with a new audience—of one or of one hundred—find out the dominant type that will be present and tailor your remarks accordingly.

SUPPORT YOUR MESSAGE

When preparing your presentation, be sure you have several ways to support and enhance your message. Great persuaders use presentation aids that will clearly, concisely, and efficiently deliver their main points. Visual aids will enhance your presentation and help keep people's attention, but visual overload will distract from your message. Find the balance between the two. When we think of visual aids, we envision the common ones like charts, graphs, pictures, or PowerPoint presentations. During your presentation, you can also use handouts, video footage, or even a physical object if it is relevant to your message.

We are finding that many audience members are developing a strong dislike for the use of PowerPoint. They see such visual presentations as a way in which you, the presenter, can read everything off the screen. They may also conclude that you are using PowerPoint to impress them with your ability to make the text fly around while simultaneously making irritating noises. The flood of information is often too much for your audience to handle.

© Randy Glasbergen.
www.glasbergen.com

**"You have been accused of cruel and abusive behavior.
Is it true you made your staff sit through
a PowerPoint presentation?"**

The reality is that average presenters use PowerPoint to make up for a lack of preparation or a lack of confidence. Sure, PowerPoint is a great tool, but understand that you, not the computer program, are the presenter. As I interview audiences, I discover that PowerPoint usually sucks the energy out of them while simultaneously destroying the presenter's spontaneity, passion, and conviction. To succeed as a persuader, you must trust in yourself and not hide behind PowerPoint. This great software and technology takes over as the major source of communication and leaves you behind to fight as the second source. You have given the control of your presentation to a machine. Presenters can become robotic, and their true personality is then buried. My rules of thumb for PowerPoint are: (1) if your presentation is under one hour, don't use PowerPoint at all, and (2) when you do use PowerPoint, don't average more than one slide every two minutes.

Visual aids are effective persuasive tools because they are optically stimulating. Most people are visually oriented, but sound, smell, touch, and taste should not be ignored. Learn to combine all the senses to increase mental involvement. The more senses you can involve, the better. Combining auditory, visual, and kinesthetic modalities will dramatically increase comprehension and retention. As a general rule, the shorter your presentation is, the simpler and fewer your visuals should be.

IT'S NOT JUST WHAT YOU SAY, BUT HOW YOU SAY IT

Words are just words and without heart they have no meaning.
—**CHINESE PROVERB**

The words we use and the way we use them can have a huge impact on how we are perceived by our audience. Different words mean different things to different people. In fact, it is hard to find a neutral word. The right words are captivating; the wrong words are devastating. Effective words make things come to life, create energy, and are more persuasive. Contrarily, ineffective words dull, alienate and repel. Numerous studies have shown that speakers who possess greater verbal skills are seen as more credible and competent. Speakers who hesitate, use the wrong words, or lack fluency, on the other hand, have less credibility and come across as being weak and ineffective.

Another way in which successful persuaders increase the impact of their message is to use vividly descriptive language. Pretend you are standing in a beautiful, sunny kitchen. You reach across the counter and grab a bright, juicy lemon. You can feel it is heavy with sour juice. You can smell the powerful lemon scent as you rub the oil of the skin on your hand. Reaching for a knife,

I refer to the skill of knowing the right words and how to use them as "Verbal Packaging." It is often not *what* you say as much as *how* you say it. For example:

Wrong Word	Right Word
Bill	Invoice
Salesperson	Representative
Price	Investment
Expensive	Top of the line
Cheap	Economical
Problem	Challenge
Pitch	Presentation

you slice the lemon in half. One of the halves drips bright, sticky lemon juice over your finger. You raise half of the lemon to your lips and take a bite. As your teeth sink into the fruit, you feel the juice burst out around your teeth and tongue. The liquid is incredibly sour! You start to cringe, and then you swallow.

Did your mouth water? Almost everyone's does. The extraordinary thing is that if I had simply instructed you to produce saliva, it would not have been nearly as effective. One of the reasons vivid descriptions and vivid images are so powerful is because the subconscious mind cannot distinguish between that which is real and that which is vividly imagined. You can use this knowledge to your advantage by helping your audience see, hear, feel, and experience exactly what you are talking about.

It's not the same to talk of bulls as to be in the bullring.
—SPANISH PROVERB

A utilities company, trying to sell customers on the advantages of home insulation, learned to use vivid verbal packaging to enhance its message. It sent auditors to point out to homeowners where energy was being wasted and to provide them with money-saving, energy-efficient suggestions. In spite of the clear financial benefits over the long term, only 15 percent of the audited home-owners actually went ahead and paid for the corrections. After seeking advice from two psychologists on how they could better sell the advantages of home insulation, the utility company changed its technique by describing the inefficiencies more vivid-ly. With the next audits, homeowners were told that the seemingly minute cracks here and there were collectively equivalent to a gap-ing hole the size of a basketball. This time, 61 percent of the home-owners agreed to improvements![1]

When choosing your words, be sure to leave out unfamiliar technical language and jargon that may not be commonly under-stood. For maximum effect, your message must be easy to under-stand, memorable, and useful to your audience.

CRAFTING YOUR MESSAGE

The voice is the second face.
—GERALD BAUER

That first thirty seconds with your audience are critical. How do you start? Great persuaders craft and design their message. There is no room to wing it. Your opening is where your audience for-mulates and settles into their impressions of you. Think of your opening or introduction as comprising no more than 10 percent of your full presentation. Budgeting your speech in this manner forces you to organize your time so that you know exactly what you're going to say and how you're going to say it.

Scrap the old fillers such as "Today's topic is . . ." or "I'm going to speak on . . . ," or worse, "I was assigned to talk about. . . ." When preparing your opener, think of ways in which you can grab your audience's attention and perk up their ears. Several of the most effective attention-grabbing approaches include:

- Using humor.

- Telling a personal story.

- Posing a thought-provoking question.

- Sharing a quote.

- Presenting a startling fact or statistic.

As you move from the opening of your presentation to the main body, it is helpful to remember the acronym TESS, which stands for testimonials, examples, statistics, and stories. Top persuaders tend to incorporate each of these elements into their presentations. Our research shows that when speaking to an audience, each point of TESS will resonate with different audience members. On average, TESS resonates as follows:

Testimonials	12%
Examples	23%
Statistics	18%
Stories	47%

Testimonials. A testimonial is a person's statement or declaration of what they believe and assert to be true. In your presentation, it can be your own, or it can come from a third party. Testimonials are a source of social validation—people assume that if others believe in it, then they should too. Great persuaders know how to use testimonials when their credibility is low. Make sure your testimonials are believable and unbiased and that they are qualified for your audience.

Examples. An example is an explanation or model that demonstrates or illustrates your point. Instead of just spouting off facts, examples make your points come alive. Examples reinforce your ideas and make them vivid and real in the mind of your audience. Examples can be taken from research studies, from articles you've read—and they can be personal anecdotes.

Metaphors are another great way to more vividly express certain points. As a subset of examples, they are effective because they use pictorial language to connect objects and ideas. On average, we use almost six metaphors per minute during spoken language.[2] Here are some common, and likely familiar, metaphors:

- I struck out.
- Money burns a hole in his pocket.
- Keys to the piano of persuasion.
- Emotional bank account.
- Tree of financial independence.
- Life is a journey.

- Seasons of life.
- Time is a thief.
- Eyes are windows to the soul.
- The bread of life.
- Your love is like an ocean.
- Your brother is a pig.
- Like a rock.

Statistics. In a consumer climate that is increasingly skeptical, I recommend using statistics sparingly. Everyone knows that you can "cook the books" and find statistics to prove almost anything; your audience wants *credible* statistics. Statistics resonate with the logical mind, and when convincing, they are very persuasive. In particular, the analytical minds in your audience will love you and want to know the source. Most statistics need to be explained and often work best with visual aids.

Stories. The most powerful of the four elements of TESS

are stories. They draw your audience in while helping them understand and appreciate your message. I'm sure you can think of a time when you were in an audience, not paying much attention to the speaker. You were probably off in your own world, when all of a sudden, you perked up and started to listen because the speaker started telling a story. When we hear a story, we automatically tune in and want to know what happens next.

Great persuaders have mastered storytelling. When you understand what essential storytelling components are and how to use them, you will be able to touch people's hearts. Since you won't always have an opportunity to build rapport and trust with every individual in your audience on a one-on-one basis, stories can answer their questions about who you are and what you represent. Do you want them to view you as funny, honest, or down to earth? Identify the main points you want to get across and select your stories accordingly. When an individual's emotions are engaged, he will be more inclined to accept you and your message. The more common ground you can establish with your audience, the more attentive and receptive they will be.

People value their own conclusions more highly than yours, so if you can make your story *their* story, you will be that much more persuasive. As human beings, we are drawn to anything that gives us answers. Use stories to help your audience members answer some of their own questions. If you are successful in doing this, your message will grow and develop in their minds and hearts. If they remember nothing else about your presentation, at the very least, your story and its underlying message will get played over and over again in your listeners' minds.

Now, what about your conclusion? Your goal as a persuader is to make your conclusion memorable. Whereas your opening comprised about 10 percent of your presentation, prepare your conclusion to take up only 5 percent. Since you have been persuading the entire time, you should need only 5 percent to wrap things up.

Your conclusion should basically be a brief, clear, and concise repackaging of your main points.

As you move through your conclusion, get right down to your "call to action." Make it short, to the point, and energetic. Think of your conclusion and call to action as the final punch, the thing you want your audience to remember most. Because you've spent so much time setting it up, you want the conclusion to be really powerful.

SPEAKING STYLE OF GREAT PERSUADERS

Now that you have some pointers for the opening, body, and closing of your presentation, I'd like to give just a few pointers on the speaking style of great persuaders. We often overlook these things, but they make a big difference.

Make sure you don't speak too fast. We tend to rush through our presentations, especially when we're nervous. Obviously, if your audience can't understand you, your whole point in talking to them in the first place is defeated. On the other hand, speaking too slowly is not a good idea, either. Don't speak so slowly that you seem sluggish. Let the tempo of your speech just be natural, with enough energy that you keep things rolling, but not so fast that you seem jittery or uptight.

Another important consideration is volume. We've all had the frustrating experience of straining to hear someone. Be sure that you project and can be easily heard, especially if you will not have the aid of a microphone.

Be sure to consider the impact of pauses and moments of silence. These gaps also add meaning and impact to your message. The sound of well-timed silence can be more powerful than a dozen words. Because of this technique's dramatic effect, however, it can be overdone. Don't use pauses or silence too much. If you do, they lose their effectiveness. Besides highlighting important points, pausing also increases comprehension. When you pause in your story, it allows your audience a moment of introspection, which helps them absorb your message, both mentally and emotionally. Whether it is a moment to reflect or to enjoy a good laugh, a lull allows your audience members to process your story on a deeper level.

During a presentation, use gestures very carefully. Certainly there is room for spontaneity, but as a general rule, rookies should plan their gestures out ahead of time. They have to fit the story you are telling and not seem awkward or thrown together. Don't overdo gestures, but do use them to keep your audience's attention, to add drama to your story, and to underscore your key points. Think of your body as a prop that serves as a visual extension of the story you are telling with your voice. Above all else, your gestures must come across very naturally. Don't be robotic in your presentations.

MANAGING EXPECTATIONS

Great persuaders know how to manage expectations. Individuals tend to behave in a manner that is consistent with how others expect them to perform, whether those expectations are positive or negative. When we know someone expects something from us, we try to usually satisfy them in order to gain respect and likeability.

Expectations are communicated in a variety of ways. It may be through language, voice inflections, or body language. Think of a time when you've been introduced to someone. Usually, if that person introduces herself by her first name, then you do the same. Likewise, if she gives you her first and last name, you do as well. Whether you realize it or not, you accept cues from others regarding their expectations and you act accordingly.

Have you ever noticed how your expectations become reality in your personal life? Expectation is literally a self-fulfilling prophecy. We become slaves to our expectations on both a conscious and subconscious level. We see this used in the business world all the time. For example, when an electronics salesman says, "You're really going to love how this TV makes your sports come alive," he is shifting the focus away from the sale and creating an exciting image in your head. He is also speaking as though you had already agreed to the sale because you wouldn't be watching the TV unless you were going to buy it. He's acting like it's a done deal—and the truth is, the more he acts this way, the more it is!

I love seeing door-to-door salespeople use expectations to their advantage. They approach a door, ring the bell, and with a big smile, tell their audience that they have a great presentation that needs to be seen. Of course, they employ this strategy while they are wiping their feet on the prospect's doormat in expectation of being let in the house. You would be surprised by how often this technique actually works. You see the persuader handing over his pen in expectation of the contract being signed. Have you ever felt bad leaving a store or situation where you did not buy something? Why do you think you felt this way? It's because the store created and imposed upon you (often through very subtle means) the expectation that you would make a purchase.

THE ELEMENTS OF MYSTERY AND SUSPENSE

Using the elements of mystery and suspense is another way to enhance communication. Great persuaders are able to get their audience members sitting on the edge of their seats, wanting more. When we feel as if we've been left hanging, it drives us crazy! We want to know the end of the story. This is also known as the "Zeigarnik Effect," named after Bluma Zeigarnik, a Russian psychologist. This effect is the tendency we have to remember uncompleted thoughts, ideas, or tasks more than completed ones.[3]

We see the Zeigarnik Effect in action on the television news and other programs all the time. Right before a commercial break, the newscasters announce some interesting tidbit that will come later in the hour. This information piques your interest, and rather than flipping the channel, you stay tuned. Movies and dramas on television also leave you hanging in suspense. By leaving something unresolved right before the commercial break, these programs draw our attention, keep us involved, and motivate us to continue watching. We don't feel satisfaction until we receive finality, closure, or resolution.

GREAT PERSUASION AND PHONE SKILLS

Communication over the phone poses unique challenges. A first impression over the phone is just as important as it is in face-to-face contact, but the first challenge is that your audience can't see your face, your body language, or your presence. Everything about you is being judged entirely through the phone.

Face-to-face presentations are usually scheduled and planned, while phone conversations are often viewed as interruptions. It is amazing how many companies are still using automated systems when one of people's top complaints is that they are not getting a live body. (The second most common complaint is that they are getting the run-around by being transferred from person to person.) You can always find out if it is a good time to talk simply by asking your audience up front if it is. You are not in a race to finish your agenda. You need to be considerate of your audience's time. Otherwise, you become the uninvited guest who becomes a pest.

What are the biggest complaints your audience has about persuaders contacting them by phone?

- The caller races to finish the script without interruptions.
- The caller rambles.
- They feel insulted by casual greetings.
- They do not like the caller's tone of voice.
- The caller is hard to understand.
- They feel rushed.
- They feel that the caller is only pretending to listen to them.
- The caller lacks empathy.
- They believe they are being treated as though they are stupid.

The best persuaders do the following over the phone:

- They prepare before the call is made.
- They know the exact purpose and desired end result of the call.
- They smile during the conversation. (Yes, you can hear the smile.)
- They are polite.
- They focus on their audience's needs and wants.
- They use appropriate humor.
- They use the phrases "please," "thank you," and "you're welcome."
- They return calls within twenty-four hours.
- They end on a positive note.
- They are brief and to the point.
- They never ask, "How are you today?" because it is a telemarketing red flag.

- They qualify early and often.

- They exemplify sincerity and empathy.

- They employ listening skills.

- They use questions to control the conversations.

- They leave clear messages on voicemail and an explicit reason to call back.

Optimal Phone Delivery

- Listen more than you talk.

- Don't speak too loudly—hold the mouthpiece an inch away from your mouth.

- Vary your rate of speech—don't speak too quickly or too slowly.

- Let your audience *know* that you're listening (for example, "uh huh," "yes," "oh").

- Don't force your audience to strain to hear.

- Vary your inflection—don't speak in a monotone.

MASTERING PRESENTATION SKILLS

Not having the skills discussed in this chapter is like taking a road trip with your family without a CD, DVD, or radio in the car. It's like having no air conditioner or heater for the trip. I'm sure you could last for eight hours without these conveniences, but you would have some pretty unhappy campers by the end of the first hour. These skills are of maximum importance. Persuasion mastery involves perfecting your communication skills.

Every day, you will make either phone calls or live presentations or both, whether to groups of people or to one person. Be careful that you don't spend all your time on the content and none on the delivery. You could have perfect material, but if the delivery is poor, it won't matter. Careful preparation of not just *what* you say, but *how* you say it, is paramount to making sure you will be persuasive. Keep in mind that your audience will usually remember the delivery more than the content itself. They are judging *you* first and your information second. Unfortunately, most persuaders have never had training in communication and presentation skills. If you're one of these individuals, now is the time to master these valuable, timeless, and priceless skills.

Do you give the perfect presentation? Do you have the skills that will make you the top of your profession? How can you become he master story teller? Go to www.persuasioniq.com and find out the crucial elements of story selling.

The Donkey in the Lion's Skin: A Fable

A donkey, having put on the fur of a lion, roamed about in the jungle and amused himself by frightening all the animals he met. When he came upon a fox, he tried to frighten him also, but the fox no sooner heard the sound of the donkey's voice than he exclaimed, "I might possibly have been frightened myself, if I had not heard your voice."

Meaning: Outward appearance may temporarily fool your audience, but your words and presentation will give you away.

CHAPTER ELEVEN

PQ Skill #9

Preplanned Anticipation:
The Secret Formulas of the Pros

Dig the well before you are thirsty.
—CHINESE PROVERB

O ne of the key distinctions of ultra-successful persuaders is that they have taken the time to prepare ahead of time, every time. Too often we take for granted that we'll be able to just "go with the flow" or "wing it." Or we decide we'll just wait and see what happens. Why not? We've done it before. After all, we want our communication to come across as natural and spontaneous rather than mechanically rehearsed. However, the persuader who has anticipated questions and concerns and done the homework ahead of time has a considerable edge. Such a persuader gives a more compelling presentation simply because his preparation enables him to feel more confident. When we're unprepared or simply going through the motions, we feel less sure of ourselves. Our audience will then pick up on this lack of self-confidence right away. If you're not confident, they won't be confident either.

Perhaps the most fundamental of all preparatory steps is knowing your audience and knowing your message. Even if they have delivered the same message hundreds of times, great persuaders still review and prepare before each encounter and every presentation. They anticipate every possibility, every potential bump in the road.

KNOWING YOUR MESSAGE

What is your message? What do you have to share that will make a difference in people's lives? What is your main objective, the key thing you hope to accomplish? You've got to understand the big picture. Then, with the big picture in mind, you have to get more specific. Do you have a clear vision of how your product, service, or idea will help your audience? You've got to know your product inside and out, its pros and cons and how it stacks up against the competition. Use the following list, distilled from the work of great persuaders, to give some direction to your process of preparing and refining your message:

- What do I want to accomplish?

- How can I ensure that my message is crystal clear?

- If I had to boil my message down to three main points, what would they be?

- How can I demonstrate my expertise?

- How can I increase my trustworthiness with this audience?

- Why should others care about what I have to say?

- What are the emotional reasons that will prompt my audience to respond?

- What are the logical reasons that will prompt my audience to respond?

- What is my "call to action"?

- What are some alternatives to my initial proposal?

- Does my plan have any potential pitfalls?

- What are the top five doubts or objections I will encounter? How will I respond?

- What information should I gather about my audience? My competition?

- Do I have product samples, brochures, order forms, and catalogs?

- Do I have additional bonuses or incentives to offer in the final moments?

- Are there other ways I can build the value of my product, service, or idea?

- How can I get my prospects involved in my presentation?

- How is what I have to offer different from the competition?

KNOWING YOUR AUDIENCE

It is critical that you understand where your audience is coming from and what their needs and wants are. What do they really want to know? What are they searching for? What information can you present to bridge the gap between what they feel and what they want? It's important to understand your audience as a general group and also to get inside their minds as individuals. Here are some of the questions they will be asking themselves as you present—and that you should be thinking about as you prepare:

- Why do I need this?

- What will happen if I follow through with this? What will happen if I don't?

- What are my options?

- How will this improve/change my life?

- Where else could I go to fulfill this need?

- What is this going to cost me?

- Where can I get the best price?

- When do I need to make a final decision?

- What will my spouse/friends say?

> *You never really understand a person until*
> *you consider things from his point of view.*
> **—Harper Lee**

Here are some questions you should ask yourself about your audience as you prepare:

- Who am I trying to persuade?

- What is the common background or interest that brings them together?

- Who are these people as individuals (business people, students, mothers, etc.)?

- What can I offer that they will universally care about and understand?

- What types of things will they be looking to get out of my message?

- In terms of my key point(s), are they likely to agree, disagree, or be indifferent?

- Do I need to be aware of their political, religious, professional, or other associations?

- What is their average education and/or income level?

- What is their general age range?

- Will they tend to be more conservative or more liberal in their life views?

- Is this likely to be an easygoing or demanding crowd?

- How long will I be likely to keep them engaged? How much time is available?

- Is what I have to offer appropriate for this audience?

- What is my audience's biggest challenge and how am I going to solve it?

KNOWING THE NUMBERS

We often hear great persuaders say, "It all comes down to numbers." Of course, as a powerful persuader, you never forget what all those numbers represent: actual, living, breathing human beings with dreams, passions, hopes, fears, and concerns.

Why is an awareness of the numbers a critical part of your preparation? There are many reasons. How many people must you market to, then actually end up talking to, who will become customers? In the sales world, it is called your "conversion rate." For example, let's say your bottom line is that you've got to have sixty people become customers—your bare minimum. How many face-to-face encounters (or phone contacts, or whatever fits your situation) do you need to yield those sixty golden people? How, who, and where do you market? Is it via the Internet, cold calling, offering seminars or workshops, running classified ads, or television and/or radio commercials? Or for your niche, is it as simple as dropping fliers off at individual homes, sending e-mails, or better yet, using word of mouth? What is your system?

Knowing these numbers directly influences how and where

you should focus your energies. It converts guesswork into concrete figures and systematizes what otherwise would be aimless effort. Knowing the numbers gives you a clear starting point, a clear ending point, and all the critical steps in between. Besides, knowing the numbers allows you to see your progress and improvement.

In baseball, the indicator of greatness is the batting average. In the world of sales, it's the closing average.
—W. CLEMENT STONE

When it comes down to knowing the numbers, you will find that a poor persuader who knows their numbers will outpersuade an average but unprepared persuader every time. This is a classic example of preparation meeting opportunity. The business doesn't always go to the most deserving or the most brilliant. It goes to those who have steadily and consistently plugged along with their well-designed and well-implemented plans in hand. They have not only defined clear and specific objectives but they have translated them into action. This is the missing piece in many persuaders' preparations. We have all heard this advice, and we know it is perfectly sound and logical, but most of us rarely do anything about it.

Another way knowing the numbers is a critical part of your success is that it keeps motivation up during discouragement. Most people just give up too soon. Reality check: If discouraged persuaders simply understood the numbers, they would know that persistence in making those extra contacts would seal the deal. Various studies reveal these numbers; although they differ in their specific findings (they were asking slightly different questions of different groups of respondents), the trend is incontrovertible:

- 40 percent of persuaders admit to making no new (weekly) contacts.[1]

- 48 percent give up after only one contact.[2]

- Of those who attempt a second contact, 73 percent will then give up.[3]

- 85 percent give up after the third contact.[4]

- 90 percent give up after the fourth contact.[5]

- The 10 percent of people who persist beyond the fourth contact end up with 80 percent of the business![6]

Let's repeat that last finding: 10 percent of the people who persist beyond the fourth contact end up with 80 percent of the business. Keep at it!

SETTING YOUR OBJECTIVES

With a clear understanding of your message, your audience, and your numbers, you're now ready to set some specific objectives or goals. Many people don't like the idea of goal setting; in fact, just the mere mention of the words makes them cringe. However, I guarantee that if you ask any highly successful persuader whether or not she uses goal setting in her game plan, she'll not only answer affirmatively, but she'll also be able to tell you exactly what those goals are, in order of priority, both long- and short-term. What's more, she'll be able to furnish a list of them in writing. There's no doubt about it: goal setting works. And for the serious persuader, goal setting is serious business. Great persuaders know that you can't hit a target if you don't even know what that target is. It is critical that you define what you're aiming at—today, next week, next month, and next year. It's also crucial that you outline how to you're going to get there.

This process of refining your goals requires some organization. You'll find that you can make your system run in a much more streamlined fashion when organized thinking also extends into organized living. What is your workspace like? Could it use some decluttering? I know that some people have untidy desktops but they still know exactly where everything is. I'm not saying your work space must always be clean and pristine for you to be an effective individual, but you've got to figure out what works best for you. The questions to ask yourself are:

1. Can I find it?

2. How long does it take me to find it?

3. Is there a better, more efficient way of organizing it?

4. Might I be losing credibility based on sloppy appearance or surroundings?

5. Is there technology/software I can use to simplify my tasks and increase my productivity?

6. Is there something I can delegate?

MANAGING YOUR TIME

Of course, if we're talking about being prepared, goal-oriented, and organized, it is inevitable that we discuss the importance of wise time management. I know—you think you've heard all there is to be said about it. But before you skip ahead, let me ask you this: would you like to work less? Most people will answer yes. A very potent little detail that often gets overlooked is that when time is well managed, you actually work less.

It's the same for persuasion—great persuaders work less then the average persuader and accomplish more. It's the old "80/20 Rule." The most highly successfully people expend 20 percent of the effort and get 80 percent of the results, while the less effective folks put out 80 percent of the effort only to get 20 percent of the results. Sound unfair? Let me give you a tip for entering the world of 20 percent work/80 percent results. Great persuaders under-

**"If we learn from our mistakes, shouldn't
I try to make as many mistakes as possible?"**

stand that time is more important than money. They are fanatical-
ly aware that while we can accumulate money, we can*not* accumulate time. This knowledge informs how they spend every
moment. They don't waste time quibbling about things that don't
matter. Every ounce of energy is allocated where it will have the
most impact. It really is that simple. It's not even a matter of intelligence. It is just being aware and being organized.

Do you realize that most persuaders are productive less than
half of the day? Let's say, for example that the wasted moments
throughout the day add up to two hours (though research shows
that for most people, it's likely more). For a five-day work week,
those two measly hours add up to forty hours a month—the equivalent of another entire work week.

> *Everything is something you decide to do, and*
> *there is nothing you have to do.*
> —Denis Waitley

I mentioned earlier that successful persuaders could show you their goals in writing. This absolutely holds true for excellent time managers, too, because their daily tasks are their short-term goals. It doesn't take too long before these short-term goals add up and significantly influence whether or not we're hitting our bigger goals. As you work to get a better handle on your time management, commit to scheduling and planning things in writing. This doesn't mean you have to be a rigid, uptight person. It just gives you a guide. So often, we waste time just because we didn't have anything else to fill that time with. If you don't assign the way you're going spend a block of time, it *will* get filled, even if the activity has no meaning.

Great persuaders never start the day until it is finished on paper. Research at the Persuasion Institute shows that only 2.9 percent of persuaders have a handle on time management and fewer than one-third plan their day in advance. This means there is definitely room for most of us to gain greater control over our time and how it is spent. The good news is, as you get organized, you will probably start to work less and achieve more.

Commit to writing out your plans and goals the night before or first thing in the morning. Make sure the most important things in your life make it onto your list. Here are some questions to consider as you reflect on how you want your time to be spent:

- What is the best use of my time throughout the day?
- What part of my day should be reserved for the most difficult tasks?
- Do I do the simple, enjoyable things first?
- Am I spending important time on unimportant things?
- Do I confuse being busy with achievement?

- Do I know my priorities? Is this knowledge reflected in the way I spend my time?

- Am I clear about what I want to accomplish?

- What unnecessary things can I remove from my life?

- Is there any redundancy in my daily activities?

At the Persuasion Institute, we discovered the following:

- 4 percent of persuaders have perfected prospecting.

- 11 percent consistently spend time each week finding more customers.

- 12 percent will ask for referrals after every visit. (Referrals should comprise the majority of your business.)

- 81 percent of average persuaders spend less than five hours a week creating new customers.

We all have the same amount of time each day. The first step in using your time more wisely is being aware of how your time is currently used. Our research has shown that persuaders waste 57 percent of the day with non-income-producing activities (i.e., traveling, paperwork, waiting, idle chit chat, etc.) Sure, some of this is necessary, but top persuaders maximize income-producing activities and limit or delegate non-income-producing activities.

Once you have a clear handle on where you stand now, you need to settle on what improvements are necessary. Comparing the two—your current use of time versus your desired use of time—will help you assess what you need to adjust. You can always use the success of others as a model for your own success. Below are some time management skills successful persuaders possess. See if you could add any of these skills or techniques to your toolbox:

- Grouping and batching similar tasks.

- Monitoring interruptions.

- Multitasking.

- Implementing deadlines and rewards.

- Restricting sleep to only what is necessary (not sleeping longer than is needful).

- Exercising.

- Scheduling all activities and events, even "catch-up" time and rest time.

- Using technology to automate your contact, email and tracking systems.

AVOIDING PROCRASTINATION

It is impossible to talk about time management and not end up talking about procrastination. Why is the tendency to procrastinate so prevalent? We know it does us no good, and yet it plagues even the best of us. Putting things off until the last minute never gives the best results. Great persuaders don't have time to procrastinate.

While there are many different psychological factors motivating a person's tendency to procrastinate, the number-one reason is fear of failure or rejection. We often exhibit avoidance, reluctance, apathy, and rationalization when we are afraid.

What are some other reasons we procrastinate? Another big one is indecision. We fear being wrong and making mistakes. As much as we want to see life as black or white, good or bad, we need to let go of the need for tidy compartmentalizing; life just isn't that way. Often, there are many ways of accomplishing the same thing, and there can be many right answers to any one question. Successful persuaders are good decision-makers. They act in the moment. They decide now, not later.

Sometimes we procrastinate because we are tired or we don't

have the energy. Other times, it's because our goals aren't big enough, and we become apathetic. It can also be the reverse: if our goals seem too big, they will overwhelm us and we'll start to shut down. When you feel overwhelmed, the key is to break tasks down into smaller, more manageable, bite-size pieces. Yet another reason for procrastination is lack of knowledge or no drive to acquire that knowledge.

All these reasons are really more correctly called "excuses." There is no reason to postpone an important activity. As President Theodore Roosevelt said, "In a moment of decision, the best thing you can do is the right thing, the next best thing is the wrong thing, and the worst thing you can do is nothing."

No matter the root of the problem—fear, indecision, apathy, lack of knowledge, or something else—there are four basic excuses people use to justify their procrastination behavior.

1. *Perfectionism.* The first excuse is when a person insists that everything be perfect, that all their ducks be in a row, before taking the next step. These people are your classic perfectionists. There is always one more thing they need to fix or fine-tune before they can get down to the business of talking to potential customers.

2. *Pessimism.* The second common excuse behind procrastination is pessimism—always entertaining worst-case scenarios and all the reasons not to proceed. There are always many excuses not to do the work, but never any good reasons. These people spend all their time worrying and negatively forecasting the future.

3. *Amiability.* The third excuse for procrastination is "amiability." These are the folks who are always afraid of being too pushy, intrusive, and annoying. They avoid anything that will put them in a situation where someone might get upset or, even worse, not like them.

4. *Credibility.* The final excuse-maker is the superficial expert. Superficial experts fear that if they let others find out that they don't really possess all the skills they pretend to have, they will lose all credibility. They like being looked up to and admired from a distance, but the thought of being in a situation where they might actually have to demonstrate their alleged knowledge and abilities is terrifying. It would also force them to have to actually do some work. Instead, it is easier to avoid the call of duty.

It is helpful to know the underpinnings, but you can look at procrastination in an even more basic way. There are many fairly surface-level giveaways that tell you if you're dealing with (or happen to be) a procrastinator. According to Dr. Joseph Ferrari, a procrastinator tends to possess these five tendencies:

1. They overestimate the time they have left to perform tasks.

2. They underestimate the time it takes to complete tasks.

3. They overestimate how motivated they will feel the next day, the next week, the next month—to do whatever they are putting off.

4. They mistakenly think that succeeding at a task requires that they feel like doing it.

5. They mistakenly believe that working when not in the mood is suboptimal.[7]

Eliminate Common Excuses

The Persuasion Institute found that the following were the most common excuses that got in the way of getting the task accomplished. Are there any that sound familiar?

- "I'm too busy to . . ."
- "They'll never talk to me."
- "I don't want to seem pushy."
- "What if they're not interested?"
- "They're always in a bad mood."
- "I need to finish the paperwork."
- "I need some coffee before I start."
- "It's lunchtime and no one will be in."
- "I left a message; they'll call me back."
- "Maybe I should do some more research."
- "They won't want this product/service/idea."
- "I need to get lunch before I can think straight."
- "I need to get some office supplies before I can start."
- "Someone may have left a message on my cell phone."
- "I have a meeting in an hour, so I can't start calling now."
- "It's Friday and everyone is getting ready for the weekend."
- "It's Monday and everyone is catching up from the weekend."
- "Someone else already tried to contact them, with no success."
- "I need to check my e-mail again in case someone has responded."

DISCOVER, DESIGN, AND DELIVER: TECHNIQUES OF GREAT PERSUADERS

After you've assessed your message, your audience, your goals, and your time management, you're prepared to start designing your presentation. This process is a simple formula: discover, design, and deliver. Here, too, your preplanning and anticipation builds your confidence so that you are more or less ready for anything. Think about the following ideas great persuaders use when they are preparing their persuasive message:

1. How much time is allotted for you to present?

2. What will the setting be (auditorium, office, classroom, etc.)?

3. How large will your audience be?

4. Will you be presenting from a platform, over the phone, in front of a microphone, or in an intimate circle?

5. What time of day will it be? Will your audience be tired, refreshed, hungry, or preoccupied? Should you/can you consider scheduling a break in your presentation?

6. Will there be any possible distractions that you can avoid by knowing about them in advance? For example, noise from neighboring rooms, outside distractions, children, traffic volume as people move from one room to another, sunlight producing too much glare, etc.?

7. Can you inspect the presentation venue ahead of time? Where will you present from and what will your audience's seating situation be?

8. What equipment will be available, such as an overhead projector, a portable microphone, a flip chart, computer, a blackboard, or a dry erase board (along with chalk or markers)?

After you've considered details about the space, venue, time of day, and so forth, it's time to zero in on designing your message—the actual words you will say. Your message should accomplish all of the following elements based on great persuaders:

1. *Create interest.* Your audience needs a reason to listen to you. You have to generate interest in your chosen topic. Why should they care? What's in it for them? How can you help them? A message that starts with a really good reason to listen will grab your audience's attention. Without their undivided attention, there is no hope of getting your message across.

2. *State the problem.* You must clearly define the problem you are trying to solve. The best pattern for a persuasive speech is to identify a problem and then relate how that problem affects the audience. In this way, you show them why your presentation is of concern to them. Why does your audience have this problem? How does this problem affect them?

3. *Offer evidence.* Evidence is the support you give to your argument. Evidence validates your claims and offers proof that your argument is right. It allows your audience to rely on sources besides you. Evidence can include examples, statistics, stories, testimonials, analogies, and any other supporting material that enhances the integrity and congruency of your message.

4. *Present a solution.* You have gained your audience's interest, described a problem, and provided evidence in support of your message. Now you must solve their problem by presenting a solution. How can your product, service, or idea meet your audience's needs and wants? How can it help them achieve their goals?

5. *Call to action.* A persuasive message is not true persuasion if your audience does not know exactly what they need to do next. In order to solve their problem, your audience must take action. Your call to action is the climax of your presentation. When planning and preparing your call to

action, remember that the process does not have to be long and painful. It will work best when you are specific and precise. Bear in mind that the prescribed actions must be feasible—make your call to action as easy as possible.

Using this structure will facilitate people's acceptance of your message and clarify what you want them to do by addressing the logical mind. If your audience doesn't sense some sort of structure, they are likely to become confused and seek their own solution. If you aren't clear, concise, and orderly, your audience will find someone else who is. A great persuader can get his or her audience to remember, retain, and respond to the message. Have your points been memorable, easy to understand, and simple to follow? Your message will boil down to what your audience remembers, not what you say or do.

MAKING YOUR MESSAGE MEMORABLE

Here are some final thoughts on ways you can make your message more memorable, thus giving it greater impact:

Offer Choices

When someone tells us exactly what to do, our natural human tendency is to reject it simply because it has been dictated to us. People feel the need for freedom and the ability to make their own choices. If forced to choose something against their will, they experience psychological resistance. They are then overcome with the need to restore their freedom—all too often by saying no. The way to avoid this rejection is to offer people a few options so they can make a choice for themselves—let them choose the details of the yes. Great persuaders prepare their choices ahead of time.

If you absolutely have to limit your audience's choice to one option, you must explain the limitation. If your audience understands why a limit has been put on their freedom, they are more likely to accept a constraint.

On the flip side, try not to give your audience more than two or three choices. If you offer too many alternatives, your audience will be less likely to choose any of them. Structured choices give your audience the experience of control. As a result, they will be more cooperative and committed. Effective use of options will really only give your audience one choice—the one you ultimately want them to make. For example, "Would you like to see the live demonstration, or do you want me to send you the DVD?" Either choice would work for you.

Use Repetition

The use of repetition is a very effective persuasion tool. We have heard that repetition is the mother of all learning; it is also the mother of effective persuasion. When something gets repeated, it gets stuck in our memory, and comprehension improves. Repetition will create familiarity with your ideas, which will lead to positive association.

You need to repeat your message several times so your audience understands precisely what you are talking about and what you want them to do. Keep in mind that you can repeat your message several times without saying the same words over and over again. Great persuaders repeat but repackage. Each time you express your point, use new evidence and new words—you don't want to sound like a broken record.

Bear in mind that diminishing returns may result from overuse of repetition. You know how you feel about someone telling you a joke or a story you've already heard or about that commercial you've seen one too many times. Keep your repetitions about each point to approximately three references, and definitely no more than five.

Brevity and Simplicity

Keep your message short and simple. This brevity will make it clearer and therefore easier to remember. Make sure your speech is articulate and intelligent, but be careful not to use obscure language. Use simple terms and jargon that are familiar to your audience. Complexity will not impress them; rather, it will jumble your message. Make your points simple, clear, and direct.

Inoculation

Great persuaders know how to inoculate. The term "inoculation" comes from the medical field. Inoculation refers to injecting a weak dose of a virus to prevent a patient from actually getting the virus. The body's immune system fights off this weak form of the disease and is then prepared in case the real disease attacks. In the world of persuasion, you prepare your audience in advance to fight off the influence of the negative things they might hear about you or your product. Your audience may also generate their own counterarguments, strengthening their opposition against your message.[8] By presenting your audience with the other side of the argument, you show them that you know how they might be feeling and what they might be thinking. You will win a great deal of respect and enhance your ability to persuade by answering questions and responding to objections before they are even asked.

Imagine that your competition is always spreading the word that your product is the most expensive on the market. You need to inoculate your audience against these attacks. For example, you could tell them that your product is the highest-quality, longest-lasting, most expensive product on the market. That way, you make the drawback an important, positive feature. This inoculation, strategically planted in the mind of your audience, will enable them to access the facts when the competition tries to badmouth you or your product.

MAKING IT HAPPEN

Not being prepared is like driving your car without a map or, even worse, without a steering wheel. You might get lucky and arrive at your destination, but most of the time you won't make it. Preparation and anticipation is the foundation of successful persuasion. It takes extra time, effort, and discipline to hone these skills, but the results are worth it. If preparation has been last on your list of what it takes to convert yourself into a master persuader (or missing from that list altogether), now is the time to reform. Careful, well-planned preparation will ensure that you hit the target every time. The time you spend preparing will return to you tenfold.

Can you set your goals? Do you really want to be a great persuader? You know deep down that creating goals will make the difference between mediocrity and success. Top persuaders have their goals in writing. Do you want the goal system? Do you finally want to achieve your main objective? Go to www.persuasion-iq.com and get your goal mastery system to achieve your goals and desires in life.

The Ant and the Grasshopper: A Fable

In a field one summer's day, a grasshopper was hopping about, chirping and singing to its heart's content. An ant passed by, struggling with a piece of corn he was taking to the nest. "Why not come and play with me," said the Grasshopper, "instead of working so hard?" "I am helping to store food for the winter," said the ant, "and I recommend you do the same." "Why bother about winter?" said the grasshopper, "We have got plenty of food right now." But the ant went on his way and continued his hard work. When winter arrived, the grasshopper had no food and found himself dying of hunger. Meanwhile, he saw the ants distributing corn and grain from the supplies they had collected in the summer.

Meaning: The time to prepare is before you need it. The time to learn how to persuade is before you require it.

CHAPTER TWELVE

PQ Skill #10

Self-Mastery and Personal Development

If we all did the things we are capable of doing,
we would literally astound ourselves.
—THOMAS EDISON

There is a story about two neighbors who lived near each other in the mountains. They were quite competitive and were always testing each other's strength. One day, the first neighbor challenged the second. They would see who could chop the most wood in three hours. The second neighbor agreed to the challenge. The first neighbor started out strong. As he chopped away, the second neighbor chopped for only ten minutes and then sat down under the shade of a large tree. The first neighbor could not believe his neighbor's laziness. To his surprise, the second neighbor continued to take these ten-minute breaks each hour for the duration of the contest. Finally the three hours passed. Not having paused to take even a single break, the first neighbor was sure victory was his. To his dismay, he found that the second neighbor had chopped twice as much wood as he had! In disbelief, he said, "That's impossible! You took a break every hour." Without batting an eye, the second neighbor replied, "I wasn't resting; I was sharpening my axe."

Great persuaders all adhere to an intensive personal development program. They know that "dull knives work the hardest," so keeping themselves sharp is of the utmost importance. Average persuaders don't consider personal training to be worthwhile. They figure working harder is the answer. They also assume that they'll figure it all out on their own sooner or later, maybe from reading a book or two. They also think it's too expensive to learn from the best. Great persuaders know that experience is the best teacher, and that there is a lot to be learned from books, but that having an expert guide them through an experience dramatically shortens the learning curve. Instead of being a painful expense, intensive training is an indispensable investment. This is why successful persuaders can work half as hard—and get twice the results. Have you ever been in the situation of breaking your back with effort and then seeing someone else hardly lift a finger, only to run circles around you? This extremely frustrating scenario can often be traced back to the more successful person having a solid training or personal development program in place.

You are not truly educated unless you are learning and growing every day—learning from others, from your experiences, your mentors, your coaches, books, training programs, seminars, and CDs and DVDs. You should spend time every day contemplating what you have learned and applying it to your future. Take time to think about what happened during the day. What did you do well and what could you have done better? Are you wasting valuable time? Failing to work on personal development and ongoing training is like putting your paycheck in the trash after you have earned it. Just like a computer, if you don't upgrade yourself, you will become obsolete to both yourself and your future.

GET THE ADVICE OF EXPERTS

"I'll figure it out on my own." This has to be one of the most common—but most impeding—attitudes of mediocre persuaders. It may eventually prove true, but only after pain, stress, time spent, money blown, and many costly mistakes. This line of reasoning may be common, but it is not how great persuaders think. They know someone else has already figured out what they need to know. They magnify their productivity by maximizing their gifts, talents, and strengths and by using other people's strengths when dealing with something outside their expertise.

Great persuaders don't squander their time and energy in their areas of weakness. They excel because they learn to leverage their areas of natural strength and leave the rest to the experts. Think of some of the most brilliantly successful people you know. Chances are they focus on what they are good at and don't waste their time on the things they are not good at. This is why they excel. For example, trying to build an amazing website when you have no computer savvy will take you forever and divert your attention from areas where you can get impressive results with significantly less effort. And in the end, it's likely that your site will not be what it could have been if you'd left it to an expert Web designer. The time spent and the money lost (loss of income because it took you so long and didn't do it right) is not worth it. There is no money saved in the long run; there is only money lost.

Early in my career, I used to say, "I will figure it out on my own. How hard can it be?" Over the years, that phrase has cost me millions of dollars. I remember going to a stock market seminar that dealt with learning how to trade. It was going to cost me over $10,000 to attend additional training, so I declined in favor of figuring it out on my own. I got burned when I lost three times the amount I would have spent on training. The students who attended the additional classes, on the other hand, invested up front, learned the proper skills, and became great traders. I lost out by not allowing the experts to teach me the right skills.

It was a great day indeed when I realized that all the problems and obstacles I was encountering in life and in business had already been solved or figured out by someone else. Someone had already found the answer to all my problems. I could either pay them to teach me, or end up paying far more in the school of hard knocks. I'd pay more, not just financially, but with my time, energy, and commitment. Successful persuaders do not care how much it costs to learn the skills; they are concerned with their return on investment.

If you wanted to learn how to fly, would you just try to figure it out on your own? Would you read the best book on learning how to fly and then hop in a plane and learn along the way? No, of course you wouldn't! This is because the stakes would be so high—you'd likely end up losing your life. But if you're always falling short, missing the mark, and experiencing pain and frustration that could have been avoided—if you never reach your goals and aspirations—isn't it time to find someone that has mastered these skills?

None of the problems we will experience in life are new. All our potential challenges have already been experienced and solved by someone else. So, why struggle to solve them yourself when you can find someone who already has? There is someone out there—a seminar leader, a coach, a mentor—who can make a difference in your life. Find people who are experts in their field, ask questions, attend seminars and workshops and take college classes. Success is an open book test; the answers are all there right in front of you when you're willing to look for them.

There is no such thing as a "self-made" man. We are made up of thousands of others. Everyone who has ever done a kind deed for us, or spoken one word of encouragement to us, has entered into the makeup of our character and our thoughts, as well as our success.
—GEORGE MATTHEW ADAMS

YOUR PERSONAL DEVELOPMENT PROGRAM

What constitutes a personal development program? Top persuaders take multi-faceted approaches that include books, audios, seminars, and coaching. Any single method is incomplete; they all reinforce each other.

Consider these painful numbers:

- 58 percent of the U.S. adult population never reads another book after high school.

- 42 percent of college graduates never read another book.

- 80 percent of U.S. families did not buy or read a book last year.

- 70 percent of U.S. adults have not been in a bookstore in the last five years.[1]

The basic foundation of a personal development program is books, just as high school is the foundation for college. Personal success expert Brian Tracy says, "If you can get yourself to read thirty minutes a day, you're going to double your income every year." Other findings suggest that if you read up on a particular topic for even just thirty to sixty minutes a day, it will take you only a few years to become an expert in that field. How do you spend your time? We know that millionaires watch less TV than those stuck in poverty. We know there is a powerful and direct connection between a personal growth program and income level.

A book tightly shut is but a block of paper.
—**Chinese proverb**

While reading is often a beginner persuader's only approach, it is rarely effective by itself. Most people will not retain and apply all that they read, but reading does reinforce principles that you're working on in a seminar or with a coach. It's definitely time better spent than watching TV! The realistic truth about books—and believe me, as an author this is hard to say—is that the chances of finishing a book you have bought *and* applying one principle from it are less than one percent.

Audio programs are another perfect way to reinforce new ideas you're working on. Think of all the time you spend commuting. Don't waste away that time listening to the radio. Instead, turn your car into a workshop by listening to educational and motivational CDs.

> *Your income can grow only to the extent you do.*
> —HARV EKER

When you are focusing on your development, you are using your mind, your knowledge, and your skills. When you employ this trio of self-assets, you'll find previously untapped motivation. You'll develop a sense of urgency and direction that will bring you to higher levels of success. You can't be successful until you decide to explode out of your comfort zone and attempt the things that stretch and challenge you. Great persuaders learn to develop their hunger for knowledge and personal development. They want to grow, improve, and accomplish things they were not able to do in the past. When our capacity for growth and understanding increase, our self-esteem, optimism, and success also increase.

Seminars and workshops are one of the most effective ways to maximize your personal development program. They give you the chance to set aside two or three days for intensive study, to really zero in on specific topics and skills. Books and audios are a great start, but in a seminar or workshop setting you can take it to the next level. There is no substitute for going out of your way to meet with other individuals who are committed to the same ideals. A group of enthusiastic and energetic individuals who have been brought together by a common interest create a unique kind of synergy that cannot come about any other way. Oftentimes a seminar gives us just what we need to get the fire burning—to obtain new and exciting ideas, strategies, and techniques. Seminars and workshops are also tremendous opportunities for networking, which serve you long after you've left the classroom. Because of the value seminars and workshops offer that cannot be acquired in any other way, top persuaders make sure they incorporate them into their annual planning, securing the necessary funds and arranging attendance often months in advance.

An even quicker, more powerful, and more cost-effective way to enhance personal development is to enlist the help of a mentor or coach. Great persuaders have multiple mentors and coaches. A mentor is an individual who has superior experience, knowledge, and awareness and who is committed to providing insight, advancement, and support to one's career or life. Why is mentoring the best option? Mentors and coaches have been there before, figured it all out, and can therefore spare you immeasurable time, money, frustration, and disappointment. They also bring detachment to the table, enabling them to give you truly objective and realistic advice.

© Copyright 2006 by Randy Glasbergen.
www.glasbergen.com

**"I'm looking for a mentor who can show me how to
get rich without boring me with a lot of advice."**

Coaching has increased in popularity in recent years, and the results have been astounding. An obvious analogy is to compare coaching in life to coaching in sports. Take Michael Jordan and Tiger Woods as examples. Even with their innate gifts, they each committed enormous time, energy, and resources to working with the very best coaches. As serious athletes, they knew that in order to realize their fullest possible potential, they needed to surround themselves with knowledgeable, experienced, and wise coaches and mentors. Whatever your field is, do you take it seriously? If you took it as seriously as Michael Jordan does basketball, or Tiger Woods does golf, how much better would you be? The bottom line is, the research shows that mentors increase performance, lower turnover, increase job satisfaction, and—obviously—increase sales.[2]

Take a look at the Personal Development graphic below, and you will see clearly how each type of personal development approach correlates with success—how soon you will see success and the level of that success.

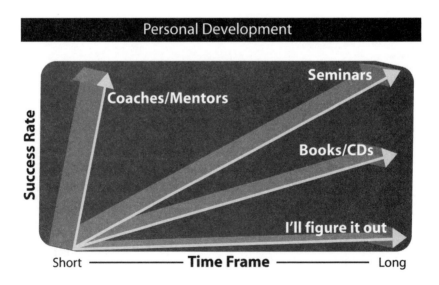

To better paint the picture of just how profound and far-reaching the effects of coaching can be, I have outlined (with feedback from top persuaders) some specific ways coaches and mentors work and enhance performance:

A great coach or mentor can:

- Role-play.
- Listen to your presentation.
- Raise your self-esteem.
- Evaluate and offer feedback.
- Hold you accountable.
- Offer support.
- Help you develop new skills.
- Encourage and motivate you.
- Help you overcome fears.
- Teach self-confidence.
- Offer encouragement.
- Give personal attention.
- Help you adapt to new conditions.
- Prepare you for the future.
- Help in negotiations.
- Assist with account planning.

Working with a great coach or mentor can result in:

- Increased revenue.
- Increased productivity.
- Accountability.
- Ego not being an issue.
- Improved self.
- Improved customer retention.
- Improved communication.
- Improved morale.
- Lower turnover.
- Increased confidence.
- Increased technical knowledge.
- Enhanced team synergy.

- Improved employee retention.

- Reinforcement of other training.

There is one last thing to keep in mind when it comes to mentors: mentors will rarely come to you and ask if you want to be mentored or coached. It's like a junior high school dance where everyone sits against the walls hoping to be asked to dance. You have to find the courage and inspiration to do the asking. You must be proactive and understand that mentorship will cost you time or money or both. All successful people talk of someone who mentored them and changed their life. The individuals that we look up to often intimidate us, but very often you'll find that they are actually quite open to sharing their thoughts and ideas, if only you would ask them. I have found that top producers are more than willing to share their secrets of success, but no one asks. Have you ever asked? You will be surprised by how willing people are to give, teach, and help take you to the next level. Just remember that they rarely will ask you if you need help. Take a top producer to lunch, pick up the tab, and pick his or her brain. People are usually quite surprised by how easy and profitable it is to learn from the best. Average persuaders tend to resent the successful while great persuaders become great by associating with great persuaders.

A single conversation with a wise man is worth a month's study of books.
—CHINESE PROVERB

Top management and sales trainer Brian Tracy says, "The fact is that the best companies have the best-trained salespeople. The second best companies have the second-best trained salespeople. The third-best companies have the worst salespeople and are on their way out of business."[3]

THE RETURN IS GREATER THAN THE COST

With all of this talk about the importance of implementing a personal development program, you might say, how is this possible? How do these people have time or resources for reading books and listening to CDs? How am I going to afford a three-day intensive workshop, or scarier yet, long-term one-on-one coaching? And if this kind of training has such an impact, not only on the individual but also on the companies they represent, why don't employers make this training easier to pursue?

Unfortunately, all too many people don't get past these questions and end up doing nothing to enhance their personal development, even on a basic level. As I mentioned earlier, most people will never even pick up a book again after graduating from high school. At the Persuasion Institute, we found that less than 5 percent of the population will ever attend a seminar in their lifetime unless it is required by the job, and even among rookie persuaders, most will attend only one.

Further aggravating the issue is that those we'd hoped would support and advocate such training do not. Many bosses and managers are so busy that they don't invest in training, even for themselves. And if they don't see the value in getting it for themselves, they most assuredly won't see the value in investing in it for employees. Often they don't believe that training will truly enhance performance, or they need assurance of a guaranteed outcome.

It is amazing to hear average persuaders say, "I already know all this stuff," or "I heard that before." Then you ask them why they are not more successful. You'd better duck as the rationalization, excuses, and blame come out. You will never hear a top persuader say, "I've heard that before." They always say, "I appreciate the review." There is always something to work on, a skill to fine-tune, or a fundamental to practice. Can you imagine a professional basketball player refusing to constantly and consistently practice the fundamentals? You will never hear, "I'm doing OK at shooting free throws—I don't need to practice anymore. I already know how to do it." Do you think there are any concert pianists who don't practice every day?

> *Men hate most what they cannot understand.*
> —MOSES EZRA

Great persuaders, on average, set aside 5 to 10 percent of their annual income for personal development. If you're skeptical about incorporating a personal development program into your own life or into your workplace, remember that personal development is a good investment—just like a great tax accountant. Great tax accountants always pay for themselves and then some. So it is with personal development. The return on investment dramatically outweighs any financial pinch you may feel up front. The Persuasion Institute found that average persuaders spend one to five hours a week on personal development. And what do they get? Average results. Guess how much time top persuaders spend on personal development? Five to ten hours per week—and it shows. In another study, we found that only 5 percent of active full-time persuaders ever invest in their own personal growth. And you guessed it—they earn the top 5 percent of income.

MASTER YOUR PRODUCT

There is no doubt that great persuaders know their product, service, or business. I have found that great persuaders use their own product or service. Through this use, they have experienced what their audience will experience. You must know every possible thing about your industry. Nothing is going to surprise a great persuader. They are up to speed on the economy, the industry, the company, and the competition. The time and energy you invest to get to this level will define your position with respect to top persuaders. Persuasion Institute statistics tell us that only 22 percent of persuaders feel they have great product knowledge. How well do you know these important aspects of your business?

- Customers
- Industry
- Trade journals and magazines
- Trade shows
- Current advertising campaigns
- Installation protocol
- Annual report

- Demonstrations
- Credit risks
- Training available
- Market trends
- Business news
- Market conditions

Do you know everything about your product or service? Do you know everything about your competition? In order to master your product, you should be able to answer the following questions fully:

- What are my product or service's weaknesses? Strengths?
- What are my product or service's advantages? Disadvantages?
- How will the economy help or hurt my business?
- What percent of the market do I have? What percent do my various competitors have?
- Why are my consumers loyal to my product or service?
- Do I know my (and my competitors'):
  - Pricing structure?
  - Delivery options?
  - Warranties?

- Maintenance care?

- Product lines?

- Finance terms?

- Service records?

- Guarantees?

- Marketing and advertising strategies?

KNOWLEDGE IS POWER

If you think education is expensive, try ignorance.
—DEREK BOK

The more you learn, the more you realize how little you know. I have found it very interesting that the opposite also seems to be true: the less you learn, the more you think you know. As the saying goes, ignorance and arrogance go hand in hand. If we're not working on ourselves, we don't realize the wealth of knowledge out there waiting for us. We are living in the information age, and if you don't spend time learning, keeping up with technology, and increasing your knowledge base, you will fall so far behind that it will be extremely difficult to catch up. Knowledge is the key to success in today's world. Studies consistently demonstrate that those who are learning and growing every day are more successful and optimistic about life.

It is interesting to compare the mindsets of average persuaders with those of great persuaders regarding ongoing training and education. Average persuaders say, "It's too expensive," "I've heard it before," or "I don't have the time," and leave it at that. They dismiss it without the careful deliberation it deserves. Great persuaders investigate, do research, and then base their decisions on the answer to that question: "What is the return on my investment?" Education and personal development are never expensive. Ignorance and lack of success are expensive.

Never become so much of an expert that you stop gaining expertise. View life as a continuous learning experience.
—**Denis Waitley**

Personal development has a great effect on your performance and output. If you are learning and growing every day, your mind is like a good bank account that is compounding interest. If you are stagnating, it is like credit card debt compounding against you.

Even if you went to college and pursued various degrees, that education will eventually become obsolete if you don't stay on top of the latest research and developments. Imagine if a medical surgeon never took the time to learn after medical school. In fact, all doctors *must* attend a certain number of medical seminars to retain their license. The world is changing and growing too fast to just sit back and think a degree makes you educated. If you are not learning, you are mentally deteriorating.

If you don't take charge of your learning, who will? Remember that you do not get paid for how hard you work. You get paid for results. Realize that learning opportunities won't just appear on your doorstep; you must seek them out and then put yourself in situations where you can learn and absorb. You must discipline yourself to find ways to expand your mind. If you are afraid to learn how to use a computer, for example, get one and use it. If you don't know anything about the stock market, get some training and begin to invest.

STOP MAKING EXCUSES

Many of us know what we want, but we still don't take the necessary steps to get it. Even when we want it very badly, we often give ourselves as many hoops to jump through as possible to put off the most painful or difficult steps. We desperately want to achieve our goals and dreams, and yet we use avoidance behavior to protect ourselves from our irrational fears. We want the perks without paying the price. We want improved circumstances without improving ourselves. We live each day waiting and dreaming and hoping for the stars to line up in our favor or for the winning lottery number. If this describes you, it's time to take a long, serious look in the mirror. That day will never come while you're waiting. It will only come when you bite the bullet and do what has to be done. I love what Richard Taylor, author of *The Disciplined Life*, has to say about this:

> "Ambition will never be realized, even when it is within the
> range of one's natural endowment, unless its possessor
> disciplines himself through the training, sacrifice, restrictions,
> inconvenience, and consecrated application which its
> realization may demand."[4]

Jim Rohn, one of America's greatest speakers and one of my early mentors, taught me a powerful lesson about accountability. When I first met him, I was sitting at a dinner table with ten other people. I grabbed a seat near him, just wanting to listen to his words of wisdom. A lull in the conversation arose, and I was caught off guard when he turned and asked me about my goals, dreams, and aspirations. In response, I began to talk about many of the roadblocks I had experienced in my pursuit of success. I listed all the reasons I wasn't able to achieve my goals and dreams. I let him know who was to blame and insisted that none of it was my fault.

I thought I had made a pretty good case for myself, and then the hammer dropped. Jim looked at me and said, "Kurt, for things to change, *you* must change, and for things to get better, you must get better." That brief moment changed my life forever. It was then that I realized that everything I wanted in life would be driven by personal change. I also realized that no matter what the excuse was—good or bad—it would not produce *results.*

Top performers know that change is the key to both their success and their ability to persuade others. When we understand how we change, we can help others change. And helping others change is a large part of persuasion. Often, however, we fiercely resist change. Why is this resistance so often present? We can only become who we want to become through change. What we do or do not experience financially, spiritually, or physically depends on whether or not we are willing to make changes. In spite of this knowledge, we still often wallow in our comfort zone. Even when achievement sits on our doorstep, we're still too comfortable to make an adjustment.

Sometimes, people are actually afraid of being "too" successful. To be brilliant or amazing might actually be a scary proposition. As success comes into sight, you might feel a lot of responsibility weighing down on you. So how successful should you be? How healthy should you be? How wealthy should you be? How strong should your relationships be? Consider the following powerful quote from Marianne Williamson:

> "Our deepest fear is not that we are inadequate. Our deepest
> fear is that we are powerful beyond measure. It is our Light, not
> our Darkness, that most frightens us. We ask ourselves, who am
> I to be brilliant, gorgeous, talented, or fabulous? Actually, who
> are you not to be? You are a child of God. Your playing small
> does not serve the World. There is nothing enlightening about
> shrinking so that other people won't feel insecure around you."[5]

In spite of the greatness that lies within us, we often program ourselves to do the least amount possible to get by. That is, we often do only what is necessary to survive. I see this tendency with my students at the local university all the time. Their mentality is: "What is the least amount of work I can do to pass this class?" They are paying top dollar to get their education, yet rarely do you see students take advantage of all the resources at their disposal. We see symptoms of the same mental laziness and resistance to change in the workplace, too: "What is the least amount of work I can do to get a paycheck and not get fired?" We will never find happiness in this lethargic mindset, and as a result, our soul starts to rust.

We are often discouraged by not seeing results fast enough, particularly after we've exerted a lot of effort. We want the quick fix, the easy way out. However, this is not how life works. If it takes someone a year to lose twenty pounds, why does someone else think he can lose the same amount in a couple of weeks? This principle also applies in reverse. We may not realize how far off course we've gotten until years have flown by, due again to the fact that consequences and results are often slow to manifest themselves. An example of this is poor dietary habits. We know that junk food is not good for us, and yet we deceive ourselves with: "Hey, nothing bad happened today after I had that burger and super-sized order of fries." The consequences of consistently unhealthy intake will take time—maybe even years—to show up in a really obvious way. In the meantime, however, the instant gratification of a fast and tasty meal *now* overpowers concerns about the future that, in the moment, seem immaterial. Imagine if every time you ate at a fast food restaurant the consequences were immediate. You took a bite and felt a new bulge near your midsection. If that were the case, it wouldn't take long before you changed your ways.

As you can see, there are a myriad of excuses one could come up with to put off a personal development program. Do any of the following ring a bell?

- "I can't afford it."
- "It's too expensive."
- "The company should pay for it."
- "I don't have the time."
- "It's hard enough just to get by."

- ■ "I can find a better way."

- ■ "It's really just luck."

- ■ "I've heard it all before."

- ■ "I'm embarrassed to admit weakness."

- ■ "My job is so specialized that no one can help me."

- ■ "It's too overwhelming—I don't even know where to begin."

BREAK OR BOUNCE

The gem cannot be polished without friction nor man without trials.
—Confucius

Another aspect of personal development is how you handle obstacles, challenges, and setbacks. Great persuaders are able to bounce back in the face of obstacles. When you get hit with a substantial challenge in your life, do you break or do you bounce? I have seen through my years of research and study that how we handle challenges and setbacks defines who we are. I believe that every challenge or obstacle you face in life can become a learning experience that you can use to take your life or income to the next level. When these defining moments hit, they will give you constant mental pain or help you tap into your passion.

It does not matter who you are; you *will* be tested. Ask yourself this question: "Will I pass this test, or will I fail and end up repeating it?" We have to remember that these experiences prepare us and strengthen us. Everything that happens in your life teaches you a lesson. No matter how pointless or painful it might seem, there is always something to be learned from your problems. How you look at challenges will dictate whether you enjoy life or merely endure it. Does your life give you excuses or give you power? Do you fall into self-pity or do you develop self-mastery? Helen Keller said, "Self-pity is our worst enemy, and if we yield to it, we can never do anything wise in the world."

> *Opportunity often comes disguised in the form*
> *of misfortune, or temporary defeat.*
> —NAPOLEON HILL

UPGRADE YOUR FUTURE POTENTIAL

I'd say now is the time to take a careful look at your personal development program. Are there ways it can be enhanced? Every day, you are either learning or deteriorating. You are either closer to or farther away from your goals. Learn to model the best in your field. Find those who excel in your industry and benchmark what will work for you. Pay the price to become an expert in your field. Don't settle for mediocrity. Change the things in your life that are holding you back. Practice your skills every day. Learn from your setbacks and mistakes. After every persuasive encounter, ask yourself what you did well and what you could do better. If you were not successful, make sure you understand why.

Go to the seminars, buy the books, find a coach, and get the CDs for your car. Remember to judge not by the cost of the program but by the return on your investment. I have heard many of the very best persuaders say that it was a seminar or mentor that changed their lives. Average persuaders say, "Tell me something new or that doesn't really work." I remember being invited to a seminar that cost $6,000. I first thought that it was too expensive, but then I saw that none of the top producers hesitated even briefly in signing up. I changed my mindset and went to the seminar. That decision ended up changing my skills, my income, and my life. The question is not "What does it cost?" but rather "What will it cost me if I don't go?" Personal development is the key to a successful future. Do you want to learn the cutting edge tools of persuasion? Are you going to treat yourself like a do-it-yourself project? Let me help with your personal development and join me for a free tele-conference on the new and improved forms of persuasion. Register at www.persuasioniq.com.

The Frog and the Ox: A Fable

"Father, Father," said a little frog to his father sitting by the side of the pond. "I have seen a huge terrible monster! It was as big as a mountain, with horns on its head, and a long tail." "Easy son," said old Father Frog. "That was only the farmer's ox. It isn't that big; he may be a little bit taller than I am, but I could easily make myself quite as large; just you see." So he blew himself out, and blew himself out, and blew himself out. "Was he as big as that?" Father Frog asked his son. "Oh, much bigger than that," said the young frog. Again, the old frog blew himself out and asked the young one if the ox was as big as that. "Bigger, Father, bigger," was the reply. So the old frog took a deep breath, and blew and blew and blew, and swelled and swelled and swelled. And then he said, "I'm sure the ox is not as big as . . ." but at this moment he burst.

Meaning: Self-conceit, denial, and blame about your current situation and lack of personal development will lead to self-destruction.

Final Thoughts

Time to Capture Your Greatness

*The story of the human race is the story of
men and women selling themselves short.*
—Abraham Maslow

Congratulations! You have just finished this book (as long as you did not skip ahead). Now comes the process of refining, learning, and mastering the skills and traits you have been exposed to in this book. Give yourself time and space, and see what your efforts will bring. Set high expectations for yourself and watch your world, your relationships, and your income change. As human beings, we need to have lofty goals and ambitions to keep us happy and inspired. What you expect, want, and desire is what you will attract.

When you have mastered these skills, you will always be successful, no matter what field or business you apply them to. You will always be able to find employment, run a business, and take control of your life and income. Great persuaders universally possess the following traits:

- Independence
- Financial freedom
- Job security
- Solid relationships
- Life mastery
- Passion
- Enthusiasm
- Love of life
- Success

I believe in you and your ability to improve yourself. I believe in your ability to improve the lives around you and make the world a better place. Before closing, I want to leave you with four universal success principles.

1. *Work on yourself first.* You cannot borrow success or the power to persuade. You have to master the skills yourself. This mastery is especially important if you aspire to help and serve those around you. Think of it as similar to being in an airplane. In the event of an emergency, the flight attendants instruct you to put on your oxygen mask first, and then help those around you. If you don't administer to yourself first, you will pass out before you have a chance to help others, and everyone loses.

It is very difficult to persuade others when you can't persuade yourself. Identify what you need to do to achieve your dreams and to fulfill your goals. Beware of the Wobegon Effect (Chapter 2), and tap into your greatness. Find your drive and the courage to change your life. It is easy to get stuck in complacency and mediocrity, but you know that you have more than just average potential inside you. Tapping into your potential means doing the thing you know you are capable of achieving. Stephen Covey said it best: "Some of the greatest acts of courage are in that instant between stimulus and response in our everyday decisions in life . . . ." It takes courage to realize that you are greater than your moods and your thoughts and that you can control *both*. Become a student of success. Customize your success plan to your talents, drive, personality, abilities, strengths, and weaknesses, and you will be perfectly positioned to persuade yourself and others.

> *First, they ignore you. Second, they laugh at you.*
> *Third, they fight you. Finally, you win.*
> —GANDHI

2. *Don't judge or criticize these principles.* We often condemn or ridicule what we don't understand or don't want to face. This tendency impedes our success. With something new, try it, test it, and use it. The principles in this book have been tried, proven, and used by successful people. Listen to the experts and use these principles—the results will speak for themselves.

This advice reminds me of a story about a group of nomads who were traveling through the desert. They stopped for the evening, ate a meal, and were preparing for bed when all of a sudden a bright light surrounded them. Their intuition told them that they were in the presence of a powerful, supreme being. As a result, they started to anticipate a message of great value, importance, and wisdom—a message intended just for them. After what seemed a long wait, they finally heard a deep, booming voice say, "Gather as many small stones as you can and put them in your saddle bags. Do this at once and at the end of tomorrow's journey, you will be greatly rewarded." The light then departed and the nomads were shocked and dismayed. Why would they do what had been requested of them? "This request has no wisdom," they thought. They began to share their frustration and anger with each other.

The nomads were expecting a profound message that would lead to a grand purpose and great wealth. Why should they perform such a menial assignment as the one that had been instructed? Although it didn't make much sense, some followed the command nonetheless and filled their bags. Others collected just a few stones, while yet others ignored the message completely. The nomads finally retired for the evening, awoke early the next morning, and traveled the whole day. As the day wore on, the messenger became a mere distant thought in their minds. As they approached their camp for the evening, they were shocked as they reached into their saddlebags. Miraculously, every stone they had collected had turned into a precious gold nugget. Those who had obeyed the messenger's command were glad to have an increase in wealth while those who had dismissed the message had few or no nuggets. Those obedient few who had followed the messenger's request had enough fortune to last them a lifetime.

Now this story may be a bit far-fetched, but the underlying message is clear. Follow, learn, listen, and reap the rewards. Listen to successful people around you, implement their strategies, and change your life forever.

> *By dismissing what could work, we dismiss*
> *our own growth. We dismiss what's possible.*
> —JOE VITALE

3. *Practice resolve, persistence, and determination.* A love-struck young couple decided to have a picnic out in the country. The young man borrowed his dad's convertible, and off they went. They had a great time, and before they knew it, it was time to head home. As they headed back, the young lady had an allergy attack and badly needed a drink of water for her medication. The young

man pulled over to get her a drink. Unfortunately, when he looked in the trunk, he saw that all the remaining water had spilled and there was nothing to offer her. By this time, she was in a bad way.

Scanning the countryside, the young man noticed an abandoned farm. As they drove closer, he could see that there was an old water pump in front of it. They drove up to the pump, and he jumped out and immediately started pumping. After five minutes had passed, beads of perspiration began developing on his forehead. After ten minutes, his muscles started to ache. He was about ready to give up when his girlfriend said, "No, no, no, don't give up. The water could be right there. Please keep pumping." Wanting to do anything to please her, the young man kept pumping for another five minutes, then another ten minutes. His arms were killing him, but he toiled away. Suddenly, without notice, without any fanfare, cold, refreshing water finally came gushing out. The young man's persistence had paid off! He was his girlfriend's hero!

I tell you this story because you'll never know the exact date, time, or circumstances when success will hit. I do know when you keep pumping, even when it hurts, even when you can't see how close the water is, and even when you are tired—the day and time will come when the waters of financial independence and success will come gushing forth. You'll see your success, you'll enjoy happiness, and you'll be able to achieve your greatest dreams. Go for it, do it, and accomplish true success.

4. *Tap into your value, find your worth, and exceed your potential.* We tend to look everywhere except in our own backyards for the answers or solutions to life's challenges. The answers are closer than you think. Russell Conwell often retold a story he first heard while on a camel caravan in Mesopotamia, the Acre of Diamonds parable. The story was about Alehafed, a Persian farmer. Alehafed was doing well enough with his life, but he had heard stories from a Buddhist priest about diamonds. Rumor had it that if he traveled far enough and searched hard enough he

could find diamonds that would produce enough wealth to purchase an entire country. Armed with such riches, Alehafed could become a person of great influence, provide thrones for his children, and live out his life in immense wealth.

Driven by this dream of endless wealth, Alehafed went to bed every night miserable and discontented. Finally, Alehafed left his family, sold his farm, and began his quest for the elusive diamonds. Years went by while he searched and searched. In the interim, he lost all his money and never did find those elusive diamonds. Upset, discouraged, and depressed, he threw himself into the ocean, never to be heard from again.

Meanwhile, back at Alehafed's former farm, one day the new owner stopped at the stream to give his camel a drink. As he looked around, the sun just happened to hit upon a large black stone to his right. From that angle, the new owner of Alehafed's farm could clearly see the colors and brilliance of a diamond. The irony of the story is that the farm Alehafed sold to fund his quest for diamonds turned out to be one of the largest diamonds mines in history. If he had looked right under his own nose, he would have found immense wealth with his own acre of diamonds.

Don't let this scenario happen to you. Change your perspective on life and see that you have diamonds in your very own mind. You don't have to look far to discover your own acre of diamonds. The greatness, talent, and potential you seek are closer than you realize. When you can see clearly, you will discover your internal potential and worth. Don't let the fogs of low self-esteem, critical friends, or the media tell you where to find your diamonds. Great wealth and success can be found in your very own talents, abilities, and experience. The challenge lies in the fact that a rough, uncut diamond does not shine like a cut, polished diamond. Many people will judge you by your unpolished past instead of your cut, shaped, polished, and brilliant future. Rest assured that your personal acre of diamonds will be unearthed and will begin to shine as you develop, learn, and change. Be ready. Learn, work smart and hard, and eventually everything will fall into place. Then, you will create an overflowing destiny of diamonds.

• • • • • • • •

Stay in touch with the Persuasion Institute's latest findings and research. Join our free newsletter, visit our free reports and participate our workshops and our coaching and training sessions. I would also love to track your success with our latest persuasion makeover. Go to www.persuasioniq.com for more information.

Appendix A

Persuasion IQ Book
Bonuses/Free Reports

CHAPTER ONE

Go to www.persuasioniq.com, and take the free persuasion skills assessment. It helps you and it helps our research. I will even give you free persuasion software ($197 value). This persuasion software systematizes the persuasion process. Wondering what to say or do next while you are persuading others? Find out and follow what great persuaders do and say during persuasion.

CHAPTER TWO

What is your personal Wobegon Effect? Do you suffer from the Wobegon Effect? Where do your talents and traits compare to the real world? If you really want to know go to www.persuasioniq.com and click on free reports.

CHAPTER THREE

The use of mental programming will sharpen your focus, make your investments of time and energy more productive. Do you want to know your strengths and weaknesses? Take your millionaire IQ at www.millionaireiq.com. If you want financial independence you need to think, act and do what millionaires do.

CHAPTER FOUR

I have identified twelve laws of persuasion that work below the radar. My book *Maximum Influence* is devoted to an in-depth study of these principles, and their mastery is critical to anyone desiring to be a skilled persuader. For an overview of the twelve laws of persuasion go to www.persuasioniq.com.

CHAPTER FIVE

Do you attract or repel people? Sure you answer in the affirmative, but it is not what you think, but what your audience thinks. Do you really want to know? Go to www.persuasioniq.com and find out the ten things you may be doing to repel your audience.

CHAPTER SIX

How trustworthy are you? Do you have the credibility to gain the trust of your audience? As you know, no credibility—no trust. Go to www.persuasioniq.com to take your credibility evaluation.

CHAPTER SEVEN

Do you want to know the top ten dark tactics of unethical people? Warning: these are not for you to use. There are for your understanding and preparation only. When you are prepared for these dark tactics you will be prepared to handle them in an honorable and ethical fashion. Go to www.persuasioniq.com to see the ten dark forms of power.

CHAPTER EIGHT

Do you have charisma? You might think so, but what do others really think about you? Do you attract people and do they want to be influenced by you? Do you repel people and don't even know it? Do you possess the ten traits of charismatic people. Go to www.persuasioniq.com and find out.

CHAPTER NINE

Motivation is a true art. When you understand human nature and the role influence plays in it, you will not only be able to motivate, but you will also have earned the right to motivate and inspire others. If you want to stay on track, download your motivation system and your will be able to stick to your goals, dreams, and passions. Go to www.persuasioniq.com

CHAPTER TEN

How do you give the perfect presentation? What are the skills that will make you top of your profession? How do you design your message? How can you become a master storyteller? Go to www.persuasioniq.com and find out the crucial elements of a perfect persuasive presentation.

CHAPTER ELEVEN

Can you set your goals? Do you really want to be a great per-suader? You know deep down that goals will make the difference between mediocrity and success. Top persuaders set down their goals in writing. Do you want a goal system? Do you finally want to achieve your main objective? Go to www.persuasioniq.com and get your goal mastery system to achieve your goals and desires in life.

CHAPTER TWELVE

Personal development is the key to a successful future. Do you want to learn the cutting-edge tools of persuasion? Are you going to treat yourself like a do-it-yourself-project. Join me for a free teleconference on the new and improved forms of persuasion. Register at www.persuasioniq.com.

FINAL THOUGHTS

Stay in touch with the Persuasion Institute's latest findings and research. Join our free newsletter, visit our free reports and partic-ipate our workshops and our coaching and training sessions. I would also love to track your success with our latest persuasion makeover. Go to www.persuasioniq.com for more information.

Appendix B

Abridged Persuasion IQ Test

How many of the over 100 persuasion and influence tools and techniques do you use during the persuasion process? Where do you rank compared to the world's top persuaders? The comprehensive Persuasion IQ test (www.persuasion-iq.com) ranks you in fifteen different areas, all critical to your ability to persuade, influence, and motivate others. You'll receive some great recommendations, analysis, and online tips by seasoned experts on what you can do to increase your IQ score (and income). Here is the abridged version of the Persuasion IQ test. Go online for the full version or take the condensed version here. Take your Persuasion IQ now and discover your strengths and weaknesses.

1. What technique creates the *most* urgency or scarcity?
   a. Deadlines
   b. Limited space

   c. Restricting freedom

   d. Might lose out

   e. Withholding information

2. When you show your products or service, what should you do to increase the perceived value?
   a. Show them the savings first
   b. Show the most expensive item first
   c. Show the least expensive first
   d. Show the average price first
   e. Show them the benefits

3. Which one is the main reason people do things they don't want to do?
   a. Fear
   b. Greed
   c. Dissonance
   d. Love
   e. Pride

4. You are trying to convince a future client (after multiple contacts) to make a decision to do business with you. What technique will be the most persuasive?
   a. Everyone has this product/service. (Social Validation)
   b. What would happen if he didn't do it. (Loss/Scarcity)
   c. What he (or company) gains. (Rewards/Gain)
   d. He is doing the right thing for his family/society. (Esteem)
   e. Show the incredible value. (Contrast)

5. What persuasion tool is constantly overused and losing its value in the mind of your audience?
   a. Finding something in common
   b. Closing tactics
   c. Sense of urgency
   d. Statistics
   e. Humor

6. When you come to the main pivotal point of your presentation you should:
   a. Increase your volume.
   b. Decrease your volume.
   c. Slow down.
   d. Speed up.
   e. Mirror and match.

7. When you know price is the biggest issue, the first thing you should do is:
   a. Talk about the guarantee.
   b. Show the most expensive product first.
   c. Show the least expensive item first.
   d. List additional features.
   e. List additional benefits.

8. People who are _____ are better at persuading.
   a. Educated
   b. Competitive
   c. Analytical
   d. Extroverted
   e. Introverted

9. 96% of small businesses will fail within 5 years because of:
   a. Lack of knowledge.
   b. Weak people skills.
   c. Lack of sales.
   d. Bad product/service.
   e. Poor location.

10. Which of the following can affect the persuasion process?
    a. Color
    b. Smell
    c. Moods
    d. Appearance
    e. All of the above

11. What is the first color to register in the human brain?
    a. Red
    b. Orange
    c. Yellow
    d. White
    e. Gold

12. What percent of people will always go against the social norm and violate social conformity?
    a. 1–5%
    b. 5–10%
    c. 10–15%
    d. 15–20%
    e. 20–25%

13. If you called six friends over the phone and needed to give them a good reason to come to a business presentation, what statement would increase your ability to persuade them?
    a. Because this will change your life.
    b. Don't you want to help me?
    c. You will see the value after the presentation.
    d. Aren't you tired of your dead end job?
    e. If you come you will see results.

14. Your main goal as a persuader is to:
    a. Close them into the deal.
    b. Help them persuade themselves.
    c. Connect and develop trust.
    d. Educate them on your product or service.
    e. Find their wants and needs.

15. What percent of the decision-making process takes place in the subconscious mind?
    a. 55%
    b. 65%
    c. 75%

d. 85%

e. 95%

16. When does your audience create mental shortcuts in their decision-making process?
    a. When the decision isn't important.
    b. When they must act quickly.
    c. When there is extensive social validation and pressure.
    d. When they are unsure of how to act, or what to do.
    e. All of the above.

17. When your audience or customer is starting to feel frustrated it is usually because:
    a. They are feeling manipulated.
    b. They are being pushed too hard.
    c. You did not meet their expectations.
    d. They had a bad day.
    e. You did not develop trust.

18. What percent of all purchasing decisions are based on price?
    a. 81%
    b. 55%
    c. 33%
    d. 21%
    e. 6%

19. During your presentation you should focus more on:
    a. Logic.
    b. Emotion.
    c. Logic and emotion.
    d. Features.
    e. Benefits.

20. People who are in a good mood:
    a. Buy more.
    b. Listen better.

    c. See the positive over the negative.

    d. Give better evaluations.

    e. All of the above.

21. When clients and customers tell us what they love about their personal persuader, which one did *not* make the list?

    a. Dependable

    b. Sincere

    c. Product knowledge

    d. Kept promises

    e. Friendly

22. What is the number one reason someone will trust you or your company?

    a. Advertising and marketing

    b. Friend/family feedback

    c. Knowledge of company/industry

    d. Personal experience

    e. Media

23. When you feel trust is low during a presentation you should:

    a. Be more bold.

    b. Ask them if they trust you.

    c. Reveal a weakness.

    d. Use more statistics.

    e. None of the above.

24. What number one characteristic is naturally found in most great persuaders?

    a. Empathy

    b. Optimism

    c. Sympathy

    d. Congruence

    e. Vision

25. Why do most people continually compare themselves to other people?
    a. Culture
    b. Media
    c. Low self-esteem
    d. Natural behavior
    e. All of the above

26. We have five senses. When you create involvement with your audience, you need to use as many senses as possible. What are the top three senses (in order)?
    a. Visual, hearing, smell
    b. Visual, hearing, taste
    c. Touch, taste, visual
    d. Touch, visual, hearing
    e. Hearing, visual, touch

27. According to your audience, what is the biggest barrier to communicating with persuaders?
    a. Listening
    b. Disorganized
    c. Lack of time
    d. A and B
    e. B and C

28. To get your audience or anyone to make a personal change in their life you must have four things happen. Which one does not belong?
    a. Overcome their fear.
    b. Find their motivation.
    c. Give them the tools.
    d. Help them see the future results.
    e. Listen to their story.

29. Which one of these skills is the most important in your ability to persuade?
    a. Passion

    b. Mindset

    c. People skills

    d. Trust

    e. Listening skills

30. Which type of evidence should be used the least?

    a. Testimonials

    b. Statistics

    c. Analogies

    d. Examples

    e. Facts

31. When you connect and find similarities with your customer or prospect, which one is the most important?

    a. Attitude

    b. Habits

    c. Background

    d. Appearance

    e. Religion

32. Which proficiency will affect how people evaluate you (more than the rest)?

    a. Smile

    b. People skills

    c. Touch

    d. Word choice

    e. Nonverbal behavior

33. When people were approached at a convention, their number-one complaint about the persuader was that he or she:

    a. Was obnoxious.

    b. Became too friendly too fast.

    c. Wasn't interesting.

    d. Had bad breath.

    e. Tried to give too much information.

34. When asking someone a question that they start to think about, if they look up it indicates:
    a. They are visual.
    b. They are auditory.
    c. They are kinesthetic.
    d. They are indifferent.
    e. They are resentful.

35. When you meet someone for the first time at their home or office you should:
    a. Look around for something in common.
    b. Talk about their hobbies or interests.
    c. Establish a need for your product or service.
    d. Make small talk until you have established rapport.
    e. Shake hands.

36. Can most human beings tell the difference between logic and emotion?
    a. Yes
    b. No
    c. 80% of the time
    d. 20% of the time
    e. Depends on their age

37. The brick wall of resistance thickens when you:
    a. List all the features and benefits.
    b. Don't respect their time
    c. Become arrogant.
    d. B and C.
    e. All of the above.

38. What is the main thing that offends your audience during your first contact?
    a. Pushiness
    b. Unsolicited small talk
    c. Did not leave relevant information

     d. Stayed longer than expected

     e. Late for your appointment

39. How do you know the moment when you have overpersuaded your audience?

     a. They suddenly have to go.

     b. You have lost eye contact.

     c. They ask you to send them more information.

     d. They say your product/service is too expensive.

     e. All of the above.

40. What is the main thing persuaders think they can cover up, but your audience can see right through it?

     a. Sincerity

     b. Poor product/service

     c. Enthusiasm

     d. Preparation

     e. Integrity

41. If your audience is inspired and motivated to do business with you, _____ will kill your ability to persuade.

     a. Scarcity

     b. Rewards

     c. Fear

     d. Pleasure

     e. Small talk

42. The biggest challenge of using desperation as a motivator is:

     a. People get angry.

     b. You get short-term results.

     c. It is unethical.

     d. It triggers the wrong emotion.

     e. Frustration.

43. What increases your power and ability to persuade more than the others?

     a. Title

    b. Empathy

    c. Uniform

    d. Public opinion

    e. External characteristics

44. What is the most important form of knowledge power?
    a. Information
    b. Resources
    c. Expertise
    d. Wisdom
    e. Contacts

45. When you come into a negotiation with a high number, you must make sure it is:
    a. Justifiable.
    b. The first offer on the table.
    c. Overwhelming
    d. 200% more (or less) than expected.
    e. Your final offer.

46. If someone attacks you personally the first thing you should do is:
    a. Ask a question.
    b. Ignore and continue.
    c. Apologize.
    d. Deny the accusation.
    e. Attack back.

47. One thing that really triggers long-term trust more than the others is:
    a. Sincerity.
    b. Predictability.
    c. History.
    d. Conviction.
    e. All of the above.

48. To be more persuasive, your speaking rate should be:
    a. Average.
    b. Slower than normal.
    c. Faster than normal.
    d. Match their pace.
    e. None of the above.

49. What percent of your audience will complain to you or a manager when you offend them or you pushed to hard?
    a. 1–5%
    b. 6–10%
    c. 11–20%
    d. 21–30%
    e. 31–40%

50. What is the best long-term motivation?
    a. Obligation
    b. Respect
    c. Fear
    d. Inspiration
    e. Desperation

PERSUASION IQ ANSWERS

1. c	11. c	21. c	31. a	41. c
2. b	12. b	22. d	32. c	42. b
3. c	13. a	23. c	33. d	43. a
4. b	14. b	24. b	34. a	44. c
5. c	15. e	25. c	35. c	45. a
6. c	16. e	26. a	36. b	46. c
7. b	17. c	27. d	37. e	47. b
8. e	18. e	28. e	38. b	48. c
9. c	19. b	29. b	39. b	49. a
10. e	20. e	30. b	40. d	50. d

SCORE

50–45	Professional
44–40	Average
39–35	Novice
34–30	Below Average
29–1	Poor

Endnotes

CHAPTER ONE

1. Antonio Damasio, "How the Brain Creates the Mind," *Scientific American* 12, 1 (2002): 4.

2. Brian Tracy, *The 100 Absolutely Unbreakable Laws of Business Success* (San Francisco: Berrett-Koehler Publishers, Inc., 2000), p. 19.

3. "The Road Best Traveled," *Success* (March 1988), p. 28.

4. "Help Wanted," *Sales & Marketing Management* (July 1998), p.14.

5. Napoleon Hill, *Succeed and Grow Rich Through Persuasion* (Greenwich, Conn.: Fawcett Crest, 1970), p. 27.

6. *New York Times* poll, September 2002.

7. Anthony Pratkanis and Elliot Aronson, *Age of Propaganda: The Everyday Use and Abuse of Persuasion* (New York: Freeman, 1992).

8. J. Maxwell and J. Dornan, *Becoming a Person of Influence* (Nashville: Dornan International, 1997), p. 47.

9. Small Business Administration (sba.gov) Dun and Bradstreet (dnb.com) and Persuasion Institute interviews (persuasioninstitute.com).

10. K. A. Ericsson, R.Th. Krampe, and C. Tesche-Romer, "The Role of Deliberate Practice in the Acquisition of Expert Performance," *Psychological Review* 100, 3 (1993): 363.

11. "Sales Know-How Is Only a Footnote For Most Programs," *Wall Street Journal*, April 11, 2006, p. B8; http://online.wsj.com/article/SB114471734001322452.html.

CHAPTER TWO

1. Garrison Keillor, *Lake Wobegon Days* (New York: Viking Press, 1985).

2. Justin Kruger, "Lake Wobegon Be Gone! The 'Below-Average Effect' and the Egocentric Nature of Comparative Ability Judgments," *Journal of Personality and Social Psychology* 77, 2 (August 1999): 212–232.

3. David G. Myers, *Social Psychology*, 5th ed. (New York: McGraw Hill, 1996), pp. 444–445.

4. L. Baker and R. Emery, "When Every Relationship Is Above Average: Perceptions and Expectations of Divorce at the Time of Marriage," *Law and Human Behavior* 17 (1993): 439–450.

5. M. D. Alicke, M. L. Klotz, D. L. Breitenbecher, T. J. Yurak, and D. S. Vredenburg, "Personal Contact, Individuation, and

the Better-Than-Average Effect," *Journal of Personality and Social Psychology* 68 (1995): 804–825.

6. Jeannine Aversa, Associated Press, "Self-employed find 'cutting cord' can be profitable," *Deseret Morning News*, Sunday May 28, 2006; http://findarticles.com/p/articles/mi_qn4188/is_20060528/ai_n 16434929.

7. William T. Brooks and Thomas M. Travisano, *You're Working Too Hard To Make the Sale!* (Bay Ridge, Ill.: Irwin Professional Publishers, 1995), p. 102, n 4.

CHAPTER THREE

1. Napoleon Hill, *Think and Grow Rich* (New York: Tarcher, 2005).

2. Earl Nightingale, *The Essence of Success*, CD-rom (Niles, Ill.: Nightingale-Conant, 1997).

3. R. F. Baumeister, "Understanding the Inner Nature of Low Self-Esteem: Uncertain, Fragile, Protective, and Conflicted." In *Self-Esteem: The Puzzle of Low Self-Regard*, R. F. Baumeister, ed. (New York: Plenum Press, 1993), pp. 201–208.

4. Jack Canfield, Mark Victor Hansen, and Leslie Hewitt, *The Power of Focus* (Deerfield Beach, Fla.: HCI, 2000); Persuasion Institute.

5. R. J. Sternberg, "A Triangular Theory of Love," *Psychological Review* 93 (1986):119–135.

6. R. Robinson, D. N. Khansari, A. J. Murgo, and R. E. Faith, "How Laughter Affects Your Health: Effects of Stress on the Immune System," *Immunology Today* 11, 5 (1990): 170, 175.

CHAPTER FOUR

1. Joseph Sugarman, Ron Hugher, and Dick Hafer, *Triggers: 30 Sales Tools You Can Use to Control the Mind of Your Prospect to Motivate, Influence and Persuade* (Las Vegas, Nev.: DelStar Publishing, 1999), p. 4.

2. Joseph E. LeDoux, *The Emotional Brain* (Simon & Schuster, 1998).

3. Vicki G. Morwitz, Joel H. Steckel, and Alok Gupta, "When Do Purchase Intentions Predict Sales?," working paper, 97-112 (Cambridge, Mass.: Marketing Science Institute, 1997); see also Gerard J. Tellis and Peter N. Golder, *Will and Vision: How Latecomers Grow to Dominate Markets* (New York: McGraw-Hill, 2002).

4. G. E. Belch and M. A. Belch, *Advertising and Promotion: An Integrated Marketing Communications Perspective* (New York: McGraw-Hill, 1998).

5. Ronald Marks, *Personal Selling: A Relationship Approach*, *6th ed.* (Saddle River, N.J.: Prentice Hall, 1997), p. 313, Figure 11.1.

6. Ibid.

7. J. D. Mayer and E. Hanson, "Mood-Congruent Judgment Over Time," *Personality and Social Psychology Bulletin* 21 (1995): 237–244.

8. I. L. Janis, D. Kaye, and P. Kirschner, "Facilitating Effects of 'Eating While Reading' on Responsiveness to Persuasive Communications," *Journal of Personality and Social Psychology* 1 (1965), 17–27.

9. R. A. Baron, "Interviewers' Moods and Reactions to Job Applicants: The Influence of Affective States on Applied Social Judgments," *Journal of Applied Social Psychology* 16 (1987): 16–28.

10. C. A. Estrada, A. M. Isen, and M. J. Young, "Positive-Affect Improves Creative Problem-Solving and Influences Reported

Source of Practice Satisfaction in Physicians," *Motivation and Emotion* 18 (1955): 285–300.

11. Gerald Zaltman, *How Customers Think: Essential Insights Into the Mind of the Market* (Cambridge, Mass.: Harvard Business School Press, 2003).

12. B. Rind, "Effect of Beliefs About Weather Conditions on Tipping," *Journal of Applied Social Psychology* 26 (1996): 137–147.

13. Brooks and Travisano, p. 51.

CHAPTER FIVE

1. Brooks and Travisano, p. 47.

2. N. Ambady and R. Rosenthal, "Half a Minute: Predicting Teacher Evaluations from Thin Slices of Nonverbal Behavior and Physical Attractiveness," *Journal of Personality and Social Psychology* 64 (1993): 431–441.

3. S. M. Andersen and A. Baum, "Transference in Interpersonal Relations: Inferences and Affect Based on Significant-Other Representations," *Journal of Personality* 62 (1994): 459–497.

4. "How Plaintiffs' Lawyers Pick Their Targets" *Bulletin* 10, 3 (Fall 2001), reprinted from *Medical Economics* magazine. http://www.aans.org/library/article.aspx?articleid=10046.

5. Murray Raphel, "Listening Correctly Can Increase Your Sales," *Direct Marketing* 41, 11 (November 1982): 113.

6. *The Wall Street Journal*, March 22, 1990, p. B1.

7. S. B. Castleberry and C. D. Shepherd, "Effective Interpersonal Listening and Personal Selling," *Journal of Personal Selling & Sales Management* 13 (Winter 1993): 35–49.

8. Albert Mehrabian, *Silent Messages* (Belmont, Calif.: Wadsworth, 1971).

9. Ray L. Birdwhistle. *Kinesics and Context: Essays on Body Motion and Communication* (Philadelphia: University of Pennsylvania Press, 1970).

10. Adapted from Leonard Zunin, *Contact: The First Four Minutes* (New York: Ballantine Books, 1985); Jerry La Martina, "Shake It, Don't Crush It," *San Jose Mercury News,* (June 25, 2000), p.4PC; and Persuasion Institute.

11. Paul Ekman, *Telling Lies* (New York: Norton, 1985).

12. J. T. Cacioppo, J. S. Martzke, R. E. Petty, and L. G. Tassinary, "Specific Forms of Facial EMG Response Index Emotions During an Interview: From Darwin to the Continuous Flow Hypothesis of Affect-Laden Information Processing," *Journal of Personality and Social Psychology* 54 (1988): 52–604.

13. Dr. Taylor Hartman, PhD.

14. Manning/Reece.

15. Robert Allen, Mark Victor Hansen.

16. Wilson Learning.

17. Stuart Atkins Inc.

18. People Smarts.

19. Myers-Briggs.

20. Disc Behavioral Style.

21. Persuasion Institute.

22. Aristotle.

23. C. P. Duncan and J. E. Nelson, "Effects of Humor in a Radio Advertising Experiment," *Journal of Advertising* 14 (1985): 33–40.; and M. G. Weinberger and L. Campbell, "The Use and Impact of Humor in Radio Advertising," *Journal of Advertising Research* 30 (1991), 44–52.

24. M. Smith, C. P. Haugtvedt, and R. E. Petty, "Humor Can Either Enhance or Disrupt Message Processing: The Moderating Role of Humor Relevance," unpublished manuscript (1994).

25. J. L. Freedman, D. O. Sears, and J. M. Carlsmith, *Social Psychology*, 3rd ed. (Englewood Cliffs, NJ: Prentice Hall, 1978).

26. J. C. Meyer, "Humor in Member Narratives: Uniting and Dividing at Work," *Western Journal of Communication* 61 (1997): 188–208.

27. W. P. Hampes, "The Relationship Between Humor and Trust," *International Journal of Humor Research* 12 (1999): 253–259.

28. Edward T. Hall, *Beyond Culture* (New York: Doubleday, 1976).

29. Michael B. McCaskey, "The Hidden Messages Managers Send," *Harvard Business Review* (November-December 1979): 147.

30. J. Frank Bernieri, "Coordinated Movement and Rapport in Student-Teacher Interactions," *Journal of Nonverbal Behavior* 12 (Summer 1988): 120.

31. I. H. Frieze, J. E. Olson, and J. Russell, "Attractiveness and Income for Men and Women in Management," *Journal of Applied Social Psychology* 21 (1991): 1039–1057; and P. Roszell, D. Kennedy, and E. Grabb, "Physical Attractiveness and Income Attainment Among Canadians," *Journal of Psychology* 123 (1990): 547–559.

32. S. Chaiken and A. H. Eagly, "Communication Modality as a Determinant of Persuasion: The Role of Communicator Salience," *Journal of Personality and Social Psychology* 45 (1983), 241–256; and K. K. Dion and S. Stein, "Physical Attractiveness and Interpersonal Influence," *Journal of Experimental Social Psychology* 14 (1978), 97–109.

33. K. K. Dion, E. Berscheid, and E. Walster, "What Is Beautiful Is Good," *Journal of Personality and Social Psychology*, 24 (1972): 285-290.

34. Ibid.; and E. Aronson, T. D. Wilson, and R. M. Akert, *Social Psychology*, 2nd ed. (Reading, Mass.: Addison-Wesley, 1997).

35. V. S. Folkes and D. O. Sears, "Does Anybody Like a Liar?" *Journal of Experimental Social Psychology* 13 (1977): 505–519; and S. J. Lynn and K. Bate, "The Reaction of Others to Enacted Depression: The Effects of Attitude and Topic Valence," *Journal of Social and Clinical Psychology* 3 (1985): 268–282.

36. Robert A. Baron and Donn Byrne, *Social Psychology*, 8th ed. (Boston: Allyn and Bacon, 1997), p. 261, Fig. 7.11.

37. Edward T. Hall, *The Hidden Dimension* (New York: Doubleday, 1966).

CHAPTER SIX

1. Gallup poll, September 27, 2005.

2. Brooks and Travisano, p.16.

3. Stephen Covey, *The Seven Habits of Highly Effective People: Restoring the Character Ethic* (New York: Simon and Schuster, 1989).

4. Sharon Begley, "A World of Their Own," *Newsweek*, May 8, 2000, pp. 53–56.

5. "Nearly Half of Workers Take Unethical Actions—Survey," *Des Moines Register*, April 7, 1997, p.18B.

6. Rosabeth Moss Kanter, "Confidence," *Selling Power* (April 2006), pp. 43–44.

7. D. K. Berlo, J. B. Lemert, and R. J. Mertz, "Dimensions for Evaluating the Acceptability of Message Sources," *Public Opinion Quarterly* 33 (1969): 563–576; and J. C. McCroskey and T. J. Young, "Ethos and Credibility: The Construct and Its Measurement After Three Decades," *Central States Speech Journal* 32 (1981): 24–34.

8. D. Joel Whalen, *I See What You Mean: Persuasive Business Communication* (Thousand Oaks, Calif.: Sage Publications, 1996) p. 159.

9. Noelle Nelson, *Winning: Using Lawyers' Courtroom Techniques to Get Your Way in Everyday Situations* (Prentice Hall, 1997), p.16.

10. S. Chaiken and D. Maheswaran, "Heuristic Processing Can Bias Systematic Processing," *Journal of Personality and Social Psychology*, 66 (1994): 460–473.

11. Gerald Zaltman, pp. 59–60.

CHAPTER SEVEN

1. David R. Hawkins, *Power vs. Force: The Hidden Determinants of Human Behavior* (Carlsbad, Calif.: Hay House, Inc., 1995), p. 133.

2. Floyd Allport, *Social Psychology* (New York: Houghton Mifflin, 1999).

3. Stanley Milgram, *Obedience to Authority* (New York: Harper Torchbooks, 1974).

4. Ibid., p. 5.

5. C. Harper, C. Kidera, and J. Cullen, "Study of simulated airplane pilot incapacitation: Phase 2, subtle or partial loss of function," *Aerospace Medicine*, 42 (1971): 946–948.

6. L. Bickman, "The Social Power of a Uniform," *Journal of Applied Social Psychology* 4 (1974): 47–61.

7. S. Lawrence and M. Watson, "Getting Others to Help: The Effectiveness of Professional Uniforms in Charitable Fund Raising," *Journal of Applied Communication Research* 19 (1991): 170–185.

8. C. K. Hofling, E. Brotzman, S. Dalrymple, N. Graves, and C. Bierce, "An Experimental Study of Nurse-Physician Relations," *Journal of Nervous and Mental Disease* 143 (1966): 171–180.

9. John Markoff, "Circuit Flaw Causes Pentium Chip to Miscalculate, Intel Admits," *New York Times*, November 24, 1994.

10. Emanuel Rosen, *The Anatomy of Buzz* (New York: Doubleday, 2000), p.16.

11. J. Sheppard and A. Strathman, "Attractiveness and Height," *Personality and Social Psychology Bulletin* 15 (1989): 617–627.

12. M. Lynn and B. Shurgot, "Responses to Lonely Hearts Advertisement: Effects of Reported Physical Attractiveness, Physique, and Coloration," *Personality and Social Psychology Bulletin* 10, 3 (1984): 349–357.

13. A. Doob and A. Cross, "Status of Frustrator as an Inhibitor of Horn-honking Response," *Journal of Social Psychology* 76 (1968): 213–218.

14. http://ecommons.txstate.edu/cgi/viewcontent.cgi?article=1014&context=honorprog.

15. John A. Bates, "Extrinsic Reward and Intrinsic Motivation: A Review with Implications for the Classroom," *Review of Educational Research* 49, 4 (1979), pp. 557–576.

CHAPTER EIGHT

1. Gerry Spence, *How to Argue and Win Every Time* (New York: St. Martin's Press, 1995), p.155.

2. Jay Conger, *The Charismatic Leader: Behind the Mystique of Exceptional* (San Francisco: Jossey-Bass, 1989).

3. M. E. P. Seligman and P. Schulman, "Explanatory Style as a Predictor of Productivity and Quitting Among Life Insurance Sales Agents," *Journal of Personality and Social Psychology* 50 (1986), 832–838.

4. Viktor Frankl, *Man's Search for Meaning* (Boston: Beacon Press, 1959).

5. Hans Werner Bierhoff, Renate Klein, and Peter Kramp, "Evidence for the Altruistic Personality from Data on Accident Research," *Journal of Personality* 59 (1991): 264–280.

6. Stephen Covey, p. 98.

7. A. Nadler and J. D. Fisher, "The role of threat to self-esteem and perceived control in recipient reactions to help: Theory development and empirical validation," in *Advances in Experimental Social Psychology*, L. Berkowitz, ed., 19 (New York, Academic Press, 1986), pp. 81–122.

8. D. G. Myers, *Social Psychology, 5th ed.* (New York: McGraw-Hill, 1996), p. 440.

CHAPTER NINE

1. S. Berglas and E. E. Jones, "Drug Choice as a Self-Handicapping Strategy in Response to Noncontingent Success," *Journal of Personality and Social Psychology*, 36 (1978): 405–417.

2. Martin Seligman, *Learned Optimism: How to Change Your Mind and Your Life,* (New York: Free Press, 1998).

3. Dr. Martin Seligman interview by Gerhard Gschwandtner in *Selling Power Magazine*, September 2006, p. 38.

4. J. Metcalfe and W. Mischel, "A Hot/Cool System Analysis of Delay of Gratification: Dynamics of Willpower," *Psychological Review* 106 (1999), 3–19.

5. M. Muraven and R. F. Baumeister, "Self-Regulation and Depletion of Limited Resources: Does Self-Control Resemble a Muscle?" *Psychological Bulletin* 126 (2000), 247–259.

6. Abraham Maslow, *Motivation and Personality* (Menlo Park, Calif.: Addison-Wesley Publishers, 1976), p. 15–26.

7. Melissa Van Dyke, *Sales and Marketing Management*, August 2007, p. 16.

8. Kenneth A. Kovack, "Employee Motivation, Addressing a Crucial Factor in Your Organization's Performance," working paper, George Mason University, Fairfax, Virginia, 1997.

9. Neal E Miller, "Studies of Fear as an Acquirable Drive: Fear as Motivation and Fear-Reduction as Reinforcement in the Learning of New Responses," *Yale University Journal of Experimental Psychology: General* 121, 1 (1922): 6–11.

10. Edward Deci, *Why We Do What We Do: The Dynamics of Personal Autonomy*, (New York: Putnum, 1995).

CHAPTER TEN

1. A. Pratkanis and E. Aronson, *Age of Propaganda* (New York: W.H. Freeman, 1991) p. 128.

2. Raymond W. Gibbs, Jr., "Categorization and Metaphor Understanding," *Psychological Review* 99, 3 (1992): 572–577.

3. B. V. Zeigarnik, "On Finished and Unfinished Tasks," in W. D. Ellis, ed. *A Sourcebook of Gestalt Psychology* (New York: Humanities Press, 1967).

CHAPTER ELEVEN

1. Persuasion Institute.

2. Graham Roberts-Phelps, "Make Persistence Pay," *Personal Selling Power*, (May/June 1994), p. 68.

3. Ibid.

4. Ibid.

5. Ibid.

6. Persuasion Institute.

7. J. R. Ferrari, "Getting Things Done on Time: Conquering Procrastination," in *Coping and Copers: Adaptive Processes and People*, C. R. Snyder, ed. (New York: Oxford University Press, 2001), pp. 30–46.

8. R. E. Petty and J. T. Cacioppo, "Forewarning, Cognitive Responding, and Resistance to Persuasion," *Journal of Personality and Social Psychology* 35 (1977): 645–655.

CHAPTER TWELVE

1. http://www.parapublishing.com/sites/para/resources/statistics.cfm.

2. Thomas Brashear, Danny Bellenger, James Boles, and Hiram Barksdale, Jr., "An Exploratory Study of the Relative Effectiveness of Different Types of Sales Force Mentors," *Journal of Personal Selling & Sales Management*, 26, 1 (Winter 2006): 7–18.

3. Brian Tracy, *Sales and Marketing Management*, Aug. 2006, p. 6.

4. Richard S. Taylor, *The Disciplined Life* (Minneapolis: Beacon Hill Press, 1962) p. 61.

5. Marianne Williamson, *A Return to Love: Reflections on the Principles of "A Course in Miracles"* (New York: HarperCollins Publisher, 1992).

Index

facial expressions *(continued)*
  recognizing, 104
failure(s)
  acknowledging, 60–62
  of businesses/products, 72
  fear of, 76
  of motivation, 187–189
  through self-handicapping,
    182–183
familiarity, rapport and, 114–115
fear
  confronting, 49–50
  in desperation cycle, 188
  in Desperation Formula, 199
  of failure, 76
  and lack of confidence, 127–129
  and procrastination, 240
  of public speaking, 209–210
  of rejection, 29–31
  of success, 267
  as tool of persuasion, 194
features, 26
Federal Reserve, 25
Ferrari, Joseph, 242
financial issues
  in life alignment, 201
  as obstacle to persuasion, 77, 80–81
finding your purpose, 51–53
first impressions, 91–92, 117, 131
Five Cs of trust, 123, 137–139, 163
force, power vs., 142
Frankl, Victor
  on attitude, 169
  on happiness, 64
Franklin, Benjamin, on appeal
    to interest, 71
Fripp, Patricia, on being
    remembered, 95
frustration, 169
functional concerns, as obstacle to
    persuasion, 77

Gandhi, Mohandas, on finally
    winning, 275
Gardner, Howard, *ix*
Garfield, Charles, 203
"gas," 2, 5
Gates, Bill, 184
genuineness, 35
Germany, personal space in, 117
Giovanni, Nikki, on understanding
    yourself, 34

Glasbergen, Randy, 109
goals
  setting, 235–236
  writing out, 238
Goleman, Daniel, *ix*
gratification
  delayed, 185–186
  instant, 181

habit(s), 55–56, 169
Hall, Edward T., 115
Hancock, John, on greatest ability in
    business, 11
handshakes, 104
Hansen, Mark Victor, 184
happiness
  created by persuaders, 85
  true, 62–64
  and use of humor, 108
harmony
  for congruence, 136
  with personality types, 106
Hawkins, David R., on power, 142
healthy habits, 55–56
hierarchy of needs, 189–191
high-pressure techniques, avoiding,
    22
Hill, Napoleon, 3
  on dominant thoughts, 47
  on opportunity, 270
  on power of speaking, 211
honesty, 36, 124, 134
hostile persons, 212–213
Hubbard, Elbert, on alibis, 59
human nature, 67, 68, 142
humor, 107–109, 163

ignorance, 264
improving yourself, 37
incentives, 156–157
income, appearance and, 113
indecision, 240
indifferent persons, 213
influence, 161–177
  and attitude, 168–170
  characteristics for, 161–162
  and charisma, 162–164
  and empathy, 170–173
  and optimism, 166–168
  and passion, 164–166
  and self-esteem, 174–176
  and vision, 173–174

statistics, use of, 220
Stone, W. Clement, on closing
    average, 235
stories, use of, 220–221
subconscious mind, 44, 46, 50
    decoding of nonverbal
        communication in, 105
    laws of persuasion for, 88–89
    and mirroring, 110
    in path to persuasion, 69–71
    and perception of competence, 126
success
    and college grades, 10
    and delayed gratification, 185–186
    determined by attitude, 168–169
    fear of, 267
    and happiness, 62
    and motivation, 180
    and objections from audience, 76
    ownership of, 183
    people skills for, 111
    principles for, 274–279
    and self-handicapping, 182–183
    steps toward, 55
"The Sun and the Wind" (fable),
    36–37
superiority, 130
support, lack of, 77
supporting message, 214–216
supportive persons, 214
suspense, in presentations, 224–225
synchronization, 110–111
synchronized beliefs, 47–48

taking action, 57–58
talking too much, 25–27, 82–83, 97,
    98
Taylor, Richard, on ambition, 266
territory, 116
TESS, 219
testimonials, 132, 219
Thoreau, Henry David, on castles in
    the air, 43
thought direction, 45–47
timeframe, in Motivation Formulas,
    199
time management, 236–240
title, authority by, 149–150
Tracy, Brian
    on dominating the listening, 99
    on people who cannot present
        their ideas, 2–3

on reading, 255
on training, 260
training, see personal development
traits of great persuaders, 12, 274
true happiness, 62–64
Trump, Donald, on art of persuasion,
    6
trust, 119–140
    assuming, 119–120
    building, 139–140
    and character, 123–126
    and competence, 126–127
    and confidence, 127–130
    and congruence, 135–137
    and credibility, 131–135
    factors in developing, 121
    five Cs of, 123, 137–139
    for power and authority, 141–142
    profession-based, 122
    and use of humor, 109
Twain, Mark, on cats on hot stoves,
    188
twelve laws of persuasion, 88–89

uncompleted thoughts, 224–225
understanding audience's thinking,
    67–89
    for closing the right way, 86–87
    and effect of moods, 85–86
    and emotions in decision-making,
        74–75
    and handling objections and
        concerns, 76–80
    and perception of value, 80–81
    and persistence, 87–88
    and power of emotions, 70–73
    and power of questions, 82–84
    and twelve laws of persuasion,
        88–89
uniform, authority by, 148–149
uninformed persons, 213
unspoken messages, rapport radar
    for, 94

value
    perception of, 80–81
    tapping into, 277–278
"vehicle," 2, 5
Verbal Packaging, 217
verbal self-representation, 103
vision
    and charisma, 162–163

About the Author

Kurt Mortensen is the internationally respected founder of the Persuasion Institute, a negotiation, leadership, and sales research firm. Kurt is one of the world's leading authorities on self-persuasion, motivation, and influence. The Persuasion Institute's training, coaching, and seminars have changed the world of persuasion and personal development. Kurt has been entertaining, educating, and inspiring audiences worldwide for the past twenty years.

Through his highly acclaimed speaking, training, and consulting programs, Kurt has helped countless people achieve unprecedented success in both their business and personal lives. He is also well known for his groundbreaking book *Maximum Influence: The 12 Laws of Persuasion*. His other pioneering work includes: *Perfect Persuasion, Power Negotiation, Persuasive Presentations, Millionaire IQ, Magnetic Persuasion, Exponential Success Skills,* and the *Psychology of Objections*. His Persuasion IQ Mastery Course is dramatically changing the way people explode their achievements.

For speaking and contact information, visit Kurt Mortensen at:
www.persuasioniq.com
www.persuasioninstitute.com
www.kurtmortensen.com

or write to him at:
Persuasion Institute
3214 North University Ave #613
Provo, Utah 84604
801-434-4022
info@persuasioninstitute.com